EMBODIED SOULS, ENSOULED BODIES

T&T Clark Studies in Systematic Theology

Edited by

John Webster
Ian A. McFarland
Ivor Davidson

EMBODIED SOULS, ENSOULED BODIES

An Exercise in Christological Anthropology and Its Significance for the Mind/Body Debate

Marc Cortez

t&t clark

Published by T&T Clark

The Tower Building
11 York Road
London SE1 7NX

80 Maiden Lane
Suite 704, New York
NY 10038

www.continuumbooks.com

All rights reserved. No part of this publication may be reproduced or transmitted in any form or by any means, electronic or mechanical, including photocopying, recording or any information storage or retrieval system, without permission in writing from the publishers.

Copyright © Marc Cortez, 2008

Marc Cortez has asserted his right under the Copyright, Designs and Patents Act, 1988, to be identified as the Author of this work.

British Library Cataloguing-in-Publication Data
A catalogue record for this book is available from the British Library

ISBN-10: HB: 0-567-03368-6
ISBN-13: HB: 978-0-567-03368-0

Typeset by Newgen Imaging Systems Pvt Ltd, Chennai, India
Printed on acid-free paper in Great Britain by Biddles Ltd, King's Lynn, Norfolk

CONTENTS

Acknowledgments		vi
1	Introduction	1
2	From Christology to Anthropology: The Ontological Determination of Humanity in Karl Barth's Theological Anthropology	16
3	Conversing with the Enemy? The Phenomena of the Human and the Nature of a Christologically Determined Dialogue	40
4	Christ, Spirit, and Covenant: A Model for Human Ontology	75
5	Physicalism, but Not Reductionism: Christological Adequacy and Nonreductive Forms of Physicalism	110
6	Across the Cartesian Divide: Christological Adequacy and Holistic Forms of Dualism	155
7	Conclusion: Making the Turn: Sharpening Our Christological Vision	188
Bibliography		198
Index		241

ACKNOWLEDGMENTS

I would like to thank Professor Alan Torrance for his continual support and encouragement throughout the process of writing my dissertation and revising it for publication. I would also like to express my sincere gratitude to the theology research seminar of St Mary's College at the University of St Andrews for the opportunity to present various parts of this project and for their warm support and insightful suggestions. In addition, I am grateful for permission to reproduce the following material that has either been published previously or is soon to appear in print elsewhere: 'Body, Soul, and (Holy) Spirit: Karl Barth's Theological Framework for Understanding Human Ontology', *International Journal of Systematic Theology* (forthcoming, 2008); 'What Does It Mean to Call Karl Barth a Christocentric Theologian?', *Scottish Journal of Theology* 60 (2007): 127–43; 'Context and Concept: Contextual Theology and the Nature of Theological Discourse', *Westminster Theological Journal* 67 (2005): 85–102.

Marc Cortez
Portland, OR 97215, July 2008

1

INTRODUCTION: RECENTERING THEOLOGICAL ANTHROPOLOGY

I. Who Are We?: The Anthropological Question and the Ontology of Human Beings

What is man that you are mindful of him, And the son of man that you care for him?

(Ps. 8.3, ESV)

On five different occasions the biblical authors raise this fundamental query, what we might call the 'anthropological question' (see also Job 7.17; 15.14; Ps. 144.3; Heb. 2.6). In so doing, they participate in humanity's ongoing pursuit to answer such basic questions as: Who are we? What are we? What are we supposed to be doing? Who are we in relation to everything else? This is a pursuit with decisive implications:

> So much depends on our conception of human nature: for individuals, the meaning and purpose of our lives, what we ought to do or strive for, what we may hope to achieve or to become; for human societies, what vision of human community we may hope to work toward and what sort of social changes we should make. Our answers to all these huge questions depend on whether we think there is some 'true' or 'innate' nature of human beings. If so, what is it? (Stevenson and Haberman 1998: 3)

Although the anthropological question thus seems a simple query, it is one fraught with tremendous philosophical and theological ramifications.

Located within this broader pursuit for anthropological insight, a long tradition of inquiry has sought to understand the ontological constitution of human persons. Thinkers of all disciplines have striven to determine the proper way to construe the nature and number of the composite elements (e.g. mental, physical, spiritual, etc.) of a human being – that is, a single, physical substance (physicalism), a single, non-physical substance (idealism), or two distinct substances (dualism).[1] While this debate, often referred to as the mind–brain or body–soul debate,[2] has a long and storied history, the implications raised by recent scientific and philosophical developments have given the ontological debate a vitality and a focus that has seldom been seen before (Jeeves 2004b). Indeed, in the latter part of the twentieth century the achievements of the 'brain sciences' (e.g. neuroanatomy, neurophysiology, cognitive science, etc.)[3] and the rapid rise of contemporary philosophy of mind to a place of prominence among the philosophical disciplines[4] were so remarkable that the 1990s were officially declared 'the Decade of the Brain',[5] and the 2000s have subsequently been dubbed 'the Decade of the Mind' (e.g. Borenstein 2001). Thus, according to Joel Green, 'quantum leaps in our understanding of the brain in the last three decades are rewriting our understanding of who we are' (2005: 6).

The tremendous possibilities, challenges, and potential liabilities generated by these and other late-twentieth-century advances like human cloning have caused contemporary thinkers to ask the anthropological question 'with renewed urgency' (Price 2002: 1–2). Spanning multiple disciplines, these implications encompass a wide range of issues – e.g. determining the relationships and distinctions that obtain between humans, other animals, and machines; understanding human agency, moral responsibility, and free will; making sense of our traditional affirmations of human dignity and

---

[1] As we will see with respect to physicalism and dualism, there are a variety of ways in which each of these can be formulated.

[2] Since a large portion of this thesis focuses on contemporary philosophy of mind, I will tend to use the more common (in that field) *mind–body* label rather than the more theologically oriented *body–soul*. For more on the shift from soul-talk to mind-talk, see Jeeves 2004c.

[3] We will briefly survey some of these developments in Chapter 6; for useful summaries see Jeeves 1998, 2004c.

[4] Although philosophical thinking about the nature of the human person and, more specifically, humanity's mental aspects can be traced to the dim recesses of ancient philosophy (cf. Humphrey 1999; Crane and Patterson 2000; Wright and Potter 2000; and MacDonald 2003), Jaegwon Kim (1998a) points out that modern philosophy of mind really begins with the publication of seminal essays by U. T. Place (1956), Hebert Feigl (1958), and J. J. C. Smart (1959). He does recognize that the origins of twentieth century philosophy of mind could be identified with earlier studies by C. D. Broad (1925) and Gilbert Ryle (1949), but he argues that neither were responsible for the shape of the modern debate in the way that these three essays were.

[5] In 1990 the U. S. Congress, followed by President George Bush, made this an official designation in an effort 'to enhance public awareness of the benefits to be derived from brain research' (see House Joint Resolution 174 and Presidential Proclamation 6158).

value; and responding rightly to the rapid technological advances on display in areas like human cloning and artificial intelligence. In addition, we must recognize that the way in which we formulate our understanding of human ontology bears directly on a variety of theological questions: What does it mean to say that humans are created in the image of God? What does it mean to be saved? What is the nature and locus of sin in human life? How does one's neurophysiological makeup affect her spiritual growth and well-being? What role does physicality play in worship and prayer? What happens to the human person after death? Philosophical, ethical, and theological questions such as these indicate the seriousness with which we should approach the task of developing a proper understanding of what it means to be a human person.

As we will see in the later chapters of this study, however, the tremendous complexity of both the relevant problems and the proposed solutions comprises a serious obstacle to providing an adequate account of human ontology. Indeed, the debate has raged for so long and the various arguments are, at times, so convoluted that one wonders whether any attempt to provide such an account is 'hopelessly ambitious' (Polkinghorne 1994: 10). Consequently, rather than attempt to unravel this labyrinthine debate in all of its philosophical, theological, historical, and scientific complexity, this study will explore the possibility of approaching the issue from a decidedly different direction.

II. 'Ecce Homo': Recentering Theological Anthropology

a. The Christocentric Turn in Theological Anthropology

Although we have seen that the biblical authors were keenly interested in the anthropological question, it is important to realize that they did not regard this as an unanswered question. Instead, these authors consistently placed the anthropological question within a theological framework that provided the basis for its answer (cf. Miller 2004). The Old Testament authors thus ask, 'What is man *that you magnify him?*' (Job 7.17), 'What is man *that you take thought of him?*' (Ps. 8.3), 'What is man *that you take knowledge of him?*' (Ps. 144.3).[6] At each point, then, the very nature of the question points the reader toward humanity's covenantal relationship with its Creator. For these biblical authors, humanity is not an undefined term awaiting conceptual clarity. Instead, it refers to a creature clearly defined and delineated by its standing in relation to God.[7]

---

[6] Even Job 7.17, where the theological reference point is not immediately stated, asks the question within the overall context of humanity's relation to God and God's righteous requirements.
[7] We will discuss the covenantal determination of humanity more fully in Chapter 2.

This covenantal answer to the anthropological question receives even sharper focus in the New Testament. In Heb. 2.6, the focal point for the question is not humanity in general but the person of Jesus Christ.[8] Paul makes a similar move; although Gen. 1.28 identifies all human persons as being created in the image of God, Paul makes it clear that Jesus alone is the proper image of God (2 Cor. 4.4; Col. 1.15); other humans share in the expression of that image only insofar as they are united with Christ and transformed into *his* image (Rom. 8.29; 1 Cor. 15.49; 2 Cor. 3.18).[9]

The significance of this christological shift in understanding the human person cannot be overstated. Indeed, a growing number of Christian theologians locate modernity's inability to understand human nature in the fundamentally misguided attempt to derive a complete picture of the human person independently of the perspective provided by the person of Jesus Christ. Such an attempt is necessarily flawed, according to these theologians, because only Jesus Christ reveals who and what human persons truly are. Thus, Ray Anderson argues, only 'the humanity of Christ . . . discloses the radical form of true humanity' (1982: 19). Echoed by a broad range of theologians, this commitment to a 'Christological perspective' (Grenz 2004: 626) on the human person has become so pervasive that theologians can speak of a broad consensus regarding the centrality of Jesus Christ in any attempt to understand the nature of human persons (e.g. McFarland 2001; Torrance 2004).[10]

Consequently, according to these theologians, failing to view humanity from this christological vantage point can only result in a distorted picture. But, as Wolfhart Pannenberg argues, this is precisely the error of 'most contributions to modern anthropology' (1985: 15). Similarly, John Haldane observes the rarity of any significant encounter between theology and philosophy of mind; a state he regards as unfortunate given the potential such a conversation would have for enlightening our understanding of human persons (1991). Robert Jenson contends that the difficulties we have with such basic concepts as death, consciousness, freedom, and even reality itself stem from a failure to understand them from the perspective provided by the Trinity and the incarnation (2003). Indeed, John Macquarrie (1979) and

---

[8] Barth thus argues that 'What is man?' is a question that ultimately has a christological answer (III/2, 20). Throughout this study, all references to Barth's *Church Dogmatics* (1956–1975) will be by volume and part number (e.g. IV/1).

[9] Although Paul can speak in Col. 3.10 of human persons being renewed into the image of their creator, it is clear from other passages (e.g. Col. 1.15) that Paul views Jesus as the one in whom the *imago* is fully realized. Consequently, others come to image God mediately through participation in him.

[10] Thus, for example, other theologians refer to Christ as 'the mystery of man' (Zizioulas 1975: 433), 'true humanity' (Sherlock 1996: 18), the 'archetype' of humanity (Nellas 1987: 33), and the revelation of 'what human nature is intended to be' (Erickson 1998: 532).

Thomas Morris (1984) have separately argued that many modern thinkers are guilty of inverting the process entirely; instead of understanding the human person in light of the incarnation, they attempt to understand the incarnation in light of a non-christological picture of the human person. Such an approach can only distort our view of both Jesus and human persons in general.

b. The Christocentric Turn and the Mind–Body Debate

Despite the widespread consensus on the determinative significance of the incarnation for understanding the human person and the tremendous impact of recent scientific and philosophical investigations into the nature of the brain and the mind, it is striking that contemporary theologians have made relatively little effort to understand the latter development in light of the former.[11] That is, while contemporary theological anthropology is marked in many ways by a commitment to viewing the human person christologically, the same cannot be said for its considerations of human ontology. Although one finds occasional assertions to the effect that Christology, especially a particular view of the incarnation, supports some anthropological ontology,[12] one rarely encounters any sustained attempt to think through the implications of this christological framework for understanding human ontology.[13] Indeed, some theologians seem more concerned with moving in the opposite direction. For example, Nancey Murphy has recently noted that positions on the mind–brain discussion may have 'implications for thinking about the person of Christ' (1998a: 23), but she never reverses the directionality of her query to consider the implications of Christology for her understanding of the mind–brain relationship. If Jesus Christ is the revelation of true humanity, however, would it not seem reasonable to consider every aspect of human existence, including human ontology, in light of his person and work?

We can certainly attribute this lack of christological reflection on the mind–body discussion to a number of different factors. For our purposes, however, three stand out as the most significant. First, although we have seen that contemporary theologians are fond of stating that Jesus Christ is the revelation of true humanity, one finds little sustained reflection on *why*

---

[11] This is particularly surprising given that many of those who are actively involved in the mind–body discussion are keenly aware of the theological issues involved.

[12] For example, some dualists argue that the incarnation provides implicit support for substance dualism (e.g. Taliaferro 1994: 242–43; and Goetz 2005: 33–34) while others argue the same for physicalism (e.g. Thatcher 1987: 183–84).

[13] Thus, for example, even a theologian like Ray Anderson, who is firmly committed to a christological approach to theological anthropology and is well aware of the significance of the contemporary mind–body discussion, makes little attempt to approach the mind–body issue christologically (cf. Anderson 1982).

this is the case, *what* it means for understanding human persons, and *how* one goes about drawing anthropological conclusions from this christological starting point.[14] Rather, such affirmations are often isolated from these methodological considerations. But, without a more robust framework for understanding the ground and methodology of a christocentric anthropology, it becomes very unclear how one should approach *any* anthropological issue, let alone one as convoluted and controversial as the mind–body debate.

Second, many theologians seem implicitly to limit the scope of the christological perspective. This is seen most clearly in the tendency to limit christological reflection on the human person to what Jesus reveals as the *exemplar* of true human living. While this exemplarist strategy has some biblical support (e.g. 1 Pet. 2.21) and a long history in both theology (e.g. Thomas à Kempis' *The Imitation of Christ*) and popular Christianity (witness the 'What Would Jesus Do?' phenomenon), it seems a remarkably limited lens through which to view humanity christologically.[15] If Jesus is the manifestation of true humanity, it would seem reasonable to consider the implications that Christology has for the full range of human existence.[16] Even when a more robust appreciation for the christological perspective is embraced, however, one finds that its scope is often limited to ostensibly theological loci (e.g. soteriology, ecclesiology, etc.) to the neglect of such issues as the nature of human consciousness, the relationship of the mind to the brain, psychophysical determinism, and other concerns raised by philosophers of mind.

And third, many philosophers and theologians would probably suspect any attempt to approach the mind–body discussion from a christological perspective as an illegitimate intrusion of theology into the domain of science and philosophy.[17] According to this objection, such an approach would require an unacceptable move toward making Christology the point of

---

[14] These issues often receive more sustained attention from those who are critical of the christocentric perspective than those who espouse it (e.g. Berkouwer 1962; TeSelle 1975; Knitter 1983; Johnson 1991; and Shults 2003; cf. also the essays in Vander Goot 1981).

[15] Indeed, the exemplarist approach itself is susceptible to critique. As Nellas rightly argues, the *imitatio Christi* should be understood primarily in terms of being conformed to Christ (i.e. '*Christification*'), rather than a merely 'external imitation' (1987: 39). Thus, he argues, imitation is more ontological than moral (see also Schwöbel 1991).

[16] This is not to say that every detail of true humanity can be positively determined through christological contemplation. As several theologians have pointed out, the nature of new being has been decisively *but not comprehensively* revealed in Jesus Christ (Sherlock 1996; and McFarland 2001). As we will see, a christocentric anthropology begins with Christology but not in such a way as to collapse anthropology into Christology.

departure for interpreting the data of the neurosciences and for arbitrating philosophical debates. For many thinkers, this is a role that theology *cannot* play without instantiating a theological ghetto, isolated from all other forms of discourse by its totalizing theological framework (Trigg 1998). In the course of this study, however, we will see that this perception is a result of misunderstanding the nature of the christocentric perspective. Indeed, we will discover that the christological perspective is well suited to engaging in significant dialogue with other disciplines. There is, therefore, no *necessary* connection between a christological approach to anthropological issues and the ghettoizing of theology. If such is the actual result of any particular theology, then, it stems from an inadequately applied Christology rather than something inherent to the perspective itself.

Together these three issues suggest that the christocentric approach to theological anthropology, indeed to reality in general, has not yet been sufficiently 'filled out and analyzed' (Nellas 1987: 27). Any attempt to understand the nature of human ontology from a christologically determined vantage point will, therefore, need to be grounded on a more adequately developed methodological framework. It is with these concerns in mind that we turn to the christological anthropology of Karl Barth.

III. Who is He?: The Centrality of Jesus Christ in the Theological Anthropology of Karl Barth

Given the concerns mentioned in the previous section, Barth's theological anthropology would seem well (or, possibly, uniquely) qualified to serve as the touchstone for our study. First, Barth's theology is well known for its 'radically christocentric' orientation (Balthasar 1992: 30). That is, he 'interprets all secular and worldly relations and realities in terms of Gods self-interpreting Word, Jesus Christ' (Balthasar 1992: 30). Barth thus seeks to ensure that his theology is 'Christologically determined' (I/2, 123) throughout. This christological orientation is vividly on display in his consideration of the human person. For Barth, 'The nature of the man Jesus

---

[17] Alternately, one might contend that this approach entails an illegitimate reliance on metaphysical speculation that is inappropriately applied to matters like these. Budenholzer rightly points out, however, that 'if the history of modern philosophy … has taught us anything it is that any understanding of reality has its own scientific presuppositions. … It is impossible to make foundational statements about the nature of physical theory without making statements about the basic nature of reality, that is, without making metaphysical assertions' (2003: 63). The question, then, is not *whether* metaphysical presuppositions are appropriate in a consideration of human nature, but *which* set of metaphysical presuppositions one will adopt and whether one will do so in an intentional manner.

alone is the key to the problem of human nature' (III/2 136).[18] Thus, according to Ray Anderson, 'Karl Barth, more than any other theologian of the church, including the Reformers, has developed a comprehensive theological anthropology by beginning with the humanity of Jesus Christ as both crucified and resurrected' (1982: 18).

Second, despite (or, more properly, *because of*) this christological emphasis, Barth does not fail to attend to the anthropological dimension. Indeed, the third volume of the *Church Dogmatics* is primarily devoted to understanding the relationship between God and humanity, the nature of human persons, and the character of human existence. The very nature of the anthropological question, however, has to be revised. Barth is keenly interested in understanding the nature of the human person, but he views this pursuit as a primarily christological endeavor. Thus, the anthropological question is significant, but it is secondary to the christological question: *Who is Jesus Christ?* Given this twofold emphasis on the centrality of Jesus Christ and the importance of theological anthropology, Barth would seem well positioned to serve as a model of the kind of christologically focused theological anthropology we have been discussing.

Third, unlike many theologians who affirm the christological perspective on the human person, Barth commits a significant portion of III/2 to considering the methodological issues involved in such an approach.[19] Barth thus addresses such issues as the impact of sin on human knowledge, the implications of Christ's particularity for understanding human nature in general, and the significance of Jesus as both fully God and fully man for drawing conclusions about human persons. In this way Barth raises and clarifies many of the obstacles that a christocentric anthropology must surmount if it is to avoid some of the difficulties and excesses to which it can be susceptible.

Fourth, in addition to thinking through the methodological issues internal to the christological perspective, Barth also considers the implications that such an approach has for interdisciplinary dialogue. Although Barth's theology has often been criticized at precisely this point,[20] we will see that he is well aware of both the need for and the difficulties involved in recognizing and interacting with the insights and perspectives of other anthropological perspectives.[21] Given the nature of the present project, Barth's willingness to

---

[18] Alan Torrance thus rightly points out the significance of the 'Who' question throughout Barth's theology (1996).

[19] Labeling Barth's christocentrism as an 'approach' should not be understood to imply that Barth believes that there are a number of different ways in which human persons, and reality in general, can be legitimately understood and that he simply adopts Christology as the clearest or most theologically tenable. Rather, as we will see in the next chapter, Barth views Christology as the *only* vantage point from which to view *true* human nature.

[20] For more on this see Chapter 3.

engage the implications of a christocentric anthropology for interdisciplinary dialogue stands out as particularly useful.

Fifth, as we noted earlier, while many theologians affirm the christological approach to anthropology, few if any take up the question of human ontology and the mind–body relationship. Barth, by contrast, devotes an entire section of III/2 to precisely this issue.[22] Taking Christ as the starting point, Barth seeks to follow 'the logic of the gospel' (Torrance 1986: 294) and to allow that perspective to determine what theology ought to affirm about human ontology. Consequently, although we will see that Barth does not approach the mind–body discussion from the perspective of an ostensive 'problem' in need of a theoretical solution, Katherine Sonderegger is right to note that his theological perspective has not 'blinded him to modern concerns in the field' (2000: 64). Barth is, therefore, well aware that his christological starting point will have considerable implications for understanding the mind–body question and directly engages many of the pertinent issues.

Finally, not only is this aspect of Barth's theology worth studying for its unique ability to raise a host of methodological and material issues that are pertinent to the present study, but also because Barth's approach to the mind–body question has been a decidedly underappreciated aspect of his theology.[23] To date there are no English-language studies of Barth's anthropological ontology. Indeed, apart from a few general surveys, very few works engage §46 in more than a cursory fashion.[24] This is unfortunate since, as we will see, the themes and ideas expressed in this section have a significant

---

[21] Of course, as Webster points out, Barth 'did not consider it the task of church theology to follow paths other than those indicated by the Christian gospel or to identify common ground between Christian faith and other views of life' (2000c: 10). But, this does not mean that Barth's theology is necessarily opposed to an open dialogue with other disciplines when their contributions touch directly on theological concerns (see esp. III/2, 71–131).

[22] Although we will see in Chapter 4 that Barth was not primarily interested in developing a particular *theory* of human ontology, the nature and extent of his discussion indicates that he was concerned to develop a proper (i.e. christologically determined) understanding of the general structure of human ontology.

[23] According to McLean, 'Barth's anthropology is buried in the doctrine of creation (CD III/2), and is, therefore, often skipped over in the reader's eagerness to get to the more central doctrine of reconciliation (CD IV). Thus is overlooked one of the richest discussions of anthropology in the western theological and philosophical tradition and also, perhaps more importantly, one of Barth's most detailed expositions of his content and method in relation to a subject available to our common experience and reflection' (1986: 115).

[24] For example, Soucek 1949; Prenter 1950; Brunner 1951; Ebneter 1952; Friedmann 1972; Frey 1978; McLean 1975, 1981; Stock 1980; Whitehouse 1949; and Krötke 2000. Among more recent studies, Price (2002) covers the mind–body relationship to some extent, but this is clearly peripheral to his main concerns.

bearing on Barth's understanding of a wide range of theological and philosophical issues.[25] In this area, then, as in many others, Barth remains 'a massive Christian thinker whose contribution to Christian theology is in many respects still waiting to be received' (Webster 2000a: 1–2).

Thus, by engaging Barth's careful commitment to a christological vantage point and the implications that it generates for understanding human ontology, Barth's theological anthropology provides a unique opportunity for developing an intriguing interdisciplinary dialogue.

IV. The Mind–Brain Debate Today, A Wide Open Field?

At this point, then, it may be useful to make some brief comments on the current state of the mind–body debate. As we noted earlier in this chapter, the latter part of the twentieth century was marked by significant scientific and philosophical developments. These developments in turn contributed to a decisive shift in the modern understanding of the human person. While previously, some form of substance dualism had been the predominant view of human ontology, from the middle part of the twentieth century on, anthropological ontologies turned in a decidedly physicalist direction.[26] The earliest forms of physicalism presented a highly *reductive* view of the human person as something that could be comprehensively understood within the parameters of the physical sciences alone (see Chapter 5). This reductive stance, however, quickly gave way to more *nonreductive* approaches that portrayed the human person as a wholly physical being, but one that exceeds the conceptual grasp of the physical sciences.[27] Despite this trend toward a less reductive understanding, the ontology of late-twentieth-century philosophers of mind retained their pervasively physicalist character. Indeed, some like

---

[25] The continued under-appreciation of Barth's contribution to understanding human ontology may well be the result of significant differences between Barth's approach to theology and the analytic tradition of philosophy that dominates contemporary philosophy of mind. In an insightful autobiographical comment, Caroline Simon states, 'I am a philosopher, trained in the Anglo-American analytic tradition. That training is little help, and perhaps a handicap, in developing the amount of sympathy necessary for understanding the theology of Karl Barth' (2004: 143). To which, John Webster can only remark, 'Where I come from, the analytical philosophers are of a rather more obdurate frame of mind when it comes to Barth, whom they regard as a joke in several volumes' (2004a: 159).

[26] For helpful discussions of this shift see Burge 1992; Boyd 1998; Kim 1998a, 2004; and Haldane 2000.

[27] Of course, reductive approaches did not give way entirely and are still promoted by thinkers like Paul and Patricia Churchland, Daniel C. Dennett, and Stephen P. Stich, among others.

INTRODUCTION

Daniel Dennett concluded that modern science had decisively refuted all forms of substance dualism such that this was no longer 'a serious view to contend with' (1978).

The end of the ontological debate, however, could not be declared so easily. First, despite the progress of philosophy of mind and the cognitive sciences throughout the twentieth century and especially in the 'Decade of the Brain', their accomplishments should not be overstated. Specifically, while these new disciplines have provided a wealth of information about the neurological underpinnings of human mentality, we remain limited in our ability to provide a theoretical framework for interpreting that information. As Steven Rose notes, 'we are still data-rich and theory-poor' (2004: 5). In other words, we have come to understand much about the nature of the *brain*, but we still possess only a very limited knowledge of the *mind*.[28] We can see this theoretical limitation at work in the variety of ontological theories claiming the moniker 'physicalism' and yet differing substantially in how human ontology should be understood – for example, nonreductive physicalism (van Gulick), dual-aspect monism (Jeeves), constitutional materialism (Corcoran), and emergent monism (O'Connor), as well as the more reductive forms that continue to have significant supporters (e.g. Dennett, Churchland, etc.).

Another reason that we should not declare the end of the debate on human ontology, however, is the simple fact that non-physicalist theories have not gone away. Shortly after Dennett's declaration of dualism's demise, other thinkers were recognizing the true complexity of the debate (e.g. Kripke 1980; Shoemaker 1984a). The latter part of the twentieth century saw a variety of philosophers step forward to defend various forms of substance dualism. Indeed, the last several decades have witnessed the development, or rediscovery, of a number of non-physicalist ontologies that continue to resist the monistic impulse of physicalism – for example, emergent dualism (Hasker), holistic dualism (Cooper), naturalistic dualism (Chalmers), integrative dualism (Taliaferro), and Thomistic dualism (Moreland), as well as other ontologies that do not fit easily into the physicalism/dualism framework like idealism (Foster), pluralism (Cartwright), and Aristotelian hylomorphism (Nussbaum). The continued vitality of non-physicalist understandings of the human person strongly suggests that even though a majority of contemporary philosophers would classify themselves as espousing some form of physicalism, the mind–body debate is still very much in question (see Corcoran 2001a; J. Green 2005).[29]

---

[28] Indeed, that is precisely why many called for a 'Decade of the Mind' to follow the 'Decade of the Brain' (Borenstein 2001).

[29] Haldane, however, points out that the debate is far more constricted than is often appreciated. He asserts, 'Anyone who reads extensively within contemporary philosophy of mind and reflects upon what they have been studying should feel the discomfort

V. *An Exercise in Christocentric Anthropology*

In this study, then, we will use the theological anthropology of Karl Barth as a springboard for exploring the implications of a christocentric anthropology for navigating the various theories involved in the contemporary mind–body debate. More specifically, the following chapters will seek to answer the following questions: What is a christocentric anthropology and what are its methodological and formal constraints? What resources does such a theological anthropology have for engaging in interdisciplinary dialogue? What implications can be drawn from a christological anthropology for understanding the ontological constitution of human persons? And, do those implications provide any assistance in understanding the complex array of proposals on display in contemporary philosophy of mind?

In Chapter 2, then, we will focus on the formal and methodological parameters of Barth's theological anthropology as expressed primarily in the opening paragraphs of *Church Dogmatics* III/2. Tracing Barth's discussion will lead to a clearer understanding of how he develops his theological anthropology on the basis of Christology, but in such a way that the former cannot be reduced to the latter. In this chapter, then, we will look at the formal and methodological implications raised by Barth's understanding of the relationship between these two doctrinal loci.

Chapter 3 advances the discussion by considering the extent to which such an anthropology can engage in interdisciplinary dialogue. Despite the concerns and objections of many theologians, we will see in this chapter that Barth's christocentric approach to theology does not necessarily preclude such dialogue. Instead, we will see that it is precisely Barth's commitment to his christological perspective that enables the possibility of a conversation in which the particularity of the various conversation partners is valued and their insights recognized.

Having established the possibility of interdisciplinary dialogue, Chapter 4 lays out the ontological implications of Barth's christocentric anthropology that will be the necessary components of any christologically adequate view of human persons. As we will see, Barth was well aware that his image of Jesus as the 'true human' should and does have a direct bearing on his understanding of what the ontology of true humanity entails. The christological commitments developed in this chapter, then, will serve as the criteria by which the christological validity of any particular theory of human ontology must be evaluated.

---

of intellectual claustrophobia. Notwithstanding that the subject is widely and actively pursued its content is remarkably confined. The boundaries of possibility are taken to stand close to one another and the available options are correspondingly few' (1991: 92). While this may be true, the divide between physicalist and dualist approaches remains a contentious one.

INTRODUCTION

Finally, the last two chapters will apply these criteria to several ontological theories that are prominent in contemporary philosophy of mind. First, in Chapter 5, we will consider a variety of proposals that view the human person as a physical being, but not one that can be reductively understood in terms of the physical sciences alone. After defining the nature of such *physicalist* ontologies and surveying some of the specific proposals that constitute *nonreductive* versions of physicalism, we will consider three ways in which these theories could be susceptible to critique from a christological perspective. Chapter 6 comprises a similar investigation with respect to *dualist* ontologies; specifically those that espouse a more *holistic* approach to the human person than is traditionally associated with Cartesian dualism. Consequently, the chapter first explores the more traditional understanding of dualism and then contrasts it with the more holistic approaches generally espoused by modern dualists. The chapter then moves into a consideration of areas of potential critique.

Through the course of these last two chapters, we will see that the christological perspective and the ontological commitments entailed by a christocentric anthropology have direct bearing on the questions being asked by contemporary philosophers of mind. We will not find any 'knock-down arguments' for or against any of the various proposals.[30] We will, however, move the discussion forward in two ways. First, we will establish on the basis of a christological analysis of human nature the paradigmatic framework within which any particular anthropological theory must function. Although the details of this framework will be familiar to anyone working in philosophy of mind, indeed, they roughly correspond to what might be considered the 'common sense' understanding of humanity, we will have established this framework on the firm theological ground of Jesus' person and work. Second, we will identify various strengths that each of the ontological proposals brings to the table as well as several prominent weaknesses that must be addressed in future proposals if these are to remain christologically viable candidates for an anthropological ontology.

Given the wide-ranging nature of this study, we will need to establish carefully the parameters of the discussion in three areas. First, a large number of studies have been devoted to the biblical material related to the ontological constitution of the human person.[31] Although the majority of recent biblical scholars have argued in favor of a physicalist depiction of the person in

---

[30] Indeed, as Joel Green argues, 'whether one is thinking, say, of Scripture or human experience, we find no knockdown arguments favoring one view to the exclusion of another' (2005: 23).
[31] Among the classic older studies are Eichrodt 1951; J. Robinson 1952; Bultmann 1955; Kümmel 1963; R. Jewett 1971; Wolff 1974; and Gundry 1976.

13

the Bible,[32] there is no shortage of scholars contending for a more dualistic conception.[33] In this study, however, since our focus will be on drawing christological implications for human ontology, we will not engage these exegetical debates directly. Without diminishing the importance of these exegetical discussions, we will concur with a number of recent scholars that the depth and complexity of the issues involved in the mind–brain debate are unlikely to be resolved at the level of biblical interpretation alone.[34]

A second set of parameters must be put into place with respect to Barth's own writings. Given the size, range, and depth of his various books, our study will focus its attention primarily on Barth's extended discussion of theological anthropology in III/2. This does not mean, of course, that we will ignore Barth's other writings.[35] On the contrary, the various aspects of Barth's theology are 'developed at such depth and breadth that it is now impossible to give a definitive exposition of any one part ... without making some reference to almost every other part' (Come 1963: 71).[36] Thus, although our study will focus primarily on III/2, we will find it necessary occasionally to draw on Barth's discussions elsewhere in his writings in an effort to present an adequate understanding of his anthropology.

Finally, the vast quantity of material written on the mind–body relationship in philosophy, science, and theology would swamp any individual study. Even the material written just in the last twenty years comprises a daunting mountain of information. The focus of our discussion in Chapters 5 and 6 must, therefore, be carefully circumscribed. To that end, we will limit our discussions to two sets of theories that together comprise the physicalist and dualist approaches adopted by the majority of contemporary philosophers, focusing specifically on several key areas in which those proposals might be seen to be in tension with a christological perspective. We will address other

---

[32] In a number of recent articles, Joel Green convincingly demonstrates and exemplifies the predominantly physicalist orientation of most contemporary biblical scholars (1998; 2002a; 2002b; 2004a; 2004c); a point that is not disputed by dualist biblical scholars (cf. Cooper 1988: 19).

[33] Among the more recent relevant studies are Osei-Bonsu 1987; Cooper 2000; and Wright 2003.

[34] As many theologians have pointed out, the Bible makes no attempt to present a theoretically rigorous view of human ontology (e.g. Cooper 1982: 15; Moreland and Rae 2000: 33; and Baker 2004: 336). But, as Barth rightly notes, 'Dogmatics must have the freedom to take up questions and concerns which cannot be answered directly either by individual scriptural phrases or by reference to specific biblical contexts of thought, and which cannot be those of exegesis, because they arise only in the Church which listens to the voice of Scripture and teaches on this basis' (I/2, 821–22).

[35] Friedmann rightly warns against the dangerous imbalance often resulting from an undue focus on just one of Barth's many writings (1972: 13).

[36] Similarly, Sykes 1979c: 2; Hunsinger 1991: 28; Jenson 1997: 28; Hauerwas 2001: 180–81; and Webster 2000c.

INTRODUCTION

issues only insofar as it is necessary to clarify the questions and concerns of our study.[37]

Fundamentally, then, this study is an exercise in understanding the nature of a christocentric anthropology and its implications for understanding human ontology. Since the approach that has been laid out will require us to devote considerable attention both to the theology of Karl Barth and to a number of contemporary philosophers of mind, this study can be appreciated as contributing (1) to the ongoing project of understanding Karl Barth by providing an analysis of an underappreciated aspect of his theology and (2) to contemporary philosophy of mind by clarifying, analyzing, and evaluating a number of recent proposals regarding the mind–body relationship. Fundamentally, however, this study aims to draw together these apparently disparate fields of inquiry by engaging both theology and philosophy in a vital dialogue on the nature of the human person as revealed in the person and work of Jesus Christ.

---

[37] Several recent philosophers have questioned the practice of adopting a physicalist/dualist framework for addressing the mind–body problem and have argued for a form of ontological pluralism that seeks to transcend the limitations of the dipolar approach (e.g. van Gelder 1998; Cartwright 1999; and Gillett 2003). Although this criticism is worth considering, this study adopts the physicalist/dualist framework for the simple reason that most contemporary philosophers still fall into one of these two categories. This does not mean, however, that ontologies which do not fit neatly into this dipolar scheme will be ignored. Rather, we will use this dipolar framework to raise the most fundamental philosophical issues involved in the development of *any* ontological theory.

2

FROM CHRISTOLOGY TO ANTHROPOLOGY: THE ONTOLOGICAL DETERMINATION OF HUMANITY IN KARL BARTH'S THEOLOGICAL ANTHROPOLOGY

I. *Christology and Anthropology: The Christocentric Shape of Barth's Theological Anthropology*

Barth's understanding of humanity in its relation to God has long attracted attention as one of the most creative, ground-breaking, and influential aspects of his theology.[1] Barth himself recognized that his theological anthropology comprised such a serious departure from traditional theology that he thought it deviated even more than his famous doctrine of predestination (III/2, ix).[2]

The point at which this divergence originates is the consistency with which Barth carried out his christocentric conviction in developing his theological anthropology. As Hartwell describes it:

> The traditional dogmatic way of thinking is here once more radically reversed. He does not start from the phenomena of the human in general

---

[1] Indeed, T. F. Torrance referred to it as 'in some ways the most arresting aspect of Barth's theology' (1990: 22) and Herbert Hartwell regarded it as 'revolutionary in content' (1964: 123).

[2] We will see, though, that the substantial departure evidenced in his anthropology is grounded in his unique understanding of election and, thus, the two departures cannot be so neatly distinguished.

as they present themselves to the philosopher or the scientist. He does not begin, as the anthropology of traditional Christian dogmatics usually does, with the problem of the constitution of man's being, of man's existence [*Dasein*] and nature [*Sosein*] in order to proceed from there to the human nature of Jesus Christ in particular. On the contrary, he derives his concept of man, of real man, from the human nature of the one particular man Jesus Christ who, because He is shown to be the revealing Word of God also in respect of the true nature of man, is treated as the source of our knowledge of man as God created him. (1964: 123)

This summary raises a number of important questions for understanding the nature of Barth's task in III/2. Why does Barth approach anthropology christologically? Does he understand this as an exclusive methodology or would he be open to other approaches to anthropological knowledge? Who is Jesus and what exactly does he reveal about the human person? How can any particular individual play this constitutive role given the tremendous diversity of human nature and reality? What is the precise relationship between Christology and anthropology as theological loci? Is this christological approach sufficient to engage the difficult questions faced by real people or is it merely an idealistic system abstracted from everyday realities? Questions like these raise some of the interesting formal and material issues that need to be answered if we are to appreciate fully Barth's christocentric theology. Although complete answers to these questions lie beyond the scope of this study, the next two chapters will explore some of the implications involved as they analyze the manner in which Barth develops and supports his understanding of human ontology in the context of the anthropological discussions of III/2.[3]

Although Barth divided III/2 into five sections, they address three main issues: the method, the form, and the content of a christological anthropology.[4]

---

[3] While Barth's anthropological discussions are found throughout the *Dogmatics* (particularly in the other parts of vol. III as well as IV/1 and IV/2), III/2 can serve as a useful staging point for any analysis of his anthropology since it is the one place where Barth develops it as a doctrinal locus in its own right. The scope of this work precludes any attempt to address or even to summarize adequately its entire presentation and all the corresponding difficulties. Indeed, as Soucek noted, 'the work is so vast, so full of complex views and illustrations and so subtly shaded, that any attempt to summarise it . . . must run the risk of inadequate and inaccurate interpretation in some respect' (Soucek 1949: 75). But, an understanding of the method and form of Barth's anthropology is absolutely necessary for understanding the content of his anthropology and thus for any meaningful engagement with his approach to human ontology. So, the next two chapters will risk the inadequacies that accompany any attempt to summarize Barth's theology as necessary for the discussions that will follow later in the study.

[4] There is a danger to characterizing Barth's theology in this way if it is understood to indicate a division rather than a distinction between form and content. As the following

In the first section (§43), 'Man as a Problem of Dogmatics', Barth lays out his basic methodological moves. Here he articulates the methodological principles that will guide the development of the entire work. The form of Barth's anthropology is the topic of the second section (§44), 'Man as the Creature of God'. There Barth considers the person and work of Jesus and the corresponding revelation of the basic criteria for true humanity. Finally, Barth lays out the content of his anthropology in the final three sections covering, respectively, humanity's essential relationality (§45), the human person as the soul of her body (§46), and the temporality of human existence (§47).[5]

In order to understand his discussion of human ontology in §46, then, it will be necessary to appreciate the formal, material, and methodological moves that he makes in the earlier sections. Consequently, in the next two chapters we will set the stage for our later discussion of ontology by first considering (1) the basic shape and methodology of Barth's christological anthropology and (2) the nature of Barth's christocentrism and its relationship to interdisciplinary dialogue.

II. The Theanthropological Twist in Barth's Doctrine of Creation

Understanding Barth's theological anthropology requires placing it in the context of his overall doctrine of creation. In developing this doctrine, Barth argues counterintuitively that the proper object of a theology of creation cannot be creation itself. There are three important steps in the way Barth formulates this proposition. First, he contends that the concept of a creation-in-itself is an improper abstraction with no concrete reality since the term *creation* necessarily implies a *creator* (III/2, 3). As Barth argues extensively in III/1, 'The Work of Creation', all creation receives both its existence and essence

---

discussion should make clear, an inseparable relationship obtains between the formal elements of Barth's theology and more material considerations. As Stuart McLean observed, for Barth 'form and content are bound up together and should be separated only for the purpose of speech. Even then, speech itself must constantly attempt to reveal that they are together' (1981: 12; see also Balthasar 1992: 47–55; and McCormack 1999: 476–77). Consequently, the distinction as used here is not intended to deny this inseparability but rather to recognize that in III/2 Barth addresses primarily formal issues (the methodology and criteria of anthropology) before moving on to more properly material ones.

[5] The discussion of the content of Barth's theology in Chapter 3 will be limited to Barth's consideration of human ontology in §46. There are a number of other studies of Barth's theology that provide useful insights into his understanding of humanity's essential relationality (e.g. Deddo 1994: 183–222; Price 2002; McLean 1981; and Miell 1989: 541–55) and his arguments for the necessary temporality of the human person (e.g. Roberts 1991; Camfield 1950; Runia 1958; and Jenson 1969).

as 'an absolute gift of God' and thus stands in a relationship of 'absolute dependence' to God and is necessarily determined by His grace (III/1, 15).[6] The essential relatedness of creation to God means that creation cannot be properly understood apart from its revelation in the Word since no phenomenological consideration of creation can reveal this necessary determination (III/1, 3–41).[7] True knowledge of creation – that is, knowledge of its absolute dependence on the Creator – is, therefore, an act of faith. Properly speaking, knowledge of God is prior to knowledge of creation.[8]

That creation-in-itself is not the proper focus of a theology of creation, however, involves a second important point for Barth: the centrality of anthropology for a properly theological understanding of creation. Barth devoted the second portion of III/1 to an extended discussion of the relationship between creation and covenant. In it, he famously argued that creation is 'the external basis of the covenant', and covenant 'the internal basis of creation' (III/1, 94–95). In other words, God's decision to establish a covenantal relationship between himself and something other than himself stands as the eternal ground for the creation and continued existence of all creaturely reality. Creation, therefore, exists as the corresponding 'presupposition' on the basis of which and the 'theatre' within which this covenantal relationship becomes a reality (III/1, 96–99). However, the covenantal love of God, though encompassing all of creation, finds its 'centre' (III/1, 20) and clearest expression in humanity, who alone was created to be God's true covenantal counterpart and thus 'represents the secret of the creature' (III/1, 18).[9] The logic of Barth's argument is rather simple: if creation can only be understood on the basis of the covenant and if the covenant centers on God's relationship with humanity, then creation can only be understood in terms

---

[6] Of course, as Balthasar points out, Barth's notion of 'absolute dependence' is markedly different from Schleiermacher's well-known approach (1992: 225; see also Webster 2001: 61–62).

[7] Barth thus argues that even one's knowledge that heaven and earth are created realities is part of the 'credo' and thus an act of faith (III/1, 3).

[8] George Hendry argues that Barth exhibits a dependence on Kant's philosophy at this point, but fails to demonstrate anything more than a formal similarity (1984: 219–20).

[9] The rest of creation has its own relationship with the creator but the 'inner mystery' of this relationship has not been revealed to humans and can only be extrapolated on the basis of the God–human relationship (III/2, 18). Some have indicated that this way of understanding the relationship between the doctrines of creation and anthropology indicates a denigration of creation (cf. Green 2004). On the contrary, however, Barth strongly affirms that other creatures have 'their own dignity and right' as they exist 'in the secret of their own relation to the Creator' (III/2, 4). Our approach to creation cannot be characterized by 'blindness, indifference, or disparagement' in a misguided attempt to abstract humanity from its essential relationship to creation (III/2, 4), even as we recognize the distinction between them revealed through humanity's role as God's covenantal counterpart.

of this theanthropic relationship (cf. Barth 1982a: 11).[10] This means that, contrary to common practice, anthropology cannot be approached as a subset of a larger theology of creation but must rather be its focal point.[11]

The theanthropic turn in Barth's argument, though, is itself grounded in the third and most fundamental aspect of his methodology; just as a theology of creation is grounded in theanthropology, so theanthropology is grounded in Christology. As creation cannot be understood apart from Creator neither can humanity be abstracted from its relationship to God.[12] This means that humanity 'is ontically and therefore noetically dependent on the fact that he is not without God' (III/2, 345).[13] But, as will be addressed later in this chapter, the relationship between God and humanity is fully revealed only in the person of Jesus, who is the unique union of true deity and true humanity.[14] Thus, it is in the person of Jesus Christ alone 'that God Himself has revealed the relationship between Creator and creature – its basis, norm and meaning' (III/1, 25). While Barth can affirm that the human

---

[10] Webster notes that, although some argue that this theanthropic turn took place late in Barth's theological development, it actually predates the *Dogmatics* by at least a decade (2001c: 58).

[11] It is at this point that Barth engages in his famous polemic against cosmological world-views (III/2, 4–13), contending that theology is not properly concerned with cosmologies (theories on the structure and dynamics of the total universe), but with the relationship between humanity and God, which is the primary theme of Scripture (III/2, 19). Although cosmological accounts are necessary aspects of our understanding of the world, even the Bible adopted the cosmological beliefs of the surrounding cultures (III/2, 7–8), theology must critically appropriate such world-views without sanctioning them or becoming overtly identified with them (III/2, 8–10).

[12] For Barth, 'man must be understood as a being which from the very outset stands in some kind of relationship to God' (III/2, 72). Barth's contention that covenantal relationality is of constitutive significance for understanding human nature plays a particularly prominent role in his understanding of the *imago Dei*. He argues that humans are made in the image of God inasmuch as they are beings-in-relationship and therefore model the intra-relationality of the Triune God (see III/1, 184–91). Humanity's creation as male and female, according to Barth, is the ultimate demonstration of humanity's relationality (III/1, 288–310; cf. also III/2, 285–324) and is thus the 'climax and conclusion' of creation (III/1, 288) as the primary model of the covenantal relationship between God and humanity (III/1, 311–21).

[13] The fact that, for Barth, ontic dependence necessitates noetic dependence is one of the key elements of his theology in general, and thus his anthropology in particular. Brown, however, disputes that there are any good exegetical, logical, or metaphysical reasons for maintaining the necessity of this connection (1980: 533–49). Though he may be correct in his contention that the connection between ontic and noetic dependence might not be as strong as Barth believes them to be, Brown's argument that this constitutes a decisive undermining of Barth's view on natural theology is less convincing. Even without basing noetic dependence on ontic dependence, it seems perfectly reasonable to maintain Barth's view that the sovereign freedom and mystery of God necessitate noetic dependency (see II/1, 63–254).

person, as God's counterpart, is 'at the heart of the cosmos' (III/1, 28), it is ultimately Jesus who is the full revelation of the God–creature relationship.[15] Jesus alone is 'the Fulfiller of the covenant' (III/1, 332) and thus 'the meaning and end of creation' (III/1, 377). This christocentric turn indicates that as creation cannot be understood apart from the knowledge of the God–creature relationship manifested in humanity, neither can humanity be understood apart from the God–human relationship manifested in Jesus Christ. So, for Barth, 'the man Jesus . . . is the source [*Quelle*] of our knowledge of the nature of man [*menschlichen Wesens*] as created by God' (III/2, 41).[16] This 'means nothing more nor less than the founding of anthropology on Christology' (III/2, 44).[17]

III. The Ontological Determination of Human Persons in Jesus Christ

Barth's conviction that anthropology must be founded on Christology is clearly evidenced in III/2 where each section begins with an explicit consideration of God's self-revelation in Jesus and its import for anthropology.[18] While the human person might be a mystery to herself, the Word provides true and reliable insight into her nature and the reality of her existence. On this basis Barth begins developing the constructive element of his theological anthropology by stating his central anthropological principle:

> The ontological determination [*ontologische Bestimmung*] of humanity is grounded in the fact that one man [*Menschen*] among all others is the man [*der Mensch*] Jesus. So long as we select any other starting point for our study, we shall reach only the phenomena of the human. We are condemned to abstractions so long as our attention is riveted

---

[14] Even a brief consideration of the substance of Barth's Christology lies outside the scope of this thesis. I will thus follow Hunsinger's account of the basically Chalcedonian nature of Barth's Christology (2000b: 131–47). Hunsinger disagrees with studies that find Barth's Christology to be essentially Alexandrian (e.g. Hartwell 1964: 78–79; and Waldrop 1984) or Antiochene (e.g. McIntyre 1966, esp. 154 f.). According to Hunsinger, Barth believes that the nature of the incarnation is such that humans cannot conceptualize both Christ's full-deity and his full-humanity at the same time. Consequently, it becomes necessary to juxtapose both Alexandrian and Antiochene approaches in an attempt to do justice to the Chalcedonian faith.

[15] Barth balances the epistemological orientation of this argument by noting that Jesus is also the ontological ground of creation as its creator and preserver (III/1, 28).

[16] Whether he is the *only* source of such knowledge is a question that will be addressed in the next chapter.

[17] For a similar perspective, see A. Torrance 2004: 205–06.

[18] See Shults 2003: 120.

as it were on other men, or rather on man in general, as if we could learn about real man [*wirklich Menschen*] from a study of man in general, and in abstraction from the fact that one man among all others is the man Jesus. In this case we miss the one Archimedean point given us beyond humanity, and therefore the one possibility of discovering the ontological determination of man. Theological anthropology has no choice in this matter. It is not yet or no longer theological anthropology if it tries to pose and answer the question of the true being of man [*des Menschen Sein und Wesen*] from any other angle. (III/2, 132)

Thus, the question of Ps. 8, 'What is man?' is answered in Christ, and he alone must be the focus of any attempt to see humanity as it really is, '*in concreto*' (III/2, 41). Human nature, therefore, is not something that can be known as 'a neutral point [*neutraler Punkt*]' but rather must be 'explained' by Jesus as it is manifested in his concrete existence (III/2, 59).

a. Grounded in the Decree: The Subject and Object of the Eternal Decree of Election

What does it mean to say that 'the ontological determination of humanity is grounded' in the man Jesus? For Barth this means first that humanity is ontologically determined by election: 'the being of man as a being with Jesus rests upon the election of God' (III/2, 142).[19] In other words, 'To be a man is thus to be with the One who is the true and primary Elect of God' (III/2, 145).[20] Understanding the ontological determination of humanity will therefore require that we spend some time considering Barth's doctrine of election.[21]

Barth developed his rather unique approach to the doctrine of election primarily in II/2.[22] His 'fundamental thesis', according to Bruce McCormack, was that 'Jesus Christ is both the Subject of election and its Object, the electing God and the elect human' (2000: 93).[23] Affirming Jesus as the 'Elected'

---

[19] Berkouwer comments that the epistemological centrality of Christ has been a common approach to theological anthropology, but that the real turn in Barth's anthropology is this turn to the ontological centrality of Christ's humanity (1962: 92). He goes on to argue, however, that Barth is not consistently christological on this point. He contends that Barth grounds his anthropology both on its ontological determination in Christ and on the idea of its absolute creaturely dependence. It is not clear, though, that Barth would be able to distinguish so neatly between creaturely dependence and christological determination with respect to the human person such that he would perceive them to be independent grounds for his anthropology. The criticism also fails to realize that Barth's christocentrism requires all anthropological thinking to *begin* with Christology, not that it must remain there.

[20] John Thompson helpfully points out that even though Barth understands election christocentrically we should recognize the significant pneumatological aspects of his presentation as well (1991: 34–35).

meant not only that the man Jesus had been elected as Messiah and that his election was soteriologically foundational to that of other human beings, who are also among the elect, but, more importantly, that Jesus was 'the sole Object [*der Gegesntand*] of this good-pleasure' (II/2, 104) such that all others are only 'elect' in so far as they are 'united in Him and represented by Him' (II/2, 105).[24] So, 'Jesus Christ ... is not merely one of the elect but *the* elect of God. From the very beginning (from eternity itself), as elected man He does not stand alongside the rest of the elect, but before and above them as the One who is originally and properly the Elect [*der ursprünglich und eignetlich Erwählte*]' (II/2, 116). Strictly speaking, then, only Jesus is the elected one; all others are elect only insofar as they are incorporated into his primal election. By affirming that Jesus is also the 'Elector' (II/2, 105), Barth

---

[21] As Ebneter rightly notes, then, Barth's anthropological christocentrism cannot be understood in isolation from his doctrine of election (1952: 11). Our task at this point, however, cannot be a detailed analysis of election itself, as this lies beyond the scope of the study. Rather, we will simply summarize Barth's understanding of election as a means of understanding how he develops and applies it in III/2. For more comprehensive discussions of Barth's doctrine of election see Cunningham 1995; McCormack 1999: 470–93 and 2000: 92–110; F. Clarke 1984: 229–45; Colwell 1989; McDowell 2003a; O'Neill 2004: 311–26.

[22] In the preface to this work, as in III/2, Barth acknowledged that his view of election left 'the framework of theological tradition to a far greater extent' than the earlier parts of his doctrine of God (II/2, x). But he felt this was necessary both because of his reading of Scripture (see II/2, 35; cf. also Cunningham 1995: 11) and because he thought that even when earlier theologians acknowledged both the importance of election and of thinking christologically about election, they failed to carry through this christological interpretation sufficiently (II/2, 60–76; 147–54). They thus ended up with a doctrine of predestination that was mired in mystery at both ends: the *decretum absolutum* of a hidden God and an unknown and unknowable (humanly speaking) number of elect (II/2, 158–61). On the contrary, he asserted that a true knowledge of both God and humanity is only possible through the theanthropic relationship grounded in the eternal election of Jesus Christ. Barth thus argued that we cannot know God properly apart from his eternal decision to relate himself to something external to himself (II/2, 6) and that Jesus Christ is himself the eternal and irreversible self-determination of this relationship (II/2, 7).

[23] See II/2, 9–11; 94–145, esp. 103–05.

[24] For Barth, understanding Jesus as the primary object of election was required by the ἐν αὐτῷ of Eph. 1.4 (II/2, 105). So he argues: 'From the very beginning (from eternity itself), there are no other elect together with or apart from Him, but, as Eph. 1.4 tells us, only 'in' Him. 'In Him' does not simply mean with Him, together with Him, in His company. Nor does it mean only through Him, by means of that which He as elected man can be and do for them. 'In Him' means in His person, in His will, in His own divine choice, in the basic decision of God which He fulfils over against every man. What singles Him out from the rest of the elect, and yet also, and for the first time, unites Him with them, is the fact that as elected man He is also the electing God, electing them in His own humanity' (II/2, 116–17).

argued for the pre-existence of the man Jesus in union with the eternal Logos and thus as the subject of God's act of election.[25] Since the man Jesus *is* the eternal act of election, he exists in an eternal union with the Logos and as such is the Subject as well as the Object of election (II/2, 94).[26]

Both of these points are important for understanding the constitutive relationship between Jesus' election and the rest of humanity. Jesus is the ontological determination of humanity because 'His election includes ours within itself and because ours is grounded in His. We are elected together with Him in so far as we are elected "in Him"' (II/2, 120). Thus, the God–human relationship that is determinative for what it means to be human is eternally grounded in 'this one man Jesus' whom 'God puts at the head and in the place of all other men' (II/2).[27] He alone is able to ground humanity in this relationship and to secure it from surrendering this essential determination.[28] The ontological decisiveness of Jesus as Elect, however, is itself grounded on his status as the Elector. That Jesus' election is ontologically decisive and not simply the epistemological manifestation of a general election is established by the fact that 'He Himself is the One who elects us' (II/2, 115). Without his status as Elector, Barth argued, we would not be able to maintain the ontological decisiveness of his election:

> Now without our first assertion we cannot maintain such a position. For where can Jesus Christ derive the authority and power to be Lord and Head of all others, and how can these others be elected 'in Him', and how can they see their election in Him the first of the elect, and how can they find in His election the assurance of their own, if He is only the object of election and not Himself its Subject. (II/2, 116)

---

[25] Barth supports the pre-existence of the man Jesus primarily through his exegesis of Jn 1.1–2 (II/2, 95–99). There he contends that the οὗτος of v. 2 refers proleptically to the incarnate Word (v. 14) about whom John testified (v. 15) and that this, therefore, identifies the man Jesus in a pre-nativity union with the eternally existing Logos (II/2, 98). For a good discussion of some of the objections that have been raised to Barth's understanding of the pre-existence of the man Jesus see J. Thompson 1976: 261–64.

[26] This is the basis of Barth's famous rejection of a *Logos asarkos* (cf. IV/1, 52–53; see also J. Thompson 1976: 256).

[27] According to Jüngel this 'primal decision constitutes the primal relationship of God to man and in this primal relationship there takes place the "primal history" in which *God already has a relationship* to man *before* all creation' (2001: 88–89; cf. II/2, 12–13).

[28] As Barth says elsewhere, 'In Christian doctrine . . . we have always to take in blind seriousness . . . that our life is hid with Christ in God. With Christ: never at all apart from him, never at all independently of him, never at all in and for itself. We as human beings never at all exist in ourselves. . . . We exist as human beings in Jesus Christ and in him alone. . . . The being and nature of human beings in and for themselves as independent bearers of and independent predicate, have, by the revelation of Jesus Christ, become an abstraction which can be destined only to disappear' (II/1, 149).

24

FROM CHRISTOLOGY TO ANTHROPOLOGY

Barth thus concludes that Jesus is 'the original and all-inclusive election; the election which is absolutely unique', but that this election is only 'universally meaningful and efficacious, because it is the election of Him who Himself elects' (II/2, 117).[29]

> To the extent that he is with Jesus and therefore with God, man himself is a creature elected in the divine election of grace, i.e., elected along with or into Jesus. He is elected to the extent that he derives from God, which means concretely that his being rests upon the election of God, namely, the election of the one man Jesus. . . . He is elected to the extent that as man he is a creature whom the election of the man Jesus . . . immediately concerns. (III/2, 145)

---

[29] A number of concerns have been raised regarding Barth's doctrine of election. O'Neill usefully summarizes three of the most common as (1) its Scriptural basis; (2) its universalistic implications; and (3) concerns about whether it vitiates human history and agency (2004: 311). With respect to the first, Cunningham correctly asserts that at the very least we must recognize that Barth's primary concern was to remain exegetically faithful (1995: cf. esp. 9–11). And as John Thompson points out, even if one disagrees with Barth's exegesis, it must be acknowledged that his interpretation is at least exegetically tenable (1976: 266). Regarding universalism, despite Barth's strong disavowals of a necessary universalism in his theology (e.g. II/2, 295, 416–19, 476–77), his theology has been consistently accused of resulting in just such a position (e.g. Berkouwer 1956: 262–96; Brunner 1951: 123–35; Ebneter 1952: 37–38; and more recently McGrath 1997: 456). A number of studies, however, have argued convincingly that Barth's doctrine of election can be maintained alongside his agnosticism regarding the *apokastasis* question (cf. esp. Bettis 1967: 423–436, Colwell 1989: 231–69, and O'Neill 2004; cf. also Torrance 1990: 319–20 and Hartwell 1964: 110–12). The final concern involves that of 'narrowing' everything to Christology such that it vitiates creaturely history and agency of real meaning (Balthasar 1992: 242; cf. also Come 1963: 152–57; Willis 1971: 236 ff.; McGrath 1986: 105–06; Muers 1999: 268–69; Deegan 1961; and Biggar 1993: 5). Colin Gunton suggests that the problem is an imbalance in Barth's theology caused by inadequate Trinitarian and pneumatological views and a certain level of unsophistication in his development of human freedom (1989: 55 ff.; cf. Macken 1990). A number of studies, however, particularly those by John Webster, have demonstrated that these concerns revolve around a failure to appreciate the dialectic involved in Barth's redefinition of human freedom as a determinate correspondence of freedom for God (see McLean 1981: 60–62; McCormack 2000: 106; and J. Webster 1995; 1998). Several theologians also argue that this criticism misses Barth's understanding of the 'enhypostatic' nature of humanity's relationship to Jesus; as Jesus' human nature exists enhypostatically in union with the Word so all human nature exists enhypostatically in union with Jesus (e.g. Dalferth 1989: 29; Webster 1998: 88–89; I. Davidson, 2001: 129–54; and Tanner 2001: 56–58). The ontological determination of the human person in Christ, therefore, does not vitiate human freedom any more than the incarnation vitiates the freedom of Jesus (see Webster 1998: 89 n. 39, for resources on the anhypostatic/enhypostatic formula).

The christological orientation of Barth's doctrine of election, thus establishes Jesus' election as the ontological determination of all humanity.

In III/2 the ontological decisiveness of Jesus' election serves as the cornerstone for Barth's christological anthropology: 'The formal definition that the being of man [*menschliche Sein*] derives from God is given a first and material content when we recall the gracious divine election of the man Jesus' (III/2, 145). Barth grounds the centrality of election for theological anthropology on the premise that since (1) Jesus is the primary object and subject of election, and thus the primary revelation of the relationship between God and humanity, and (2) Jesus alone has lived a sinless life in response to and fulfillment of that relationship, then Jesus is the sole revelation and guarantor of human nature. Having already unpacked the first of these premises to some extent, we shall move on in the next section to consider the significance of the second.

b. Continuing in Sin: The Covenantal Faithfulness of Christ as the Guarantor of Human Nature

Barth's understanding of Christ's ontological decisiveness involves more than just his doctrine of election. Jesus is also ontologically decisive in that his sinless human nature provides the epistemological and ontological basis for the postlapsarian continuity of human nature.

Barth is very clear that all humans are sinners and thus stand in contradiction to their created essence; the human person is a 'corrupter [*Verderber*] of his own nature' (III/2, 26). The 'perversion and corruption' [*Verkehrung und Verderbnis*] (III/2, 26) produced by sin affects human nature at such a deep level that no aspect of human existence can escape its influence and, consequently, must be addressed in any attempt to understand humanity: 'The fact and knowledge of sin are far too important for us to try to abstract from it in any way . . . .. To do so we should have to see human nature very differently from the way in which it is disclosed to us by the divine revelation' (III/2, 36).

However, Barth is also very clear that despite the overwhelming reality of sin, God's gracious love ensures that humans are and will always remain human. Because human nature has been created by God for relationship with himself, it cannot be destroyed and made 'unreal' – human nature is thoroughly corrupt, but it cannot be annihilated. The gift of humanity cannot be 'blotted out' by sin as though sin were capable of destroying God's creation and making some new creature (III/1, 53). And therefore

> if we are attentive and loyal to the Word of God, we must not suppose that in describing him as a sinner we have spoken the first and final word about this real man. For it is not the case that because the creaturely being of man may be known by us only in its sinful determination,

it is not real and knowable in any other way, as though human nature had been changed into its opposite, and by sinning man had in some sense suffered a mutation [*umgeschaffen*] into a different kind of creature. (III/2, 37)

Barth was always careful to affirm that sin is more than a merely accidental attribute of human nature.[30] For Barth, however, the grace of God always remains the primary category for understanding humanity; sin is always secondary (III/2, 32). Though we must consider humanity in its sinfulness, 'we must not absolutise sin' (III/2, 37). God's gracious love thus ensures that humanity continues to be humanity even after it has fallen into the 'self-contradiction [*Selbstwiderspruch*]' (III/2, 31) of sin.[31]

The emphasis on grace for the postlapsarian continuity of human nature, however, leads ultimately to the incarnate Christ as the ultimate expression of God's grace. The continued existence of human nature, despite its pervasive sinfulness, is grounded in the faithfulness of the man Jesus to the covenantal relationship for which he has been eternally elect. Regardless of the ramifications of sin, Jesus remains the one human who has not fallen into the self-contradiction of sin and thus continues to be rightly related to God as his covenantal partner (i.e. human).[32] 'Thus', Barth argues, 'human nature in Jesus is the reason and the just foundation for the mercy in which God has turned to our human nature' (III/2, 48).

---

[30] Barth was thus in basic agreement with Matthias Flacius that sin could rightly be viewed as a substantial rather than a merely accidental characteristic of the human person (III/2, 27). Although we will see that Barth was careful not to conclude from this that postlapsarian humans were of a different nature and that sin had thus 'created' a new entity (something that sin is completely unable to do), he nonetheless wanted to view sin as having serious ontological (rather than merely existential) ramifications (III/2, 28; Ebneter 1952).

[31] Although Barth affirms the ontological continuity of human nature after the fall, this does not constitute its epistemological availability and thus cannot be used as the basis of a natural theology. As we will discuss later in the chapter, the problem of sin constitutes a humanly insurmountable block to human self-knowledge (cf. III/2, 29–41).

[32] Barth does not see Jesus' sinlessness as an ontological difference between his humanity and ours – such a difference would mean that he was not human as we are – but rather affirmed that Jesus took on our human nature as it stands under the contradiction of sin (I/2, 151 ff). Nevertheless, Jesus, as empowered by the Holy Spirit, lived a truly human life in relationship to God as his covenantal partner and so lived a sinless life, though standing in solidarity with the human race under God's judgment on sin, (see Thompson 1986a: 29). Von Balthasar notes that the sinlessness of Jesus thus 'guarantees human nature an unbroken continuity' and ensures that man does not fall into irredeemable chaos (1992: 116). It is, therefore, the continuity of human nature manifest in the covenantal faithfulness of Jesus Christ that ensures the continued availability of real human nature for theological consideration.

Christ's sinlessness has both epistemological and ontological significance for the determination of true humanity. Epistemologically, Jesus is the one in whom we see true humanity unspoiled by sin: 'Always and in every respect it is primarily and originally in this man that we see God's attitude to sinful man to be of such a kind that it maintains and discloses the interrelation of sin and grace' (III/2, 42). Similarly,

> [t]he attitude of God in which the faithfulness of the Creator and therefore the unchanging relationship of the human being created by Him are revealed and knowable is quite simply His attitude and relation to the man Jesus; His election of this man; His becoming and remaining one with Him. (III/2, 41)

So, 'true man, the true nature behind our corrupted nature [*die Natur in unserer Unnatur*], is not concealed but revealed in the person of Jesus, and in His nature we recognise our own, and that of every man' (III/2, 43). The sinlessness of Christ thus establishes him and the sole source of any real knowledge about the nature of true humanity.

His sinlessness, however, has ontological significance as well. As 'the penetrating spearhead [*eingedrungene Spitze*] of the will of God', Jesus is not only the one in whom 'the will of God is already fulfilled and revealed' but also the one who guarantees that there will be a 'wider fulfilment of the will of God and its final consummation' (III/2, 43). Jesus became the guarantor of a humanity that is free of the self-contradiction of sin and is, therefore, 'secure from non-being [*Nichtsein*]' (III/2, 144) as it rests in the ontological determination of Jesus' election. 'He alone is the archetypal man [*der Erste*] whom all threatened and enslaved men and creatures must follow. He alone is the promise for these many, the Head of a whole body' (III/2, 144). Jesus, therefore, does not simply reveal the will of God and the nature of true humanity, but guarantees, despite the depravations of sin, that these will be realized. 'In virtue of the exoneration from sin validly effected in Jesus, we may count on this nature of ours and its innocence as we could not otherwise do. This judicial pardon gives us the courage and shows us the way to think about man as God created him. It is the true ground of theological anthropology' (III/2, 49).

c. Confronted by the Other: The Summons to Being

There is one last factor that must be taken into account in understanding the ontological decisiveness of Jesus Christ for all human beings. Not only is he the 'primarily and originally' elected human being (III/2, 42), and the one human being who maintained the covenantal faithfulness of his relationship to God and thus secured human nature against the threat of non-being, but he is also the summons by which God encounters human beings and constitutes them as his covenantal co-partners.[33]

Jesus is the incarnation of the Word of God.[34] As such, he is in his very existence the 'divine Counterpart [*Gegenüber*] of every man' (III/2, 134) and the declaration of God's gracious response to the danger of non-being surrounding humanity (III/2, 148–49). That 'this One' has entered the sphere of humanity means that all humans 'are confronted by the divine Other [*Gegenüber*]' in an ontologically decisive way (III/2, 133–34).[35] Thus, 'To be a man is to be in the particular sphere of the created world in which the Word of God is spoken and sounded' (III/2, 149). This means that our understanding of humanity has to be oriented around the fact that, 'When we say "man" [*Mensch*] we have to remember above all that there is one man among many who is this Word, and in respect of the many that it is in their sphere that this Word is to be found' (III/2, 149). The divine summons that is an inseparable aspect of Jesus' existence claims all humans as the sphere within which they are encountered by the divine Other. Humanity must, therefore, be defined as 'the creaturely being which is addressed, called and summoned by God' (III/2, 149).

For Barth, the ontologically decisive nature of this summons is such that humanity must be understood from the very beginning as that which has been summoned:

> Man *is* the being which is addressed in this way by God. He does not become this being. He does not first have a kind of nature which he is then addressed by God. He does not have something different and earlier and more intrinsic, a deeper stratum [*tiefere Schicht*] or more original substance of being [*ursprüngliche Substanz*], in which he is without or prior to the Word of God. He is from the very outset, as we may now say, 'in the Word of God'. (III/2, 149–50)

Humanity cannot be properly understood, then, apart from properly recognizing the subject and content of the divine summons. The subject being God himself as the one who addresses humanity through His Word, and the content as the declaration of God's graciousness and covenantal faithfulness

---

[33] To be sure, Barth's exposition of the summons and its determinative significance occurs entirely within his discussion of the *content* of anthropology and is an issue that he does not at all raise with respect to its methodological or formal implications. But, given what he says about the summons and its relationship to election, it seems proper to include a brief discussion of this topic here.

[34] Eschewing *ensarkos* and *asarkos* language, Barth describes the incarnation in terms of an *analogia relationis*: 'All this is concretely expressed in the fact that the man Jesus is the Word of God; that He is to the created world and therefore *ad extra* what the Son of God as the eternal Logos is within the triune being of God' (III/2, 147).

[35] According to Barth, this encounter means that 'every man in his place and time is changed, that is, he is something other than what he would have been if this One had not been man too' (III/2, 133).

in his desire to establish a relationship with that which is other than himself in and through Jesus Christ.

In Barth's theology, then, Jesus Christ is of decisive significance as the determination of all human beings.[36] He grounds this in (1) the primordial election of Jesus Christ as both Subject and Object in which other humans are included insofar as they are in union with him; (2) the covenantal faithfulness and corresponding sinlessness of Jesus Christ which establishes, both epistemologically and ontologically, the postlapsarian continuity and security of human nature; and (3) the summons of the divine Word by which humans are constituted as humans insofar as they are the recipients of the divine address. Having thus arrived at an understanding of what it means for Barth that Jesus is 'the ontological determination of humanity', it remains in the next section to consider how this proposal shapes Barth's actual approach to theological anthropology.

IV. *The Methodological Framework for a Christological Anthropology*

This christocentric orientation constitutes the basic theological and methodological presupposition of Barth's theological anthropology. But it still remains to determine the precise nature of Barth's anthropological methodology. This section will thus seek to determine the significance of Barth's christocentrism for the actual construction of his theological anthropology. Since the task of the next chapters will be the specific application of this methodology, this section will merely provide its basic outlines as a framework for understanding the later discussions.

a. Like Us, but Different: Jesus' Unique Relation to the Father

Throughout the *Dogmatics* Barth consistently maintains that Jesus Christ is both fully divine and fully human.[37] The full and true humanity of Jesus and its ontological decisiveness for all humans, as we have seen, is the guiding idea of Barth's theological anthropology, the heart of his entire exposition. Methodologically, however, Barth must address the fact that 'there can be no question of a direct equation of human nature as we know it in ourselves

---

[36] It should be clear from this discussion that the 'ontological connection' between Jesus and humanity holds for all human persons and not simply those who are members of the Christian community (IV/2, 275).

[37] Barth has occasionally been understood to mean that Jesus' full humanity was a general rather than a particular human nature (e.g. Muers 1999: 265–80). I. Davidson attributes the origin of this interpretation to F. W. Marquardt, but he contends that Barth's depiction of the autonomous character of Jesus' humanity precludes such an interpretation 2001: 144–45; cf. also Diem 1976: 121–38).

with the human nature of Jesus, and therefore of a simple deduction of anthropology from Christology' (III/2, 47). Although Jesus is fully human, theology 'must not fail to appreciate how different are His nature and ours' (III/2, 49).

Barth grounds this difference ultimately in the fact that the human nature of Jesus 'is determined by a relation between God and Himself such as has never existed between God and us, and never will exist' (III/2, 49). It is true that God has eternally chosen to exist in relationship with human beings and that this relationship is decisive for human nature, but that relationship is mediated through Jesus such that our fellowship with God utterly depends on our fellowship with Jesus Christ. As discussed earlier, Jesus alone is 'primarily and truly' the elect of God who fulfills the covenantal relationship to which all humans have been summoned; thus, 'If we too are elected, we are only the members of His body' (III/2, 49). So, Jesus stands in a relationship with God that is completely unique to him and not shared, except mediately, by any other human being.

Barth traces the difference between Jesus' humanity and ours established by this unique relationship along three lines. Since each of them is based on considerations addressed in previous sections, we will deal with them rather briefly. First, since our essential relationship with God, and thus our very nature as humans, is mediated through Jesus, he stands as the original of which we are merely copies (III/2, 50).[38] It is with respect to Jesus that

---

[38] Berkouwer objected to Barth's presentation of the ontological decisiveness of Jesus on the basis of the biblical portrayal of the incarnation: 'The Incarnation is described as consanguinity *with us*. Barth, however, formulates the matter in the opposite way, so that Jesus does not participate in our nature, but *we in His*' (1962: 95). He probably raises this objection in light of Barth's statement that Jesus does not 'partake of humanity' but that 'humanity must partake of him' (III/2, 59). But Barth elsewhere states rather explicitly that the incarnation 'means first and generally that he became man, true and real man, participating in the same human essence and existence, the same human nature and form, the same historicity that we have' (I/2, 147). Even after his assertion in III/2 he speaks of Christ assuming human nature in its historical and sinful existence (IV/2, 25). It thus appears that Barth has no problems speaking of the Word assuming and participating in 'our' nature. The important point is to realize that Barth understands human nature primarily in terms of a being's concrete relationship to God (cf. W. Johnson 1997: 157). To become human, then, is to enter into the history of God's covenantal relationship with that which is other to himself. Barth's concern in III/2, however, is to be clear that Jesus cannot be understood in terms of the 'specific determinations and features of humanity' as though they formed 'a neutral point' from which we can understand him. Contrarily, he is the one who 'reveals and explains' that those features constitute the possibility of true humanity. Barth, then, is not denying what he elsewhere affirms so clearly, that is, that Jesus assumes true human nature. What he is denying is that this assumption can be construed in such a way that Jesus is understood through an 'objective' and therefore abstract analysis of human nature.

'the decision was made who and what true man is' and he is thus the 'prototype [*Vorbildlichkeit*]' of true humanity (III/2, 50).[39]

Second, Jesus' humanity is differentiated from ours by virtue of his sinlessness. Human nature as we know it is characterized by 'self-contradiction' and 'self-deception' (III/2, 47) while human nature revealed in Jesus demonstrates 'the peace and clarity which are not in ourselves' (III/2, 48). In the incarnation, the 'rent' in our human nature is healed and 'there now remains only the pure and free humanity of Jesus as our own humanity' (III/2, 50).

The difference signaled by Jesus' sinlessness, however, does not signify 'any special quality of His humanity by which He is as it were physically incapable of sin' (III/2, 51). He is not protected from sin by virtue of some 'special capacities or potentialities . . . such as must make Him a totally different being [*andersartigen Wesen*] from us' (III/2, 53).[40] Instead, what preserved Jesus in his sinlessness was the eternal mercy of God which 'wills to maintain itself in vulnerable human nature' (III/2, 51). Thus, although his humanity is of the same nature as ours, it is differentiated from ours in virtue of his unique relationship with God.

Third, Barth contends that Jesus' human nature differs in virtue of its revelatory function: 'in Him human nature is not concealed but revealed in its original and basic form [*urbildlichen und ursprünglichen Gestalt*]' (III/2, 52). Jesus is 'the true Word about man as well as God' (III/2, 52) that becomes available to us, not through our interpretations, but as 'He discloses and explains Himself to us' in his encounter with us (III/2, 53). Barth maintains, then, that Jesus' human nature is different from human nature as we know it in that he is the sinless prototype who reveals true humanity whereas we are the sinful copies who hide true humanity in self-contradiction.

From all of this, then, we must conclude that Barth maintains both the 'complete equality of His manhood with ours' (IV/1, 131), while still maintaining that he is 'man in a different way from what we are'. The difference does not vitiate the similarity since he is 'utterly unlike us as God and utterly like us as man' (IV/1, 131).[41] But this means, 'All the otherness to be noted here is rooted in the fact that as man He is also God; his humanity, therefore, has 'a different status but not a different constitution' than ours (III/2, 53).

---

[39] Barth's use of 'prototype' language suggests that at this point he is very close to the Eastern Orthodox depiction of Jesus in terms of an 'archetype' as 'that which organizes, seals and gives shape to matter, and which simultaneously attracts it towards itself' (Nellas 1987: 33).

[40] Barth argues that any attempt to view Jesus' human nature as constitutionally different from ours is a docetic position that ultimately denies his true humanity (III/2, 54).

[41] Trevor Hart seems to miss Barth on this point when he argues that 'the primary reason for Jesus' humanity being essentially other than ours' is 'not that it is a snapshot of God, and made-over to "look like" God; but rather that it is the first fruits of a new, redeemed humanity in correspondence with God' (1999: 22). If the difference lay

b. The Starting Point, but Not the Ending Point: The Impossibility of Reducing Anthropology to Christology

The similarities and dissimilarities mentioned in the previous section carry methodological consequences. Positively, the similarities indicate that we can derive an understanding of true humanity by considering the humanity of Jesus. Since being fully human means to be like Jesus, theologians must focus on this unique individual, seeking to understand human nature in the light of his distinct reality. Anything incompatible with this picture is '*ipso facto* non-human' (III/2, 226). This methodology can be easily traced through the rest of III/2 as Barth begins each section with an explicit consideration of who Jesus is and the significance that this carries for our knowledge of human nature.

There is a negative dimension, however, that must also be considered. Since Jesus' humanity is substantially dissimilar to ours by virtue of its unique relationship to the Father, it is not possible to move directly from an examination of his nature to truths about the rest of humanity. 'There can be no question, therefore, of a direct knowledge of the nature of man in general from that of the man Jesus' (III/2, 71). So, Barth states explicitly, 'Anthropology cannot be Christology, nor Christology anthropology' (III/2, 71).

For Barth, then, anthropology must be founded on Christology but 'it cannot be deduced from it directly' (III/2, 512).[42] We must rather 'infer from His human nature the character of our own' (III/2, 54) as we seek 'to know indirectly who and what we are from the fact that we live in the same world and

---

solely in the fact that Jesus' humanity was 'a new, redeemed humanity' and ours is not, it would be possible to derive an understanding of true humanity *directly* from Christology. But Barth clearly argues that the 'irremovable difference' between the man Jesus and other humans is 'primarily and decisively the mystery of His identity with God' (III/2, 71). While Jesus is different from us by virtue of his status as the new human and this difference must be taken into account, the primary difference that necessitates an indirect inference from Christology to anthropology is his divine identity.

[42] Because of Barth's emphasis on the methodological implications of Jesus' unique humanity, Gibbs argues that Barth's theology should be viewed as having two foci: Christology *and* anthropology (1963: 132–35). He contends that Barth's way of maintaining the unlikeness of Jesus' humanity is to note, through a comparison of human persons with each other, the ways in which Jesus is different from humanity in general. Thus Barth's anthropology must focus on both Jesus and other humans in order to function effectively. While it is certainly true that Barth's methodology requires that attention be paid both to Jesus and other humans, Gibbs argument downplays the fact that the two moments in Barth's methodology are sequential and hierarchical. The christological move holds ontological, epistemological, and methodological primacy over the anthropological move and we should, therefore, be very cautious about picturing them as two foci in the same elliptical system.

have the same humanity as this man' (III/2, 71–72).[43] This means that Barth's anthropological methodology always involves an indirect extrapolation from Jesus' humanity comprising two moments:

> in our exposition of the doctrine of man we must always look in the first instance at the nature of man as it confronts us in the person of Jesus, and only secondarily – asking and answering from this place of light – at the nature of man as that of every man and all other men. (III/2, 46)

Jesus' humanity is different from ours but it is in that very difference – that is, in virtue of his unique relationship with God – that the likeness is 'disclosed' thus making a christological anthropology possible (III/2, 54).

Barth's christological methodology is thus grounded on the humanity of the man Jesus insofar as it stands in continuity with all other human beings by virtue of their common human nature, and yet in discontinuity by virtue of his unique relationship with God. A properly theological anthropology, therefore, though beginning with a consideration of Jesus' humanity, cannot remain there. In a second move, theological anthropology must extrapolate from truths so derived to truths about the nature of true humanity in general.[44] In the final section, we will see how Barth works through these two moments to establish the basic criteria of a properly theological anthropology.

V. The Criteria of a Christological Anthropology

With §44 Barth moves from the more explicitly methodological concerns of §43 into his exposition of 'the outline and form' of his anthropology. His intent is to develop 'the minimal requirements essential in all circumstances for a concept of man which can be used theologically' (III/2, 72). Given the sinful obscurity of human nature, these minimal requirements cannot be ascertained through any 'known and accepted picture of man' (III/2, 226) but only 'by our Christological basis' (III/2, 72).[45] Recognizing, however, that the uniqueness of Jesus' humanity necessitates an indirect approach to ascertaining the basic criteria of humanity in general, he sets his sights on developing a christological 'foundation' (III/2, 71) from which he can derive 'the criteria' by which we can 'pose the question of the nature

---

[43] For Barth, this is less interpretation than revelation: 'It is not that we interpret Him, but that He discloses and explains Himself to us, that through and in Himself He manifests His nature to us as our own true nature' (III/2, 53).

[44] Barth's commitment to the primacy of the particular over the general is what Hunsinger refers to as Barth's *particularism* and notes as one of the fundamental motifs of his theology (1991: 32–35; cf. III/1, 602).

of man' (III/2, 72). In this section, we will follow the two moments of his christological methodology as he first considers the person of Jesus and then infers from his existence to the existence of human nature in general.

a. Christological Discernment: The Person and Work of Jesus Christ as the Framework for Theological Anthropology

The basic premise by which Barth analyzes Jesus' humanity in order to determine the criteria for a theological anthropology is that the nature of humanity

> is to be observed and established in its history as determined by Him, in its continuous progress as resolved and executed by Him, through a series of conditions, actions, experiences, in the recurrence and confirmation of its identity through all these active modifications of its being. (III/2, 55)

So, the question 'Who is Jesus?' (along with the corresponding question 'What is humanity?') is best answered by looking at the person of Jesus as revealed 'in His work and history' (III/2, 58).[46]

For Barth, however, a consideration of Jesus' work means specifically his saving work since 'the work of Jesus is the work of the Saviour' (III/2, 58). This is because the scriptural portrayal of Jesus' life focuses almost exclusively on its soteriological dimensions, indicating that his work as Savior comprises the entirety of his existence (III/2, 63–64). He does not deny that other aspects of his human existence including his 'inner life' (e.g. his thoughts, emotions, desires, etc.) and his 'physical life' (e.g. his birth, development, everyday activities, etc.) are necessary and important to his humanity (III/2, 328–31). Nonetheless, they can never be an 'autonomous theme in the New Testament' because they are only disclosed to us through his public activity in his work as Savior (III/2, 209).[47] As a result, Barth derives the

---

[45] Barth thus rejects any of the contemporary non-christological accounts of the human person as valid pictures from which we can 'read off that which corresponds and is similar in the man to the humanity of Jesus' (III/2, 226). Such a methodology would imply that the picture of humanity is 'the constant and certain factor' against which we juxtapose 'a variable and uncertain' interpretation of Jesus (III/2, 226). By contrast, Barth consistently maintains that the humanity revealed in Jesus is 'the primary text' that judges and invalidates all other pictures (III/2, 226).

[46] Barth is very cautious with the traditional division between Christ's person and his work (cf. III/2, 61–62). While he recognizes that the distinction is useful 'for the purposes of exposition' he is concerned that theology often acts 'as if this were a real distinction' thereby losing the inseparable relation between them (III/2, 61).

[47] Barth has been repeatedly criticized on this point for so stressing the soteriological work of Christ that he ignores Jesus' human life and thus diminishes the validity and significance of everyday realities. So Baillie famously characterized Barth's theology as

christological criteria of true humanity primarily, if not exclusively, from a consideration of what Jesus' work as Savior reveals about the nature of his humanity.

On this basis, Barth derives six criteria that will comprise the foundation of his christological anthropology (III/2, 68–71):

1. Jesus is 'the one in whose identity with himself we must recognize at once the identity of God with Himself'.
2. God's presence in union with this man is not an abstract state but is 'an action with meaning and purpose' directed toward the salvation of humanity.
3. God's action toward humanity in union with this man 'does not infringe His own sovereignty' but is rather 'an exercise and demonstration of His sovereignty'.
4. Since God's action in union with this man is an expression of His divine sovereignty, the man Jesus 'exists in the Lordship of God . . . in the fulfilment of the divine act of lordship which takes place in it'.

---

a 'Logotheism' because he emphasized primarily the Word of God rather than the 'the Word made flesh' (see Deegan 1961). This same criticism has been leveled more recently by Ng'weshemi who thinks Barth goes so far in this direction that his theology ultimately leads to a docetic understanding of the incarnation (2002: 146; cf. Gunton 1989: 60; and J. Thompson 1986a: 75). While such criticisms may well have been true of Barth's earlier theology (cf. McCormack 1997: 321), they should take into account more carefully Barth's later comments on the significance (albeit of a secondary nature) of the particularities of Jesus' human existence (cf. Deegan 1961: 125). They also fail to consider Barth's understanding of humanity primarily in terms of its covenantal relationship with God where the particularities of human life (e.g. eating, drinking, sleeping, sex, religion, thought, emotion, etc.) serve as the 'field on which human being either takes place or does not take place as history, as the encounter of I and Thou' (III/2, 249). These particularities are important and may be analyzed in their own right. But they cannot contribute to a definition of true humanity, only to a definition of the possibility of true humanity. Finally, these criticisms fail to appreciate the significance of Barth's statements about the particularities of humanity as 'the gift' of God which comprises its special endowment from God with which humanity's election stands in continuity and not contradiction (cf. Barth 1982b: 52–54).

On a similar note, John D. Zizioulas questions whether such an exclusively christocentric orientation can provide any real help for 'each man in his particular existential situation' (1975: 440). While it is true that III/2 focuses primarily on the formal and material development of an account of true humanity rather than its application to existential realities, we must recognize the close connection between this account and its ethical application in III/4. Zizioulas is apparently not convinced that Barth was successful in making this application vitally useful, but we must recognize that existential concerns are not lacking from Barth's anthropology and we should note, along with a number of more recent studies, the prominent role that such concerns played through Barth's theology in his consideration of ethics (e.g. Biggar 1988a; 1993; Webster 1995; 1998).

5. As the one who 'lives within the lordship of God', the man Jesus is himself the history of God's gracious action towards humanity.
6. This man is thus the one who is supremely 'for God' in the totality of his existence.

These six principles thus form the first moment in Barth's christological methodology: a consideration of the unique humanity of Jesus Christ.[48]

b. Anthropological Inference: Moving from Christology to Anthropology

Barth's christological methodology has now provided the basic criteria by which an exposition of human nature in general may properly take place. These criteria are thus 'the limits within which we shall always have to move in our search for a theological concept of man' (III/2, 74). So, he is now ready to move into the second moment of his methodology whereby he seeks to extrapolate from the human nature of Jesus to human nature in general. In the case of each of these six criteria, he thus moves from the criterion unique to Jesus' human nature to the formulation of a criterion that will be true of all other humans. Given the prominent role that these criteria of human nature in general will play in the development of Barth's anthropology, his criticism of other anthropological perspectives, and our own examination of his understanding of human ontology later in the later chapters of this study, it may prove useful to quote these criteria more fully.

1. If it is the case in relation to the man Jesus that in His humanity we are confronted immediately and directly with the being of God, then necessarily ... every man is to be understood, at least mediately and indirectly, to the extent that he is conditioned by the priority of this man, in his relationship with God.
2. If it is the case in relation to the man Jesus that the presence and revelation of God in Him is the history of the deliverance of each and every man, then necessarily ... every man is a being which is conditioned by the fact that ... every man as such must exist and have his being in a history which stands in a clear and recognisable relationship to the divine deliverance enacted in the man Jesus.
3. If it is the case in relation to the man Jesus that in the divine action in favour of each and every man in Him it is also a matter of the freedom,

---

[48] Although it is clear that Barth feels these principles to be biblically justified, and they certainly fit coherently within his theological framework, one unfortunately has to turn elsewhere for the biblical support since he does not address the biblical texts in this context.

the sovereignty and the glory of God, then necessarily ... the being of every man ... is not an end in itself, but has its true determination in the glory of God.
4. If it is the case in relation to the man Jesus that He exists in the lordship ... then necessarily ... it must be said of every man that it is essential to him that as he exists God is over him as his Lord and he himself stands under the lordship of God the Lord.[49]
5. If it is the case in relation to the man Jesus that his being consists wholly in the history in which God is active as man's Deliverer, then necessarily ... the being of every man must consist in this history. Not only his actions but his being will consist in his participation in what God does and means for him. His freedom will be his freedom to decide for God; for what God wills to do and be for him in this history.
6. If the man Jesus is for God ... then necessarily, the being of no other man can be understood apart form the fact that his existence too ... is an event in which he renders God service, in which he for his part is for God (III/2, 73–74).

On the basis of these six criteria we can say that, for Barth, true humanity must be understood as (1) being constituted by the ontological priority of Jesus in his relationship with God; (2) being conditioned by the salvation enacted by Jesus; (3) having its 'true determination' in the glory of God; (4) existing under the Lordship of God; (5) freely corresponding in its proper action to the divine deliverance; and (6) freely rendering service to God as a being who is *for* God.

These six criteria will serve as the standard by which Barth critiques other approaches to anthropology (§44.2) and various ways of construing human ontology (§46). They also constitute the basis upon which Barth develops his understanding of the human person as the being who exists in relationship with God and his fellow-human (§45) as the soul of his body (§46) in his allotted time (§47). The extent to which Barth has been successful in developing a christological anthropology will, therefore, depend significantly on the extent to which he is successful in applying these six criteria to both their critical and constructive tasks.

---

[49] The concept of obedience plays a prominent role in Barth's understanding of true humanity. Grounded in the election of Jesus to be the 'Royal Man' (IV/2, 154–264; cf. Jüngel 1986: 127f.), Barth understands humanity to be 'actualized by faith and obedience' (McCormack 2000: 107) as realized primarily in prayer (cf. also Webster 1995: 208–12). To some extent, then, Barth can argue that we 'choose and realize' ourselves in and through our actions (III/4, 13; cf. also Johnson 1997: 81 and Sonderegger 2000: 258–73). But, as Webster argues, we must also realize that Barth's understanding of the determinacy of human nature and agency 'relativises our acts, preventing them from assuming absolute status in the definition of personhood' (1995: 75).

VI. Conclusion: The Assumption behind All Assumptions

In III/2, Barth has endeavored to develop an anthropology that is based only on Christology as 'the assumption behind all our other assumptions' (III/2, 571). This is not an assumption that we can make based on our experiences or our recognition of the inherent liabilities of all other presuppositions, but instead 'it ought to be clear by now that we can recognize and accept it and count on it and start from it, only as one which has already been made for us' (III/2, 571). As the presupposition that has been revealed to us in the Word, a properly theological anthropology must rest on this presupposition and seek to develop its account of the human person from that perspective alone.

We have seen how Barth develops his understanding of this presupposition through his ground-breaking approach to election and his corresponding understanding of the ontological decisiveness of Jesus Christ for all humanity. On this basis, theology cannot help but recognize the need to ground anthropology on Christology and seek knowledge of ourselves from the one source where true humanity has been revealed.

This does not mean, however, that theology can make a facile move from the human nature of Christ to the nature of humanity in general. Theology can not resolve the problems of anthropology 'merely by introducing the word "God" into the discussion and treating it as an Open Sesame to every problem' (III/2, 551). The hard work of developing a theological account of true humanity lies in the twofold inferential movement from the person and work of Jesus Christ to general truths of human nature. Both moments are essential. Lacking either, theological anthropology fails to be properly theological.

Barth is convinced that this christological approach to the human person not only reveals the nature of true humanity but also 'gives rise to a definite anthropology' (III/2, 552). The christological form of Barth's argument is not an empty shell that merely adopts a christological framework within which the theologian can develop largely non-christological elements. Rather, Barth understands this christological form to be inseparably related to the christological content of a theological anthropology. The remaining sections of III/2 bear out this conviction as Barth seeks to develop the content of his anthropology through a consideration of humanity's essential relatedness with both God and other human beings, the ontological nature of the human person as one constituted as the soul of his body by the Spirit, and the necessary temporality of human life as it has been determined by the eternal God. It remains for us in the next chapters, then, to consider the extent to which the implications of Barth's christocentric anthropology come to bear on contemporary attempts to understand the human person.

3

CONVERSING WITH THE ENEMY? THE PHENOMENA OF THE HUMAN AND THE NATURE OF A CHRISTOLOGICALLY DETERMINED DIALOGUE

I. Engaging the Persistent Rivals of a Christological Anthropology

In the previous chapter we explored Barth's basic anthropological thesis that as the 'ontological determination of humanity' (II/2, 132) Jesus is 'the source of our knowledge of the nature of man as created by God' (III/2, 41). This, however, brings to the forefront of our study the question of the proper source(s) for theological anthropology, and thus the relationship between theology and the non-theological disciplines.

These other disciplines, for Barth, constitute 'a very persistent rival' for theology which utilize significantly different methods, sources, and results (III/2, 21). Aware of the implications raised by these potential rivals, Barth himself poses the question as to whether theological anthropology can 'profit' by the 'methods and results' of these other disciplines (III/2, 22). He thus devotes an entire section (§44.2) entitled 'The Phenomena of the Human' to summarizing and analyzing the contributions and insights of various other approaches to understanding the human person.

The question to ask here, then, is whether Barth views these other approaches merely as 'rivals' against whom a christocentric anthropology can only declare a decisive 'No', or whether there remains a possibility for meaningful dialogue. That is, does Barth's christocentric approach entail that a properly theological anthropology must derive everything that it has to say about the human person from its christological premises, and that it therefore has very little room for significant dialogue with other anthropological perspectives? Given Barth's christological focus, what can we say about other attempts to understand the human person?

Given that many non-theological disciplines have devoted considerable attention to the ontological issues that we will address in the following chapters, the goal of this chapter will be to come to grips with Barth's understanding of what role, if any, the methods and insights of these other disciplines should play in developing a properly theological account of the human person. This chapter will thus comprise three main sections. In the first, we will take a closer look at exactly what it means to refer to Barth as a 'christocentric' theologian. By clarifying this term in the face of some significant ambiguity, we will come to a better appreciation of his christocentric methodology and the opportunities for interdisciplinary dialogue that his theology might offer. In the second section, we will look directly at Barth's discussion of 'the phenomena of the human', paying particularly close attention to his analyses of non-theological anthropologies in §44.2. Finally, having viewed how Barth actually interacts with these other disciplines, we will draw some conclusions regarding the implications of this paragraph for understanding (1) how Barth actually uses his christological criteria in interacting with and evaluating the contributions of non-theological anthropologies and (2) the extent to which Barth is open to dialoging with and learning from these other disciplines.

II. The 'Radically Christocentric' Nature of Karl Barth's Theology[1]

Given the clear emphasis that Barth placed on the centrality of Jesus Christ in Christian theology, describing him as a 'christocentric' theologian would seem like a fairly straightforward proposition. To serve usefully as a prominent characterization of a particular theology, however, as it does with respect to Barth's theology, one would reasonably expect that the term be fairly well defined and understood. But, as J. K. Riches points out, there is an unfortunate ambiguity inherent in the term, which, unless clarified, hinders its usefulness as a theological descriptor and, with respect to Barth's theology especially, results in widespread misunderstanding (1972).

Consequently, in this section we will address the nature of the ambiguity that underlies the application of this term to Barth's theology. We will see how any attempt to identify Barth's theology as christocentric must address both the ambiguity of the term and the specific characteristics of Barth's particular form of christocentrism.

---

[1] This section has been published in a slightly modified form; see Cortez 2007b.

a. Clarifying the Center: The Ambiguity of the Term 'Christocentric'

As Bruce McCormack points out, understanding any form of christocentrism requires that we take into account the difference between its formal and material aspects:

> Formally, it simply means that a Christology stands at the approximate centre of a particular theology, giving to it its characteristic shape and content. That much is true of all so-called 'christocentric theologies'. Materially, however, the meaning of the term can differ widely for the simple reason that the doctrine of Christ which is placed at the centre of theology differs from one 'christocentric' theologian to the next. (1997: 453)

Thus, there may be theologies that could be designated christocentric in a formal sense that is not reflected in their more material considerations (e.g. Schleiermacher).[2] Equally, there may be multiple theologies with equal right to the christocentric label on both the formal and material levels but still differing markedly in terms of their material development. The significance of this can be seen in the fact that christocentric is a term commonly associated not only with Barth's theology, but also with that of Ritschl, Harnack, and Herrmann.[3] In addition to the differences that can arise with respect to formal and material centricity, one should also note methodological variations – for example, the differences between a central starting point that enables one to incorporate other modes of discourse and a more deterministic center that establishes a definite circumference beyond which one may not reach. Clearly, then, merely labeling of some theological system as 'christocentric' will lead to significant ambiguity unless some attempt is

---

[2] As Hunsinger points out, Schleiermacher's theology (and arguably that of most nineteenth-century theologians) was 'formally but not substantively christocentric' (2000d: 283; see also Torrance 1990: 35). Balthasar (1992: 37) and Johnson (1997: 110) also argue that Schleiermacher's christocentrism is undermined by his methodological and material commitment to religious awareness as the basis of theology.

[3] TeSelle largely glosses over the significant differences between these various theologians in his attempt to characterize twentieth century christocentric theologians as offshoots of nineteenth century German idealism (1975). Sykes argues that although there is a formal similarity between the christocentric approaches of Harnack and Barth, they are distinguished by substantial material differences (1979a: 28–29); for a similar point with respect to Herrmann see Mangina 2004: 8–9. Thus, while there is a formal parallel between Barth's christocentrism and that of eighteenth and nineteenth century German theologians, their influence on his christological concentration should not be overemphasized. Hunsinger convincingly argues that a more fruitful background for understanding Barth's theology and his christocentrism in particular can be found in the theology of Luther (see 2000d).

made to clarify the extent to which this 'christocentrism' may or may not be applied to these formal, material, and methodological issues.

The ambiguity of the term becomes particularly prominent when we consider some of the different ways in which Barth's christocentrism has been interpreted. The scope of Barth's christocentrism has repeatedly led to charges that Barth's theology is christomonistic – that is, a theological system that reduces everything to Christology.[4] Barth, according to this interpretation, focuses so completely on the ontological and epistemological centrality of Jesus Christ for the entire cosmos that the particularity, significance, and, ultimately, even the reality of humans and other creaturely beings are lost as everything is subsumed under the totalism of Barth's Christology.[5] Similarly, Barth is critiqued for developing an isolationist approach to theology.[6] From this perspective, Barth's christological concentration involves a methodological christomonism that precludes any significant engagement with non-theological disciplines.[7] According to Bruce Marshall, then, the most common complaint against Barth's theology is its apparent isolationism

---

[4] Such criticisms have not dissipated (e.g. Rosato 1981: 145; Thiemann 1981: 120; Richmond 1986: 404; Roberts 1991; Milbank 1999; and Frei 2005) and remain particularly common among American evangelicals (e.g. Packer 1975; Muller 1991: 130ff.; and Lewis 2003).

[5] For example, Balthasar 1992: 242; cf. also Deegan 1961; Come 1963: 152–57; Willis 1971: 236ff.; McGrath 1986: 105–06; Biggar 1993: 5; and Muers 1999: 268–69.

[6] For example, Williams 1947: 253; Ebneter 1952: 36; Crawford 1972: 327; Dorrien 1997: 338–43; Milbank 1999: 2; Webb 1991: 504; and Roberts 1991: 59–79.

[7] For example, Cobb 1969. Riches notes that the term *christocentric* itself has come to be associated with an anti-intellectual rejection of natural theology and human reason (1972: 223–24). Sykes suggests that Barth is at least 'partly responsible' for such interpretations (1989b: 7). In a number of places Barth makes comments that might indicate a real reticence to engage in any such dialogue. As early as I/1, Barth cautions that theology should restrict itself to 'its own relevant concerns' (I/1, xvi) and refuse to learn anything methodologically from other disciplines (I/1, 8), as it must retain its 'autonomy' and protect itself from 'corruption' (I/1, 285). Particularly well known along these lines are Barth's famous statements regarding the practical non-existence of a *philosophia christiana* (I/1, 6), the dispensability of the natural sciences for developing a theological account of creation (III/1, ix), and the incompatibility of theology with any world-view (cf. III/1, 340–44; III/2, 4–11; and IV/3.1, 255–56). Unfortunately, such comments are often abstracted from the rest of Barth's theology and, indeed, from the context in which they were written. Thus, Barth's comments in I/1 are interpreted in isolation from his extensive discussions regarding the close relationship that exists between theology and the non-theological disciplines (I/1, 5–6, 84, 284), the possibility of revelation coming through any medium (I/1, 55), his rejection of anti-intellectualism (I/1, 200–01), and his assertion of the 'dignity' of other disciplines as they seek to carry out their own task (I/1, 256). Barth's statements must also be understood in light of his qualified affirmation of the possibility of a *philosophia christiana* (I/1, 5377–78; cf. Barth 1981: 33–38; 1986: 27, 32), the validity of future theologians interacting more extensively with the natural sciences in a theology of creation (III/1, x; cf. Webster 2000a: 111), and the impossibility of doing theology independently of some particular world-view (I/2, 728–29;

(1983: 445).[8] Thus, Barth's theology is routinely interpreted as involving a 'christological constriction' (Crawford 1972: 327) that remains isolated from other disciplines as it seeks to derive all knowledge from its christological starting point.[9]

More recently an alternative reading of Barth's christocentrism has arisen as scholars have attempted to understand the relationship between Barth's theology and postmodernism.[10] Rather than understanding the center of Barth's theology as a determinative center that encompasses all creaturely reality within its totalizing framework, this approach prefers to understand

---

III/2, 6–8). While this is certainly not sufficient to establish that Barth was in fact open to interdisciplinary dialogue, it at least suggests that his interpreters should be careful in appealing to his writings selectively to establish their point.

[8] Several scholars indicate that this criticism has been particularly common among Protestant scholars in the English speaking world (cf. Riches 1972: 223–24; Sykes 1989b: 7, 1979c: 12–13; and Mangina 2003: 437, 2004: ix).

[9] See Williams 1947: 253; Crawford 1972: 327; and Come 1963: 140. Two areas in which this criticism has been particularly prevalent are the use of the natural sciences and empirical data in theology, theological anthropology in particular, and the relationship between theology and philosophy. So, Barth is regarded as having little or no interest in the natural sciences and what they have to say about humanity (Pannenberg 1985: 16; McGrath 2001: 176; and Krötke 2000: 159). (McGrath does argue, however, that T. F. Torrance's systematic retrieval of Barth's theology with respect to the natural sciences demonstrates that while Barth's theology was limited in this regard, 'the Barthian heritage has considerable potential as a dialogue partner between Christian theology and the natural sciences' [2001: 177]). This seems to raise the possibility of a purely abstract theological anthropology disengaged from the hard realities of human existence and unable to speak meaningfully to the significant needs of contemporary society at a time when questions about the human person are becoming particularly prominent (Krötke 2000: 159; and Ng'weshemi 2002: 147). Comparable criticisms have been raised with respect to Barth's understanding of philosophy. Kincade thus accuses him of having a 'recalcitrant attitude to philosophy' that is characterized by 'ambivalence' and 'distrust' toward all philosophical contributions (1960: 161–69) and that refuses to allow any 'substantive role to philosophy within dogmatics' (Willis 1971: 103–09), resulting in a naive denial of the necessary relationship between the two. Indeed, Barth's understanding of the relationship between theology and philosophy played a prominent role in the divisions that arose between him and the other dialectical theologians (McCormack 1997: 400–10; and Ford 1979a: 59). His theology is thus derided for its subjectivity (cf. esp. Pannenberg 1991), its positivistic approach to revelation (see Fisher 1988), and its pervasive irrationalism (e.g. Blanshard 1964; and Trigg 1998). Lying at the root of many of these criticisms is Barth's well known rejection of natural theology (see Barth and Brunner 1946; Torrance 1947, 1970; Brown 1980; O'Donovan 1986; Barr 1994; Thiselton 1994; Dorrien 2000; J. Hart 2001; Hauerwas 2001; Holder 2001; and McDowell 2002) and his corresponding refusal to engage in an apologetic defense of theology (McGrath 2001: 177; Kincade 1960: 162; and Crawford 1972: 321; for more on Barth's rejection of apologetics see Pinnock 1977; Hunsinger 1991; Clausen 1999; and Ward 2004).

the center of Barth's theology indeterministically. These theologians tend to emphasize Barth's awareness of the necessary finiteness of humanity and human language, and thus the generally indeterminate nature of theological discourse. According to William Stacy Johnson, then, there is a strongly 'theocentric' strand to Barth's theology that focuses on 'the hiddenness and mystery of God' (1997: 1). Consequently, Barth's theology is understood to be largely 'nonfoundational' and 'de-centered' in the sense that the center of Bath's theology is like the 'opening at the center of a wheel' (Johnson 1997: 3–5).[11]

While there may be a measure of truth in each of these different interpretations of Barth's theology, the sheer distance between these proposals suggests that greater clarity is needed. Thus, McCormack correctly notes, 'All of this is to say that the customary description of Barth's theology as "christocentric" has very little explanatory value unless one goes on to define concretely what "christocentrism" meant in his case' (1997: 454). Well aware of some of these problems, Barth himself rarely used the term, even warning against a theology that is *too* christocentric (Barth 1991: 91). It would seem, then, that further clarification is necessary before the term *christocentric* can be used in a meaningful way to characterize Barth's theology.[12]

b. Determining Karl Barth's Brand of Christocentrism

This leads us to the question with which this section is primarily concerned: What exactly do Barth's interpreters mean when they describe him as a christocentric theologian? To answer this question it will prove helpful to adopt and expand on a definition of christocentrism offered by Bruce McCormack. According to McCormack, Barth's particular form of christocentrism can be defined as

> the attempt . . . to understand every doctrine from a centre in God's Self-revelation in Jesus Christ; i.e. from a centre in God's act of veiling and unveiling in Christ. . . . 'Christocentrism', for him, was a methodological rule . . . in accordance with which one presupposes a particular understanding of God's Self-revelation in reflecting upon each and every other doctrinal topic, and seeks to interpret those topics in the light of what is already known of Jesus Christ. (1997: 454)[13]

---

[10] See Freyer 1991; Andrews 1996; Ward 1993a, 1993b, 1995; W. Lowe 1988, 1993; Smith 1983; Johnson 1997; and Thompson 2001.

[11] While this section will make some evaluative comments with respect to such postmodern readings of Barth's christocentrism, it will not attempt a broader evaluation with respect to its adequacy as a way of understanding Barth's theology. For some studies on this topic see Ward 1993a; and Thompson and Mostert 2001.

[12] For a broader study of christocentric theologies see Vander Goot 1981.

[13] TeSelle points out that christocentrism can be applied to epistemological, anthropological, or ontological concerns (1975: 1). Barth's theology can properly be considered christocentric on all three points.

Three things about this definition stand out as being particularly important for understanding the unique form of Barth's christocentrism: a veiling and unveiling in Christ, a methodological orientation, and a particular understanding of God's self-revelation. In addition, we will need to consider the implications for Barth's christocentrism of his Trinitarian orientation and his emphasis on incorporating both divine and human realities into any properly Christian theology. These five qualifications will help us understand more clearly what it means to attribute 'christocentric' to Barth's theology.

1. (Un)veiling Christocentrism: No Simple Given

First, McCormack notes that Barth's christocentrism is one that involves both 'veiling and unveiling in Christ'. As Barth repeatedly argues, God's Word is never merely given, as though it were the possession of human beings and under their control, but is an *event* whereby God manifests or unveils himself to human beings while remaining veiled in the sovereignty and mystery of his being.[14] Though Barth firmly asserts that the incarnate Christ is the revelation of God in a human being and thus the *unveiling* of God, he nevertheless denies that this humanity is intrinsically revelatory, but is so by the gracious act of God.[15] Thus, the incarnation is the supreme manifestation of the *deus revelatus* who at the same time remains the *deus absconditus* (I/1, 320 ff.). As a result, Barth's christocentrism rejects (1) an entirely apophatic approach to theology that voids it of any meaningful content (thus denying the 'unveiling' of God's self-revelation) and (2) an illegitimate systematization of theology based on some theological concept from which the rest of the system can be logically deduced (thus denying the 'veiling'; I/2, 868 ff).

Webster argues that it is at this point that '[m]uch of the material which seeks to relate Barth to postmodernism has often lost its way' in that it overemphasizes the negative aspects of this presentation to the detriment of his 'churchly positivity' (2001a: 15). His concern, then, seems to be that many postmodern readings of Barth focus on the hiddenness of God emphasized by his language of veiling, but are not adequately balanced by an equal treatment of the givenness and objectivity of 'God's freely taking form in the incarnation of the Son', which 'bestows upon Christian dogmatics a specific kind of positivity' (2001a: 18).[16] Webster's criticisms thus point out the potential for mistake that arises whenever either pole of Barth's christocentric theology, the revelatory veiling or unveiling, are emphasized to the neglect of the other.

---

[14] See I/1, 169, 174, 315–25; II/2, 54–57, 179–203.
[15] See I/1, 173, 323–24; Barth 1991: 1, 157.

2. Methodological Christocentrism: Moving from Christ to Theology

Second, McCormack's definition presents Barth's christocentrism as 'a methodological rule'. This, of course, is not to argue that it is *merely* a methodological rule, since, as we have seen, Barth is well aware that this rule is itself based on the ontological reality of the incarnation and the constitutive nature of Jesus' eternal election. Rather, here we simply acknowledge the significance of the methodological role that Barth's christocentrism plays.

Two important aspects of Barth's christocentric methodology require our attention. First, he argues that the directionality of all theological thinking must move *from* Christ *to* any given theological formulation. Barth recognized that the directionality of theological thinking has important consequences for the content of our theologies, and consistently maintained that theological thought must always begin with Christology (cf. Tanner 2000: 111). Second, this methodological principle not only affirms the *directionality* but the *universality* of christological thinking. As indicated above, Barth maintained that properly theological thinking, whether addressing doctrine or some other mode of discourse, must begin with Christology.

This methodological christocentrism, however, cannot be interpreted as necessitating the theological isolationism with which Barth is often associated. If one wants to focus exclusively on the proper *point of departure* for theology, then it must be conceded that Barth is christomonistic, but only in this narrow sense. This does not mean, however, that his theology is, therefore, methodologically isolated from other disciplines. A number of useful studies have recently appeared arguing that Barth's theology is quite open to interacting with and learning from a broad spectrum of non-theological disciplines.[17]

---

[16] Although he is also somewhat critical of William Stacy Johnson's study, suggesting that he presents 'a rather strained reading' which tends to overemphasize the 'mystery' motif in Barth's theology (Webster 2001a: 16), Johnson at least recognizes the importance of affirming its positive dimensions in addition to its 'countermelody', that is, mystery (cf. Johnson 1997: 1). Any tendency to overemphasize the latter is probably the result of Johnson's attempt to counter the significantly more common overemphasis on the all-consuming determinateness of Barth's christological concentration. One can rightly question, however, whether Johnson's use of the terms theocentric and christocentric as the most appropriate for identifying the hiddenness and givenness of Barth's theology.

[17] For example, Stock 1980; Torrance 1990; Price 2002; McDowell 2003b; Mangina 2003, 2004; and Migliore 2004. Webster makes a similar argument with respect to Barth's openness to historical dialogue (2004b). Although several have argued that this openness was more of a theoretical than an actual reality (e.g. Johnson 1997: 8–9; and Ford 1979b: 196), we will see in the next section that his actual practice was more open than is often acknowledged.

Indeed, Barth's emphasis on the relativity of theology,[18] the importance of fellowship and solidarity with all people (III/2, 250–74),[19] the need for addressing the contemporary situation of the theologian,[20] his willingness to consider all people as potential members of the church,[21] and his openness to extra-ecclesial revelation[22] all provide significant resources for supporting interdisciplinary dialogue.[23] Rather than irrationally isolated from other forms of discourse, his theology is thus understood as critically open to engaging the ideas and insights of these other approaches – but always in such a way that the interaction is determined by the christological perspective.[24]

Indeed, John McDowell argues that Barth's clear affirmation of his presuppositions and commitments enables a more effective and meaningful engagement (2003b). After criticizing theologians who view theological conversation either as pre-determined and closed to insights from other perspectives or as completely open and thus constituted by the conversation itself, McDowell offers an understanding of conversation grounded in the particularity of the conversation partners. In such a conversation, the participants are neither fully constituted by the conversation itself, having identities that are already established by their historical particularities, but neither are they completely determined and closed to new insights, as they are willing to entertain the genuinely new insights and ideas of the other.[25] Conversation, rightly understood, thus 'involves difference, and the awareness of difference' (McDowell 2003b: 491).[26] In other words, for a conversation

---

[18] According to Barth, all theology is necessarily relativized by its character as a human response to the sovereign revelation of God (I/1, 11–24) and its temporally limited nature (cf. Frei 1988: 84).

[19] Cf. Biggar 1993: 148

[20] IV/3.2, 735; Barth 1979: 161; 1982b: 54. Barth's famous criticism of German theology in the early nineteen to twentieth century theology as capitulating to contemporary culture should not be read as indicating that Barth did not recognize engagement with culture as one of the tasks of theology, but as resisting any move to ground or validate theology in the ideas, needs, and/or questions of a particular culture (see Barth 1982a: 17–19). For other studies of Barth's understanding of human culture see Palma 1983; Gorringe 2004; Metzger 2003.

[21] III/4, 484–85; IV/3, 117, 494–96.

[22] I/1, 54–55; IV/3.2, 38–164; cf. Dorman 1997; Sonderegger 1992: 82–83; and Gill 1986.

[23] As Mangina points out, however, we should be careful about stressing the role of dialogue in Barth's theology to the extent that we neglect his emphasis on the primacy of Scripture and theology's task as witness (2004: 176). We must also heed Barth's warnings against theologians 'yearning for the fleshpots of Egypt' and losing sight of theology's true concern in their aversion to theological solitude and the need to 'swim against the stream of fellow theologians and nontheological opinions and methods' (1979: 118).

[24] See Hartwell 1964: 53–58; Freyer 1991; Balthasar 1992: 218–19, 240; McDowell 2003b; and Boyd 2004: 26. For studies countering the charges of irrationality, subjectivism, and fideism in Barth's theology see Urban 1964: 218–22; Molnar 1995: 315–39; Smith 1983, 1984; Dalferth 1989; and Mangina 2003, 2004: 48–53.

to be valuable, the participants must understand their own presuppositions and approach the conversation with something different to contribute.[27]

An important part of legitimate conversation, then, is the willingness to argue. Rather than viewing argument and disagreement as a sign of failure it should instead be viewed as an indicator of commitment to a conversational process that values the difference between one's own particular location and that of the other.

Based on this understanding of conversation, McDowell argues that, rather than viewing Barth's strong commitment to his christological presuppositions as resulting in his virtual isolation from other perspectives, it is precisely this awareness of his own particular identity that enables Barth to engage in meaningful conversation with other people.[28] As indicators of this conversational openness McDowell points to Barth's willingness to interact with 'specifically "extra-ecclesial" elements' like philosophy and culture (McDowell 2003b: 494–97).

3. Particular Christocentrism: No Mere Conceptual Construct

Finally, McCormack's definition stipulates that Barth's christocentrism operates on the basis of 'a particular understanding of God's Self-revelation'. Barth's rejection of any attempt to ground theology on a particular principle or idea is well known. He asserted that truth is not

> an idea, principle, or system. . . . Nor is it a structure of correct insights, nor a doctrine, even though this be a correct doctrine of the being of God, that of man, their normal relationship to one another and the establishment, restoration and ordering of this relationship. (IV/3.1, 375)[29]

---

[25] In a similar manner, J. Taylor defines 'dialogue' as 'a sustained conversation between parties who are not saying the same thing and who recognize and respect the differences, the contradictions and the mutual exclusions, between their various ways of thinking' (1981: 212).

[26] McDowell's argument thus parallels Kenneth Surin's criticism of pluralism as a merely 'cosmetic' commitment to difference which ultimately subsumes all differences in its pursuit of 'universal uniformity' (see Surin 1990).

[27] See also Webster 2001a: 24–26.

[28] From a similar perspective, Grenz calls for a renewed commitment to 'generous orthodoxy' that seeks to recognize the crucial and legitimate differences and contributions made by alternate perspectives while at the same time remaining committed to certain theological presuppositions (2000: 325–326).

[29] Similarly in III/2, he states, 'In Jesus God is not just a word or a systematic principle, but the reality and *prima veritas* which of itself sets itself at the head of all other thoughts and gives them a specific direction and content' (III/2, 552). This was the basis of his disagreement with Berkouwer's evaluation of his theology in *The Triumph of Grace in the Theology of Karl Barth* (1956). Barth objected to Berkouwer's title and subsequent exposition on the basis that he was 'not concerned here with the precedence,

According to Eberhard Jüngel, Barth's christological concentration centers theology not on 'a principle from which a system can be deduced', but on 'the concrete existence of Jesus Christ' (1986: 128). So Barth understood his christocentrism to center on 'an actual encounter with the reality to which theological presentation can only point'; which, for Barth meant primarily 'the divine act of the atonement' (III/2, 553).[30]

As with the discussion of veiling and unveiling above, then, the postmodern interpretation of Barth can, at times, fall short on this point. Although Barth does describe his theology using his famous metaphor of 'the opening in the centre of a wheel' (I/2, 867), he does not mean to suggest that this center is indeterminate or without particular content. Rather he affirms that knowledge of the center can only be provided through the revelatory *event* and cannot be *possessed* by conceptual knowledge.[31] Barth's christocentrism thus involves 'a particular understanding of God's self-revelation' that reveals the center of theology to be the relationship between God and man revealed in Jesus Christ through his concrete existence.

Stephen Sykes, however, finds Barth's argument inconsistent on this point. According to him, Barth denies that any 'central doctrine, concept, or idea' lies at the center of theology; an approach he associates with Barth's rejection of neo-Protestant attempts to define the 'essentials' of Christianity (1979a: 25).[32] Thus, Barth's focus is not on 'the centrality of a doctrine of the Atonement, but the centrality of the act of the Atonement in which God is God' (Sykes 1979a: 40). But Sykes thinks Barth is unaware that this actualistic center

---

victory or triumph of a principle, even though this principle be that of grace. We are concerned with the living person of Jesus Christ' (IV/3.1, 173). '[C]hristological thinking,' for Barth, 'in this sense is a very different process from deduction from a given principle' and he thus contends that theology does not develop from 'a Christ-principle', but from 'Jesus Christ Himself as attested by Holy Scripture' (III/2, 175). Therefore, Barth rejected Berkouwer's characterization of his theology on the basis that *any* principle used systematically to *determine* God's revelation is an illegitimate imposition on the divine freedom. Cushman describes it as an imposition of 'man-made constructs on that which transcends man' (1981: 11).

[30] As Barth describes it, the 'heart of the Church's dogmatics . . . has a circumference, the doctrine of creation and the doctrine of the last things, the redemption and consummation. But the covenant fulfilled in the atonement is its centre' (IV/3.1, 3). This actualistic centering of theology on the atonement has particular significance for this project as it indicates that theology cannot remain 'only a doctrine of God' but must involve the relationship between God and man (II/2, 5; cf. Webster 1998: 79–80 and Johnson 1997: 13). On this theme Barth is thus very much in line with and perhaps influenced by Eastern Orthodox anthropologies (cf. Nellas 1987: 120).

[31] Cf. W. S. Johnson 1997: 11–66. Barth thus contends that the conceptuality of doctrine can 'participate in' the truth of the Word but that the Word 'cannot be enclosed or confined in any doctrine…not even the most correct Christology', since He is the Lord as well as 'the measure and criterion' of all doctrine (IV/3.1, 376).

[32] Cf. also Sykes 1988.

[33] Cf. McGrath 1986: 107.

'demands a special Christology, which, although it is comparatively unspecific compared with the degree to which two-nature Christology was eventually developed in the post-patristic era, is nonetheless identifiably non-Docetic, non-Ebionistic, and non-Arian' (Sykes 1979a: 41).[33] Therefore, he argues that the center of Barth's theology is a particular christological *doctrine* and not merely the divine act itself. Barth's assertions to the contrary are mere rhetoric that disguise the reality of this conceptual core. Sykes, by contrast, agrees with Barth's actualism but contends that theologians should explicitly utilize some idea or theological construct to render conceptually the actuality of the atonement.

Sykes' criticisms, however, should be responded to on three points. First, even though he acknowledges that Barth's concern is primarily with forced systematization, he unaccountably fails to consider the significance of Barth's understanding of a more legitimate systematization.[34] Theology, for Barth, can be systematic so long as it is an expression of the *ratio* of its object, that is, God revealed through Christ.[35] While Barth rejects any attempt to place a principle or idea at the center of Christian theology, he fully affirms that the story of God's encounter with humanity in the incarnation can and must play this role.[36] As John Webster argues, Barth's theology 'is, then, striking above all for its *narrative density*, its ceaseless vigilance against conceptual takeover, its refusal to go beyond the simple "It came to pass"' (1995: 83–84).[37] Because of 'the absolute and self-positing character' of this divine–human event 'Barth locates the bridge between Jesus' history and our own not in some cognitive or interpretative or experiential processes, but in the self-manifestation of the risen Jesus in the power of the Spirit, as a reality which we can only acknowledge' (Webster 1995: 87–88). Thus, Barth is fully aware that the actualistic center of his theology has its own *ratio* from which a system can be developed. Second, Sykes fails to bring into the discussion Barth's awareness of the inseparability of form and content in any discussion of methodology.[38] This inseparable relationship makes it questionable at best to charge Barth with being unaware that the formal center of his theology could not be divorced from its material content. Finally, although Sykes is well aware of Barth's concern that any move toward conceptualizing the center of theology will result in the theologians

---

[34] Cf. I/2, 868 ff.
[35] On the development of Barth's use of the *ratio* concept through his interaction with Anselm see Torrance 1962: 182–93.
[36] Cf. Ford 1979a: 74.
[37] See also Webster 2001b: 41–43.
[38] As McLean observed, for Barth 'form and content are bound up together and should be separated only for the purpose of speech. Even then, speech itself must constantly attempt to reveal that they are together' (1981: 12); see also Balthasar 1992: 47–55 and McCormack 1999: 476–77.

attempting to control the object of theology – he even notes that the history of theology bears out these concerns – but he casually dismisses Barth's actualistic methodology without providing in his alternative approach any substantive response to this concern.

It may be that at times Barth does not differentiate clearly enough between the illegitimate systematization that seeks to develop an entire theological system on the basis of an idea or principle with the pragmatic adoption of some given conceptual perspective that is necessary for any given theological formulation. But Barth clearly recognizes the legitimacy of this latter move stating that

> truth certainly can and should be reflected in such a doctrine, and secondarily attested in this form. It demands to be taught as such, i.e., to be grasped, considered and understood with the greatest possible consistency, and to be expressed in tolerably correct, clear and logical thoughts, words and sentences. (IV/3.1, 375–76)

But we must recognize the limitations of these conceptualizations in that 'even in the doctrine which is most correct, and most conscientiously attained and fashioned, we are already or still in the sphere of man and not yet or no longer in that of the truth of God which encounters him' (IV/3.1, 376).[39]

Contrary to both Sykes and some postmodern readings of Barth, then, Barth is fully committed to *both* the actualistic center of theology and its material particularity. The two can be differentiated for heuristic reasons but should never be separated as though they can be independently critiqued.

4. Theocentric Christocentrism: A Trinitarian Orientation

Besides the three principles brought out by McCormack's definition of Barth's christocentrism, two other factors must be recognized. First, it seems that the most likely reason Barth thought the concept of christocentrism should be used carefully in theology is because Barth's christocentrism was always intended, as Geoffrey Bromiley observes, 'to point to (and not away from) the centrality of the triune God' (1979: xi).[40] Similarly, Johnson says,

> It is commonplace to interpret Barth as a 'christocentric' theologian. Yet this simple designation does not end the matter. One cannot focus on Jesus Christ in himself, according to Barth, without understanding his life as caught up in a more dynamic Trinitarian movement of God's Word and Spirit. (1997: 13)

---

[39] Cf. I/2, 731.
[40] See Barth 1991: 91.

Indeed, the significance of the Trinity is reflected in the entire structure of the *Church Dogmatics* and its individual expositions.[41] Unlike some contemporary theologians who seek to place *christocentric* and *theocentric* in opposition to one another (e.g. Knitter 1983), Barth would regard any such move as singularly inappropriate. Rather, Barth always intended the christocentric orientation of his theology to lead to and support his primarily *trinitarian* concerns. As John Thompson noted, for Barth, 'Christology and Trinity are distinguishable but inseparable' (1986a: 13). A christocentric theology that was in tension with, let alone in opposition to, its trinitarian orientation would ultimately fail to be Christian theology.

5. *(The)anthropological Christocentrism: The Divine–Human Relation*

Finally, as Barth's christocentrism does not reflect a denigration of the Trinity, neither does it indicate a promotion of christological concerns at the expense of creaturely realities. Barth was very clear that theology cannot be about God alone but must include humanity as well:

> A very precise definition of the Christian endeavour in this respect would really require the more complex term 'the-anthropology'. For an abstract doctrine of God has no place in the Christian realm, only a 'doctrine of God and of man', a doctrine of the commerce and communion between God and man. (1982a: 11)

The significant attention that Barth devoted to human concerns (e.g. ethics, culture, agency, etc.) demonstrates the keen interest in creaturely realities Barth exhibited through his christocentric theology (cf. Mangina 2001).

---

[41] At this point one must acknowledge the extensive discussions that have taken place regarding the adequacy of Barth's pneumatology and its implications for understanding his christocentrism. John Thompson argues that despite the apparent paucity of pneumatological material, the very structure of the *Dogmatics* suggests an inherently Trinitarian and, thus, strongly pneumatological orientation (1991: 42; cf. also Hunsinger 2000c: 127–42). T. Torrance even goes so far as to say that no one has given the Trinity a greater role in theology than Barth (1962: 176). Others have been more critical citing Barth's weaknesses in Barth's theology as underlying apparent weaknesses in his understanding of gender (Rogers 1998: 43–82; 2004), human freedom and history (Rosato 1981; Willis 1971; and Gunton 1989), and the relationship between Christ's humanity and ours (Davidson 2001) among others. But it should be noted that most of these arguments have more to do with the manner in which Barth presented his pneumatology and do not in any way weaken Thompson's point that the structure and intention of Barth's theology reflects an inherently pneumatological interest. In addition, the proposed fifth volume on redemption, which was to have focused on pneumatological issues, may well have ameliorated some, though not all, of these concerns.

Some have argued that this openness to creaturely reality is a fairly late development, not surfacing until volumes III and IV of the *Dogmatics*. According to Webster, however, it is more appropriate to speak of a richer expression in these later writings of a concern that has its roots in the earliest phases of Barth's theological development (1998: 37–38).

As we have seen, however, many interpreters contend that this aspect of Barth's theology actually involves some form of ontological or epistemological christomonism that denigrates and subsumes creaturely realities. This despite the fact that Barth's rejection of christomonism could not have been clearer. In the posthumously published fragment IV/4 he asserted that 'a true Christocentricity will strictly forbid us' from pursuing christomonistic lines of thought (IV/4, 19). Even more clearly, he argued in another late article that '[t]he Gospel defies all isms' which fail to unite God and man and that 'sound theology' eschews christomonism as a failure to appreciate the affirmation and union of both God and humanity (Barth 1962). These concerns have also been effectively responded to by a number of recent studies which demonstrate rather convincingly that such criticisms revolve primarily around a failure to appreciate the dialectic involved in Barth's redefinition of human reality, particularly human freedom, as a determinate correspondence to God.[42]

Additionally, several scholars have argued that the christomonist objection fails to appreciate Barth's understanding of the 'enhypostatic' nature of humanity's relationship to Jesus.[43] Thus, as Jesus' human nature exists enhypostatically in union with the Word, so all human nature exists enhypostatically in union with Jesus. Barth's christocentricity, then, is more properly understood as the proper ground, rather than the subsumption, of creaturely reality.

c. A Properly Delimited Christocentrism

Given these caveats, one might begin to wonder whether it is still appropriate to speak of Barth as a *christocentric* theologian. Since it is necessary to qualify the term so carefully, maybe we would be better served by finding some other descriptor that is less susceptible to such confusion. While it is true that the breadth and depth of Barth's theology make it amenable to a variety of descriptions, there remains, nonetheless, a particular aptness to this label. As indicated at the beginning of this chapter, Barth clearly emphasized that Christian theology must be determined at every stage by the incarnation. He thus argued that

> within theological thinking generally unconditional priority must be given to thinking which is attentive to the existence of the living person of Jesus Christ . . . so that *per definitionem* Christological thinking

---

[42] See esp. Webster 1995, 1998.
[43] For example, Dalferth 1989; Webster 1998; Davidson 2001; and Tanner 2001.

forms the unconditional basis [*begründende*] for all other theological thinking . . . It is thus quite out of the question to start with certain prior decisions (e.g. concerning God, man, sin, grace, etc.) and then to support these christologically. . . . The only decisions which can have any place are those which follow after [*Nachentscheidungen*], which are consistent with thinking which follows Him [*folgsamen Denkens*], which arise in the course of Christological thinking and the related investigations, definitions and conclusions. (IV/3.1, 175)

The consistency with which Barth carried out the christological determination of theology suggests that, despite the potential for confusion and mischaracterization, the christocentric label may still be justly, though carefully, applied. Indeed, one might well respond to Barth's critics by asking, along with Barth, if the incarnation is a reality, if the sovereign God of the universe has in fact become incarnate in the person of Jesus Christ, can theology be anything but christocentric?[44]

From this discussion we can see that *christocentric* is not a generic label that can be usefully applied irrespective of the unique particularities of individual theologians. Any attempt to understand Barth as a christocentric theologian must therefore bear in mind that his unique brand of christocentrism always involved (1) both a veiling and unveiling of knowledge in Christ, (2) a methodological orientation, (3) a particular Christology, (4) a Trinitarian focus, and (5) an affirmation of creaturely reality. We may continue to describe Barth's theology as a christocentric theology so long as we bear these caveats in mind.

III. Seeing the Human, in Part: The Phenomena of the Human

Having clarified the nature of Barth's christocentrism and its implications for understanding its character as both determinate and open, we are now in a position to ascertain the precise manner in which Barth actually participates in such dialogue. To do this, we will first consider Barth's understanding

---

[44] This would seem to be an apt response to those who are concerned about the 'well-nigh incredible consistency' of Barth's Christology (Frei 1993: 175); a concern that apparently led to Colin Brown's criticism that Barth developed a speculative theology that is 'more christocentric than the Bible' (1978: 108). Contrary to Brown, as we have seen, the consistency of Barth's christocentrism is not based on systematic speculations but on a commitment to the reality-defining significance of the incarnation. Brown's comment also betrays a lack of sensitivity to Barth's christological hermeneutic; which would raise serious questions about what it means to be *more* christocentric than the Bible (for good comments on this aspect of Barth's hermeneutic see Baxter 1986 and Higton 2004).

of the 'phenomena of the human [*Phänomene des Menschlichen*]' in III/2 and how such phenomena relate to the various anthropological disciplines.[45] After developing this concept, we will take a brief look at three crucial dialogues in which Barth engages other disciplines on their interpretation of these phenomena.

a. Science and Speculation: A Phenomenological View of Humanity

In §43.2 Barth considers two distinct approaches to understand the human person, each of which begin with that which can be ascertained about human nature from observing humanity as it currently appears. That is, they begin by observing the phenomena of human life.

Despite this common starting point, however, Barth makes a sharp distinction between speculative and scientific approaches to anthropology. A speculative approach involves the development of 'axiomatic principles' from which a theological anthropology may be developed (III/2, 22).[46] The second type, 'the exact science of man', differs in that it develops hypotheses from its research but, '[t]o the extent that science is exact, it will refrain from consolidating its formulae and hypotheses as axioms' (III/2, 23). Hence, the primary difference between the two is that the scientific approach understands the tentative nature of its hypothetical investigations while the

---

[45] At first glance Barth's discussions in §44.2 seems oddly placed given the overall structure of III/2. The subject matter of this section follows very naturally on the heels of the discussion in §43.2, with its critique of non-christological approaches to anthropology. And it also fits rather awkwardly in its own context separating as it does §44.1, with its discussion of Jesus as the revelation of the basic form of humanity, from §44.3, where that basic form is used to develop an understanding of true humanity as the divine counterpart. Closer examination, though, indicates that Barth intentionally postponed his more extended critique of non-christological anthropologies until after he had developed his christologically derived principles of true humanity in §44.1. §44 can thus be understood as (1) the christological development of the basic form of humanity; (2) the basic form of humanity critically applied to evaluate non-christological starting points; and (3) the basic form of humanity constructively applied to develop an understanding of humanity. So, sections §43.2 and §44.2 share the same basic concerns, but the more complete discussions of the latter section had to wait for the christological arguments of §44.1.

[46] According to Hunsinger, 'Speculation designates, in the Barthian lexicon, just that procedure which seeks to move from the general to the particular, from an a priori understanding of what sorts of things are generally possible and actual (as established by reason apart from faith) to an understanding of what sorts of things are possible and actual in theology. . . . More broadly, speculation is a term used to designate the deriving of doctrine from anything other than the biblical witness to Jesus Christ as the center and norm of God's self-revelation' (1991: 51).

speculative approach attempts to develop an axiomatic foundation upon which to build a theory of humanity.

Consistent with the christocentric orientation of his theology, Barth's comments about the speculative approach are unsurprisingly critical. He accuses this approach of being mythical, unbiblical, and arrogant. His primary concern, though, is with the arrogant self-confidence of this view whereby it attempts 'to see the essence and nature of man apart form the Word of God', and instead seeks to develop an autonomous perspective from which to develop its anthropology (III/2, 22). Whether this approach affirms some concept of God is irrelevant in Barth's analysis since either way the foundation of the anthropology is not the Word of God, but is instead the autonomous attempt by the human person to understand himself. Against this perspective, Barth can only maintain that 'we are not able to see the essence and nature of man apart from the Word of God' (III/2, 23).

The scientific approach, however, receives a much more positive evaluation from Barth insofar as it remains true to its scientific orientation. As such it will recognize that its purpose is to investigate the phenomena of humanity and not try to develop comprehensive theories regarding the essential nature of humanity.

Scientific anthropologies so understood can actually be quite helpful as they provide 'precise information and relevant data which can be of service in the wider investigation of the nature of man, and can help to build up a technique for dealing with these questions' (III/2, 24).

Despite this positive evaluation, Barth's discussion precludes any possibility that knowledge of true humanity could be derived in this way. Though the exact science of man may be adept at analyzing the phenomena of humanity, it is unable to deal with the creature in relation to God and, consequently, with the inmost reality of the human person.[47] Even scientists who are 'obedient hearers of the Word of God' cannot use the scientific approach to ascertain true humanity in its relationship with God. This is because such a move would necessitate that they 'look beyond the phenomenal man who is the object of exact science to the real man perceptible in the

---

[47] Similarly, P. Jewett observes, 'Knowledge of the outer world of the universe where we live and the inner world of the mind by which we perceive where we live – knowledge of the "phenomena of humanity", as Barth calls it – gives us genuine knowledge about ourselves. Such knowledge, however, will never disclose the ultimate mystery of our humanity; it will never tell us what it means to say "I"' (1996: 16–17). Barth's approach is thus markedly different from the more common method espoused by Zizioulas where even a humanistic approach to anthropology recognizes that 'the actual man of our experience' transcends empirical investigation, but that such endeavors, nevertheless, provide '"the raw material" for the conception or creation of the real man' (1975: 401, 402; cf. also Macquarrie 1982: 3–4). While Barth would affirm the usefulness of such 'raw material,' he would not allow that they are necessary for an understanding of true humanity.

light of God's Word' (III/2, 25). There is no reason why a person should not seek to look beyond that which is phenomenologically available but, in so doing, they should recognize that they are no longer developing a scientific but rather a theological anthropology. The scientific approach thus remains 'a good work' only insofar as it recognizes its limits and avoids becoming 'axiomatic, dogmatic and speculative' (III/2, 25).

For Barth, then, both the speculative and scientific approaches are inherently flawed when viewed as starting points for achieving an understanding of true humanity. The speculative approach fails, in Barth's estimation, to provide real knowledge of any kind with its hyper-inflated sense of its absolute vantage point; while the scientific approach, though valuable in its own right, is incapable of seeing beyond the phenomena of humanity to the nature of true humanity.

b. The Phenomena of the Human vs. the Symptoms of Real Humanity

Barth's understanding of the 'phenomena of the human', however, is somewhat more complicated than it first appears.[48] In his opening discussion of the phenomena (§43.2), Barth seems to equate the phenomena of the human with whatever is accessible to 'exact science' (III/2, 23) – for example, 'physiology, psychology, and sociology' (III/2, 24). Thus, the phenomena of humanity are understood to be the ostensibly 'external' features of humanity accessible to the exact sciences. Any anthropological approach that fails to limit its investigation to these empirical phenomena and seeks instead to develop a system for understanding *true* humanity becomes a speculative attempt at constructing a philosophical world-view. Thus, it would appear that this first discussion limits the phenomena of humanity to the 'exact' sciences and specifically excludes any speculative or philosophical consideration of human being.

This apparently scientific account of the phenomena, however, is clearly expanded in §44.2. His explicit engagement with both scientific and philosophical perspectives on the human person in this paragraph require a much broader understanding of the phenomena which he defines here as 'certain human characteristics' (III/2, 76) that are a part of humanity's creaturely nature and consequently place human beings in basic continuity with all other animals (III/2, 76–79). Later in the work, Barth explicitly defines these human characteristics that are ostensibly open to phenomenological analysis as including biological, relational, intellectual, volitional, emotional, political, cultural, and even religious dimensions of human existence.[49] For Barth, then, the 'phenomena of humanity' can be defined as any aspect of

---

[48] Thus Stock complains about the 'bewildering way [*verwirrender Weise*]' in which Barth presents this distinction (1980: 528).

human existence that can be observed and analyzed from some limited human perspective (e.g. philosophy, biology, sociology, history, etc.) independent of an awareness of the true humanity revealed in Jesus Christ.

At this point, Barth draws a helpful distinction between the 'phenomena of the human' and the 'symptoms of real man [*Symptome des wirklich Menschlichen*]' (III/2, 75).[50] In contrast to the phenomena, which can be studied independently of a christological perspective and can only result in a 'phantom man [*Schattenmenschen*]', the 'symptoms of real man' are indicators of true humanity and, as such, can only be discerned when the phenomena are viewed from the vantage point provided by the true humanity of Jesus (III/2, 75). To understand the relationship between these two views of humanity, we will have to consider the limitations of the phenomenological method.

c. Partial Perspectives: The Limitations of a Phenomenological Viewpoint

These phenomena, though useful, are inherently limited from a number of directions. First, as we discussed above, no purely phenomenological analysis of creation in general or humanity in particular can ever lead to knowledge of humanity's essential relationship to God. Since this relationship is basic to any proper knowledge of humanity, the phenomena are necessarily precluded from resulting in knowledge of true humanity.

A second limitation, however, stems from humanity's sinful condition. Theologians have consistently noted the problem of sin not only as it impacts human existence and experience but also as it affects our ability to understand humanity itself and therefore the proper methodology for approaching that study. As John Zizioulas points out, sin constitutes 'a fundamental methodological problem' for any theological anthropology (1975: 401). Theologians either affirm, on the one hand, that true humanity can be discerned through actual humanity's sinful state, thus implying that sin and redemption do not 'essentially alter our view of man' or, on the other hand, that true humanity cannot be discerned in this way, thus problematizing any

---

[49] The inclusion of religion in Barth's understanding of the phenomena is reinforced in his subsequent discussion of the theology of Emil Brunner under the same category (III/2, 128–32). For Barth, even religion and theology remain merely phenomena of humanity when they fail to regard humanity in light of its historical relationship with God grounded in its ontological determination in Christ. Elsewhere, Barth explicitly affirms that the phenomena include those things not 'perceptible to our senses' and thus not amenable to empirical study (III/2, 91).

[50] Frey critiques Barth at this point for failing to provide a 'methodologically precise account [*methodisch präzise Rechenschaft*]' of this distinction (1978: 217). Freyer, though, points out that Barth's distinction is more precise than often recognized (1991: 195).

approach to anthropology (III/2, 20–21). Hence, the methodological implications of the sin problematic are such that any theological anthropology must address them.

Barth is keenly aware of these methodological issues. According to Barth, the Word reveals humanity as 'a betrayer of himself and a sinner against his creaturely existence' (III/2, 26). Though the 'real creaturely nature of man' (III/2, 38) persists through the gracious love of God and the faithfulness of Jesus, humanity's sin means that human persons are incapable of penetrating the sinful perversion he has become and seeing the true human nature that God created. So Barth asks,

> In these circumstances how can we possibly reach a doctrine of man in the sense of a doctrine of his creaturely essence, of his human nature as such? For what we recognize to be human nature is nothing other than the disgrace which covers his nature.... But if we know man only in the corruption and distortion of his being, how can we even begin to answer the question about his creaturely nature. (III/2, 27)

We ourselves are blinded by sin and can only wonder if our understanding of humanity is mere delusion, but in Christ we see the reality.[51] Barth thus rejects the traditional approach to theological anthropology 'which was to try first to establish generally what human nature is, and on this basis to interpret the human nature of Jesus Christ in particular. Our whole approach to the relation between human sin and human nature has led us irresistibly in the opposite direction' (III/2, 44).

Interestingly, though, Barth brings sin into the discussion *after* he rejects the possibility of speculative and scientific starting points for theological anthropology. As the previous discussion shows, this is not because Barth does not appreciate the significance of the sin problematic. The order of his argument shows that his primary concern is to demonstrate that any proper theological anthropology must begin with the relationship between humanity and God. Any anthropology that begins in some other place is necessarily flawed regardless of the questions posed by sin.[52]

---

[51] In his analysis of the second edition of Barth's Romans commentary, McCormack, following Michael Beintker, identifies a similar distinction between reality theologically perceived and reality as 'it appears to men and women living in history', which he classifies as the 'ontic' and the 'phenomenological' levels of reality (1997: 266).

[52] Additionally, Barth critiques non-christological approaches for their inherently circular and self-referential nature: 'For the point at issue is who is the man who wants to know himself and thinks he can? How does he reach the platform from which he thinks he can see himself' (III/2, 75, 178)? Moltmann raises a similar concern with his observation about the necessary circularity involved in any attempt by a human person to understand his own subjectivity (1974: 2).

As a third limitation, Barth contends that the phenomena are inherently 'neutral, relative and ambiguous' (III/2, 76). While these phenomena are certainly capable being symptoms of real humanity, one wonders about the criteria by which it is possible to determine which phenomena indicate true symptoms and which only apparently do so. Thus, they are unable *on their own* to establish a picture of true humanity. What is needed is some criterion outside the sphere of the phenomena themselves by which the phenomena can be evaluated and understood in their proper order. And, of course, the only possible criterion for such a task according to Barth is the true humanity of Jesus Christ.[53]

The final limitation of any phenomenological approach to humanity is that such accounts are necessarily constrained by the current state of human knowledge. Scientific and philosophical studies of humanity offer 'only a modest degree of certainty' because their certainty can only be that of 'the competent observer' who is necessarily limited by the knowledge available in her field (III/2, 88). The insights of these disciplines, while valuable, can only provide 'modest, i.e., limited, conditioned and relative certainty, and definitely not the certainty which life demands of man' (III/2, 88). A properly theological account of the true human, by contrast, seeks to ground knowledge of humanity in its eternal relationship with God and thus a knowledge that is not affected by the ephemeral nature of human knowledge.

We can see, then, that despite Barth's affirmation of the validity of phenomenological investigations of human existence and their ability to produce true insight into human phenomena, he thinks that this endeavor is inherently limited by its christological inadequacy, the sinfulness of humanity, the ambiguous nature of its results, and the finite limitations of phenomenological knowledge.

IV. Joining the Dialogue: Karl Barth at the Anthropological Roundtable

Having considered the nature of these phenomenological investigations and their corresponding limitations, we are finally in place to determine the precise nature of Barth's approach to interdisciplinary dialogue. Consistent with Barth's aversion for general principles, however, we find that he does not give any specific guidelines for such dialogical interaction. Rather than

---

[53] Thus, in Barth's discussion of Polanus, he concludes that the idea of the human person as a rational animal is a phenomenon of humanity that can be rightly viewed as a symptom of true humanity, but only if it is seen in light of humanity's 'definite history grounded in God's attitude to him' (III/2, 77). If not, it can only be 'an indifferent phenomenon, which can be established and observed as such, but which does not shed even the smallest ray of light on the true nature of man' (III/2, 77).

provide us with an abstract account of how to deal with the phenomena, he presents several concrete examples.[54] The bulk of §44.2, then, is devoted to Barth's engagement with these various ways of understanding the human person and his repeated contention that each provides insight into the phenomena of the human, but not true humanity itself. In this section, then, we will (1) consider the nature of the three dialogue partners Barth engages, (2) determine the extent to which Barth can affirmatively engage these alternate perspective, and (3) analyze the process by which he critically interacts with each.

a. Biology, Moral Agency, and Existential Subjectivity: The Conversation Partners

The Biological Dialogue: The first of the discussions, concerning a biological account of humanity (III/2, 79–90), actually involves two separate perspectives: one theological and one more properly scientific. In the first, Barth summarizes the historical development of apologetic efforts by modern theologians to defend the uniqueness of humanity from naturalistic attempts to view it as no different from other creatures.[55] He discusses how this apologetic endeavor moved from arguments asserting a high level of discontinuity between humans and other creatures to a greater appreciation for the similarities between them and a greater use of, indeed dependence on, evolutionary accounts of human development. In each case, the theologians in question sought to establish true humanity on the basis of some distinction particular to human beings. In the second account, Barth addresses Adolf Portmann's attempt to determine 'the singularity of man in his non-human environment' (III/2, 87). Writing with more properly scientific, rather than theological, concerns, Portmann did not seek to establish humanity's absolute uniqueness but rather its relative singularity – that is, the extent to which humanity is both similar to and different from other creatures. His work is thus distinct from the previously mentioned theologians primarily in the scope of his intent; methodologically the procedures are identical.

---

[54] Barth actually deals with four different anthropologies in this paragraph. Since our concern is primarily with the manner in which Barth interacts with *non*-theological anthropologies, however, we will not address his treatment of Brunner's anthropology in the fourth dialogue.

[55] Barth affirms the intentions of these theologians even while denying that their apologetic endeavors were well grounded. He thus argues that they were right to resist the 'levelling down' of a naturalistic world-view that was prone to a 'forgetfulness and denial of the specifically human' (III/2, 84). Nonetheless, Barth believed that these theologians were constrained to confront this problem on grounds established by their opponents because of their failure to see the christological basis of humanity as the only secure starting point (III/2, 79–80).

The Ethical Dialogue: Barth's second dialogue moves beyond the realm of what is apprehensible by the senses to the person as the subject of particular volitions and actions. Thus, anthropology moves beyond the merely biological and into the realm of ethical behavior. Here Barth engages this ethical/idealist viewpoint in the philosophy of Johan Gottlieb Fichte.

Barth summarizes Fichte's presentation as moving through three phases.[56] In the first, Fichte stipulates that the scientific view of humanity plunges the human person into doubt. While it seems to the person that she is free, she comes to realize from the results of the exact sciences that her life is fully determined in every respect. She is thus cast into doubt about the reality of her existence and the conflict between two basic ways of understanding herself (i.e. intuitively known freedom and empirically established determinism). The second portion of the work resolves the dilemma through an idealistic presentation of human knowledge. Everything 'external' to the human person is viewed as an idealistic projection of that person's knowledge. The subject and the objects of which the person is aware are actually one and the apparent division between them created by the conflict addressed in the first section is dissolved. A problem remains, however, in the possibility that the subject, the *ego*, is itself merely the product of thought. While transcendental idealism can solve the dilemma posed by scientific materialism, it is inadequate for grounding the real presence of the individual subject. So, Fichte moves into the third section: faith. Here Fichte maintains that we are directly aware of ourselves as individuals who have an impulse to act. This knowledge is not derived in the sense posited by the previous section (i.e. knowledge of objects) but it is established as knowledge, nonetheless, as I 'voluntarily decide to acquiesce in the view which naturally forces itself upon men in my impulse to affirm myself in action' (III/2, 99). The reality of the *ego* is thus grounded in practical reason – that is, knowledge of the self as it freely wills itself in its own action. The human person is both a spiritual being who can posit himself by an expression of 'a pure will' and a sensual being who can act through particular deeds (III/2, 100). In these three moves (doubt, knowledge, and faith), then, Fichte seeks to establish human existence on the basis of humanity's freedom and moral agency.

The Existential Dialogue: In the third section, Barth moves from those anthropological approaches that perceive humanity as 'a self-contained reality [*geschlossene Wirklichkeit*]' (III/2, 109) to one which addresses more clearly the problem of the human person's subjective existence in relation to something other than himself. Rather than approaching the human person

---

[56] We will not be concerned in this section, or in any of the subsequent discussions, with the question as to whether Barth summarizes and interprets his various conversation partners adequately. We will simply deal with the ideas and works as he has presented them in an effort to determine the manner in which he handles their ideas.

as an object of scientific enquiry or moral action, this third approach begins from the human person's existence as a personal subject. Barth thus engages existential philosophy, primarily as espoused by Karl Jaspers, as an example of this type of approach.

According to Barth, this existential approach comprises four key moves. (1) Existentialism recognizes that a complete anthropology must transcend mere objectivity and address the ground of human subjectivity itself. (2) The human person thus lives in a tension between his objective reality and his subjective quest for himself as that which lies beyond that objectivity. Lest this collapse into vicious circularity, the existentialist posits an external ground for human subjectivity in the subject's relation to something that is 'other' than herself. (3) The fundamental ground of human subjectivity, however, cannot itself be objectifiable (that is, not simply as another human person), but 'will undoubtedly elude all objectification, materialisation, or even spiritualization; indeed every kind of definition' (III/2, 112). (4) This transcendent other, though necessarily mysterious and remote, comes to us in 'those paradoxical situations of suffering and death, conflict and guilt' in which 'existence is transformed from a mere possibility into a reality . . . in the moments when in these unavoidable and inexplicable situations we have to wrestle with them, or rather with the transcendent which encounters us in them' (III/2, 112). The real subjectivity of the human person is thus constituted as she meets the transcendent 'other' in the most difficult circumstances of life.

b. Seeing the Phenomena: The Affirming Conversation

Barth is very clear on his appreciation for all three of these approaches to the phenomena of the human. He affirms that those thinkers who have addressed the biological phenomena have 'applied themselves seriously and fundamentally to the question of human phenomena' and have seen much that was 'both incontestable and important' (III/2, 85), pointing specifically to their recognition that humanity is at least relatively distinct from other creatures. He expresses particular appreciation for Portmann's work as indicating that humanity's 'biological singularity consists in the indissoluble connexion (peculiar to each individual) between his inherited tendencies and development on the one hand and his experience of history on the other' (III/2, 87). Such insights are important and '[i]t would be obstinate to disregard and ungrateful to ignore them' (III/2, 88).

Barth expresses a similar appreciation for the insights generated by the ethical approach, considering it a necessary improvement on the merely biological. Indeed, the ethical view's emphasis on humanity's freedom and agential activity indicates something that 'may well be supremely symptomatic' and 'may well be significant for the whole further development of our theological anthropology' (III/2, 94).

The existential approach is likewise treated favorably for its recognition of a phenomenon that is not only 'decisively important' but may even be 'the most genuine symptom [*echtestes Symptom*] of the human' (III/2, 113). Although he rejects the suggestion that the existentialist approach is essentially Christian, it still surpasses the previous accounts in its ability to 'show the being of man dynamically and in its basic openness as his act in relation to another than himself and in encounter with this other rather than self-grounded, self-resting and self-moving' (III/2, 114). Transcending the self-contained objectivity of naturalism and idealism, this account highlights what is for Barth one of the essential elements of true humanity, its necessary relationality and extrinsic determination.

In all three accounts, then, Barth fully affirms that legitimate human phenomena are recognized and analyzed from these non-theological perspectives in such a way as to contribute valuable insights. These insights must, therefore, be taken into account in our attempts to understand human nature.

c. Veiling the Phenomena: The Critical Conversation

1. The Christological Critique: Anthropological Myopia and Failing to See the True Human

Barth, however, also presents a critical evaluation of the actual accomplishments of these various approaches. First, in each dialogue, he contends that each fails to consider the human person from a christologically determined vantage point. Barth's six criteria for true humanity explicitly indicate the determinative significance of humanity's relationship to God in Jesus Christ. The nature of these three non-christological approaches, however, fails to take into account the attitude of God to man and man's relationship to God and are, therefore, definitively precluded from achieving any account of true humanity. Thus, although the biological account sees 'something of his aptitudes, capacities, and possibilities', it does not see true man (III/2, 89). The ethical account is superior in that it advances beyond 'the narrowness of naturalism', but we cannot think that we have thus 'attained to real man, to his uniqueness in creation. All our six criteria for the discovery of real man forbid this' (III/2, 94).[57]

It is important to realize at this point that Barth's christological criteria are not merely formal principles depicting the bare shape of human existence, which can then be filled with whatever data might be provided by some other discipline.[58] Instead, they designate both the form and (at least some of)

---

[57] Barth does not reiterate this specifically christological objection with respect to the existential account, but it certainly undergirds the entire discussion.

[58] Thus, Barth would not appreciate the suggestion that theological anthropology provides only the 'general categories [*die Grundkategorien*]' (Stock 1980: 537) for anthropology

the content of true humanity.[59] He is thus particularly critical of the ethical view's understanding of moral freedom. Humanity, in this approach, is not only viewed as theistically independent but also morally neutral. The human being of the ethical account is free to will both for and against God. It thus presents a picture of humanity that includes the human person standing in sinful contradiction to his existence in Christ as though it could be included in a depiction of true humanity. For Barth, this simply cannot stand as a valid anthropology, contradicting as it does the christologically determined picture of humanity as existing for the glory of God (criteria #3), under his lordship (criteria #4), with the freedom to will for God (criteria #5) in his service (criteria #6).

Although Barth expresses the greatest appreciation for the existential approach, he maintains that it too fails as an account of true humanity. Thus, it rightly points out that the subjectivity of human life is grounded in a historical encounter with an 'other'. Nonetheless, such an approach falls necessarily short of true humanity by abstracting humanity's existentiality from its determinative relation in Jesus Christ. Barth thus concludes that this approach fails to show us 'a genuine symptom of real humanity' because it does not know 'what true humanity is' (III/2, 121).

For Barth, then, each of the perspectives is fundamentally limited in its ability to understand the phenomena of the human by its non-christological starting point.[60]

2. Beyond the Christological Critique: Determining the Coherence of an Anthropology

In addition to these explicitly christological concerns, Barth also demonstrates his willingness to engage the coherence and consistency of these other approaches. Thus, he argues that the biological approach has sometimes

---

and, consequently is 'blind' without the insights of scientific anthropology (Price 2002: 500–29.

[59] That Barth does not derive all the material elements of his theological anthropology directly from his christological premises will become clear in the course of this discussion.

[60] It is worth noting at this point that throughout these discussions Barth avoids using the individual criteria in particular criticisms, rather, he wields them *en toto* to challenge the basic christological adequacy of some other perspective. Since he does not discuss his methodology with respect to using the criteria, it is difficult to establish whether he does this for pragmatic reasons (e.g. space and time) or more theoretical reasons (e.g. a concern about abstracting one criterion from the others). There does not, however, appear to be any particular theoretical reason to prohibit using the criteria individually for a more nuanced interaction with some particular perspective so long as their essential interconnectedness of all the criteria remains in view.

been used to interpret the biological phenomena as indicating the unique identity and value of the human person (III/2, 85–87). But, as Barth points out, the phenomena of the human demonstrate humanity to be only relatively distinguishable from, and in no way demonstrably superior to, other animals. Indeed, a comparison of human capabilities to those of the other creatures reveals that all animals have their distinctive attributes and that those of some of the animals far surpass those of human beings (III/2, 89).[61] Consequently, any attempt to interpret these phenomena as indicators of humanity's truly unique identity in relation to the rest of creation actually transcends the limits of the biological methodology. Value judgments that seek to establish humanity's identity on this basis are themselves not phenomenologically ascertainable and, consequently, lie beyond the proper scope of this approach (III/2, 89). Transcending the limitations of their perspective, these thinkers have misinterpreted the phenomena that were rightly theirs to consider.

Similarly, Barth presents an extended critique of the coherence of Fichte's moral philosophy (III/2, 103–09). First, Barth contends that Fichte attempted to develop an indeterministic view of human freedom and that such an approach is fundamentally flawed in its inability to provide the human person with the boundaries within which true freedom must operate. Second, he thinks that Fichte's idealistic grounding of human knowledge leaves the human person without any real knowledge of himself; he is thus not even free to know that he exists as more than a mere concept.[62] Third, the idealistic conception of human knowledge means that the human person is ultimately no different than the rest of creation and thus robs humanity of the differentiation so important, for Barth, to any valid understanding of humanity. Fourth, Fichte's attempt to ground the self in freely willed action is undermined and ultimately invalidated by the premises contained in the first two stages of his own argument. If the move to faith and understanding the person as act in the third stage of the argument is valid, Barth contends that it necessarily impacts the argument at a much earlier stage and calls into question the validity of the doubt and idealistic knowledge

---

[61] As Barth says, 'If it is clear that human possibilities as compared with those of the animals closest to man are far wider, yet it must also be remembered that not only these higher animals but that others also, which according to the usual scale of values are perhaps much lower in the ladder of creation, have possibilities which put those of man in the shade. And for all we know there may be animal possibilities which do not make us think merely because we do not perceive them.'

[62] So Barth contends, 'Man as Fichte understands him has no other source of knowledge. There can be no knowledge from without because there is no "without" anyway. This type of thinking is ended before it has even begun. Hence we can only note that he appears to speak of a supposedly free man about whom he is nevertheless obliged to report that he knows nothing of himself and can know nothing' (III/2, 106).

of the earlier discussions.[63] And finally, Barth thinks that Fichte's conclusion, humanity as the triumphant determiner of her own reality, means that his argument ultimately leaves the human person in the same condition as in deterministic naturalism – that is, no different than her environment.[64] While we cannot take the time to unpack each of these criticisms, it seems clear that Barth is willing to critique Fichte on logical as well as christological grounds.

This same approach can be seen in Barth's criticism of Jaspers' existentialism. First, Barth thinks that Jaspers has provided an insufficient account as to what makes particular situations meaningful as a 'frontier [*Grenze*]' situation (III/2, 114). Although man is 'everywhere involved in suffering and death, conflict and guilt', why should these negative situations be viewed as more existentially decisive than any other (III/2, 114)? The existentialist merely asserts their distinctive quality without providing any real assurances on the matter. Likewise, this approach provides no account of the character of the other itself: 'could it not equally well be a demon which fools us at that frontier as the ostensible and illusory goal of our search' (III/2, 116)? Although the existentialist provides us with 'solemn assurances' that this is not so, the nature of the other is so key to the system that the question is not so easily avoided. Third, Jaspers' account presumes that the human person will respond appropriately to the other in the frontier situation. At the most, the existentialist allows for the opposite response, rejection of the other. But what if the human person responds with complete indifference? Jaspers' system, according to Barth, does not seem to allow for this since the encounter with the other in the frontier situation is too dynamic to ignore in this fashion.

---

[63] Barth thus asks, 'Are the doubter and the knower so presented by Fichte that he can now legitimately introduce the same person as a believer in a mode of self-contemplation in which what was formerly invisible is now visible and what formerly seemed unreal suddenly becomes real, and therefore the former mode of self-knowledge is completely shattered and transcended? How can Fichtean man make this leap when there is nothing outside himself, so that he cannot be induced by any outward cause to make any such radical transformation in his mode of self-contemplation?' (III/2, 106). Even if such a move were possible, Barth argues that it should inform the argument from the beginning: 'How could the doubter and the knower speak as Fichte makes them speak if his believer must speak in this way? If what is here said about man is fundamentally and intrinsically valid, how can it fail to have been stated earlier?' (III/2, 107).

[64] Again Barth critiques Fichte with a question, 'Does not this really bring us back to the point from which the whole essay started, to the vision, as it appears to uncritical knowledge. Of the one in the all, of the all in the one, of the great life stream in which man is only a tiny drop?' (III/2, 107). Although Fichte attempts to reverse this by focusing on the human person rather than external realities, 'In the last resort does it not amount to the same thing whether we see the one which is the all, the all which is the one, from the standpoint of its universal structure or any other part, or from that of man himself?' (III/2, 107).

But this neglects the harsh realities of human life, which is more often characterized by apathy and lethargy. Finally, and most decisively, Barth argues that Jaspers' account does not really transcend the human individual at all. This system requires that the human person be capable of placing unconditional trust in the other. But this means that 'the unconditional trust and therefore the transcendence which we supposed him to lack . . . is already within him' (III/2, 118). Since he already has the capacity for a trust that transcends himself, he possesses a transcendent dimension within himself. 'Thus man does not really need to ask concerning transcendence. Indeed, in the strict sense he cannot. What he can and must do is simply to understand that he himself is the answer to his question' (III/2, 119).

V. Dialogue vs. Monologue: We Are Talking but Is Anyone Listening?

Having developed a better appreciation for Barth's christological criteria, it remains to determine the extent to which these interactions can be considered a dialogue in which Barth is actually willing to learn and be challenged rather than a mere monologue that has been pre-determined by Barth's christological presuppositions. Through each of the three discussions, we have seen that Barth remains firmly committed to his christological criteria and that he uses them with relentless consistency to establish the inadequacy of these alternate anthropologies for depicting true humanity. Viewed from one angle, this could easily be understood as an indication that these are not true dialogues and that the outcome has been determined from the beginning. However, as we saw with McDowell's discussion of theological conversation earlier, a commitment to one's own particularity, including one's particular presuppositions, is necessary to engaging in meaningful conversation. Consequently, refusal to identify and embrace one's presuppositions is actually a refusal to participate in conversation. Thus, simply noting that Barth is committed to his christological presuppositions is insufficient for determining that these interactions do not qualify as legitimate conversations. Additionally, although Barth would not entertain the possibility that the christological center of his theology could be overturned through any dialogical encounter, his commitment to the relativity of all theological formulations leaves him at least theoretically open to the transformation of his understanding and articulation of theological realities through such conversational events.[65] Thus, although the center of his presuppositional structure

---

[65] Price thinks that Barth's refusal to allow for the possibility that science could 'invalidate the findings of theology' ultimately severs any real contact between them (2002: 10–11). Similarly, Webster suggests that Barth's theology is characterized by 'a perverse kind of idealism, an isolation of theological language about human nature and history

is not open to critique, Barth's particular formulation of it may be. Even at this level of encounter, then, Barth is not necessarily an isolationist.[66]

Barth's openness to significant conversation becomes even more apparent when we move to the level of particular phenomena. At the end of §44.3 ('Real Man'), which Barth devotes to a development of true humanity as it stands 'in the divinely initiated history of his self-responsibility before God the Creator' (III/2, 199), he returns to a consideration of the phenomena. He argues that now, with a well-established understanding of true humanity, he is in a position 'where a radical reconsideration of these aspects is possible' (III/2, 198).[67] Although a knowledge of true humanity is a necessary presupposition for this phenomenological analysis to have genuine significance for theological anthropology, that does not change the fact that this is still a genuine extra-ecclesial source of information that can lead to 'a non-theological but genuine knowledge of the phenomena of the human' (III/2, 199).[68]

Thus, all three accounts provide insights into human phenomena that Barth finds enlightening about the nature of real humanity: the biological account of humanity in its 'interconnexion with other cosmic phenomena' (III/2, 200), the ethical depiction of the human person 'in his freedom to rise above the organic chemico-biological process into the free field of a history initiated and experienced by himself' (III/2, 201), and the existential description of

---

from the "phenomena of the human" to which he grants no real definitive role in discovering what he calls "real man"' (1995: 68). His concern seems to be, then, that Barth's refusal to allow the phenomena to inform his understanding of true humanity necessitates some level of isolation between the different modes of discourse. Although it seems that the way Barth actually formulated his theology can be criticized along these lines, there are resources in his distinction between revelation and theology for handling this objection (cf. I/1, 47–87). While Barth would never allow the possibility that God's sovereign revelation could be subjected to a scientific critique, there seems to be no reason why his theology could not be open to a scientific or philosophical critique of some particular theological formulation given its necessarily human limitations (cf. Johnson 1997: 281–82).

[66] This is true at least in theory although one could certainly challenge whether Barth consistently demonstrates such theoretical openness in practice.

[67] Johnson argues that it is only at this point that Barth is able to address the phenomena positively (1997: 79). As we have seen, though, the positive aspects of Barth's evaluation have been clear throughout his discussion. What this later section allows him to do is to indicate some of the ways in which these insights can be appropriated when they are viewed *retrospectively* from the perspective of true humanity. His earlier positive evaluations are thus strengthened and clarified by showing how these insights can be incorporated into his christological anthropology in the concluding section.

[68] Price seems to think that this implies a shift from I/1 where Barth proposed 'that theology can learn little from other sciences with regard to its own method' (2002: 108; cf. I/1, 8–10). He does not make it clear, though, how this critical and *ad hoc* use of non-theological insights constitutes a weakening of his prohibition against methodological dependence.

'man in his openness towards a without ... of true transcendence which proclaims itself only in the fact of the limitation of human existence' (III/2, 201).[69] Thus, it is clear that, as Marshall argues, Barth does not think that theology needs to derive all of its anthropological insights from that which is '"immediately derivable" from scripture's talk of God in Christ' since this forms theology's 'primary orientation, not its exhaustive source' (1983: 457).[70]

For Barth, then, there can be no final separation between theological and non-theological modes of discourse.[71] Although there are significant differences between the various disciplines that must be recognized and respected, they should not be understood as occupying distinct and unrelated spheres.[72] By contrast, Barth understands all truth to be God's truth and thus to lie within the purview of theology.[73] Theological anthropology, therefore, cannot be separated from other anthropological approaches, but, as the 'exhaustive and superior' presupposition, it actually has the task of understanding and critically appropriating, whenever useful, all other presuppositions.[74] Marshall thus argues that Barth's theology is properly understood as 'totalistic' in that

---

[69] An important question that is often raised at this point is whether this is an indication that Barth's later theology exhibits a change in his position on natural theology (cf. Brunner 1951: 123–35; Crawford 1972: 320–21; and Anderson 1986). There can be no question, though, of a weakening on natural theology here. Throughout III/2 Barth has retained his negative evaluation of natural theology (III/2, 29–41, 79, 321, 520). Although he is open to the theological use of insights from other disciplines, this can only take place when these insights are understood in light of a *prior* knowledge of humanity's relationship to God through Jesus that can *only* be known through revelation (cf. Torrance 1962: 22–23 and Pannenberg 1991: 102–03).

[70] In his review essay of III/2, Brunner questions whether this does not amount to the same as his espousal of 'eristics' (1951: 130–31). Barth's interdisciplinary dialogue, however, never seeks to be an apologetic engagement for the purpose of preparing, positively or negatively, a point of contact amenable to revelation.

[71] T. Torrance thus argues that, for Barth, theology and science are closely related spheres of inquiry in that they share 'important problems and questions' but that they never surrender their distinct characteristics (1990: 51, 60).

[72] I/1, 1–11; Barth 1979: 113–14; cf. Price 2002: 105–07. Marshall thus argues that Barth 'seems concerned to deny rather than assert that there are "spheres" of discourse "external" to theology (as the first two theses of the Barmen Declaration perhaps most succinctly insist). Since theological discourse has no abiding "outside", distinctions between discourse "internal" and "external" to theology, while in some respects perhaps provisionally useful, can in principle never be binding' (1983: 456). Price affirms the same idea although he expresses some frustration that Barth failed to indicate the relationship between these various modes of discourse more clearly (2002: 109–15).

[73] Cf. Hartwell 1964: 43; McLelland 1974; and Schwöbel 2000.

[74] Hunsinger describes this process using the distinction between 'analytic' truths derived 'by way of inference from beliefs ... established as doctrinally warranted' and 'synthetic' truths derived 'by way of critically rethinking or reconstructing concepts first devised elsewhere in order to make them compatible with Christian theology' (1991: 61). Thus, when Barth adopts the existential concept of a determination of the person

it includes everything within the scope of its inquiry 'and so necessarily engages in critical dialogue with, rather than staying at "one remove from", the spirit (or spirits) of its time' (1983: 456–57).[75]

Before concluding this section, one final question needs to be addressed. Barth has routinely been criticized for neglecting empirical realities in his theological anthropology.[76] If his theology is open to interdisciplinary dialogue as argued in this chapter, one might wonder why his theology is not characterized by greater practical engagement with their empirical insights. First, we must recognize that Barth's theology was limited by the scope of his primary interests and concerns. Barth repeatedly indicated that the primary concern of his theological anthropology was to develop an account of true humanity as it is (and can only be) revealed through the person of Jesus Christ. Although he was 'open' to the possibility of other sources of anthropological knowledge, he fully admits that it was not his purpose 'to give even an indicatory or encyclopaedic exposition of this knowledge' (III/2, 199).[77] Criticizing his 'neglect' of empirical phenomena, therefore, may well be an example of faulting him for failing at something he never intended to accomplish. Second, Barth's account of humanity in III/2 must not be divorced from the ethics of creation in III/4; as integral parts of Barth's doctrine of creation, the two volumes must be read together.[78] Barth's extensive engagement with

---

through encounter with an 'other', he notes that he does so only as a concept that has now been filled with a specifically christological content (III/2, 134). There can, therefore, be no question of 'an exact correspondence and coincidence between the Christian statements and these others which rest on very different foundations,' but we should not be surprised of or unwilling to make use of the 'approximations and similarities' that inevitably arise (III/2, 277).

[75] According to Hunsinger then, we can make a useful distinction between conceptual frameworks and their material contents (2000d: 293). The former necessarily conflicts with Christianity in that two 'comprehensive organizing frameworks' are by definition incompatible. With respect to the latter, however, much of the material content of these systems is 'not only compatible with the gospel, but useful, in certain circumstances even necessary, for the Christian community to adopt' (2000d: 293).

[76] Biggar provides a useful summary of several such critiques (1993: 156–61).

[77] Thus Eberhard Busch states that his theology 'does not try to avoid problems but has, at the same time, the courage to leave otherwise much discussed "issues" aside because it believes that it has to deal with more urgent and important things' (2004: xii). Similarly, Johnson notes that despite Barth's reticence to indicate and explore specific examples of such secular sources of truth, there are a wide variety of ways in which such sources could be theologically useful (1997: 41).

[78] This is in accord with Barth's general commitment to maintaining the essential relationship between ethics and dogmatics (cf. I/1, xvi). Webster argues that neglecting the integral importance of Barth's ethical discussions 'attracts all manner of misinterpretations which can be corrected only by attending to what Barth has to say in its completeness' (2004b: 14). For a brief discussion of some thematic and structural connections between III/2 and III/4 see Preece 2001: 147–70.

the hard realities of human life in the latter part-volume (e.g. family life, abortion, war, etc.) must be seen, therefore, as the practical outworking of his more theoretical treatment in III/2.[79]

VI. Conclusion: Open and Closed – A Properly Delimited Conversation

Properly understood, Barth's christocentric approach to theology involves *neither* an unnecessary constriction of theology resulting in its isolation from all other forms of discourse *nor* an indeterministic openness that undermines the positive and objective nature of the divine self-revelation. Instead, Barth's insistence that Christian theology can *only* be grounded in the person and work of Jesus Christ constitutes a determinate starting point that grounds the possibility of any meaningful interdisciplinary dialogue. In this way, Barth's theology can be viewed as enabling a christologically determined engagement with non-theological disciplines.

In the three dialogues that we considered in the second half of this chapter, Barth exhibits the shape that he thinks such a dialogue should take, one that involves both a positive and a negative moment. Negatively, Barth presents a dialogue in which the theologian must remain firmly committed to the exclusiveness of the christological vantage point as the only perspective from which to view true humanity. On this basis, the theologian enters into a critical engagement with the inherently limited starting points adopted by other anthropological disciplines and the various ways in which their material development fails to cohere adequately with the christologically determined view of humanity. Additionally, the theologian must analyze the extent to which these other anthropological approaches present a coherent account of humanity. Barth thus devotes a fair portion of each section to pointing out various methodological and logical inconsistencies in these proposals.[80] The negative moment of Barth's interdisciplinary dialogue, then, can be summarized as: (1) a christological critique of its formal presuppositions; (2) a christological critique of its material interpretations; and (3) a rational critique of its methodological consistency and logical coherency.

This negative moment, however, should not be allowed to obscure the essential positive moment. Thus, we have seen that Barth fully appreciates

---

[79] McLean (1981: 40) and Preece (2001: 163–64) likewise argue for the theoretical strengths that Barth's theology has for engaging empirical realities despite his occasionally minimalist treatment of such issues.

[80] It is thus clear that Barth's christological criteria are necessary but not sufficient for establishing the validity of any account of human phenomena. Elsewhere in III/2 Barth also uses a pragmatic criterion for evaluating non-theological disciplines (e.g. III/2, 382–90).

the valuable contributions of these non-christological perspectives. While we cannot encounter real man through these limited vantage points, they can nonetheless provide insightful glimpses into the nature of human phenomena within their own frames of reference. As Johnson affirms, 'Even though secular knowledge provides no firm basis for a so-called natural theology of God, there is still something worth discovering and knowing in all these various ways of being human' (1997: 80).

Consequently, having discussed and evaluated three different, non-theological approaches to anthropology, each of which has sought to understand the human person 'in his own strength and by his own resources,' Barth concludes, that 'we have not encountered real man in this way' (III/2, 121). He acknowledges that this is because he set out from the very beginning determined to refuse any conception of true humanity 'which is neutral, indefinite or obscure in respect of God's attitude towards it and its own attitude towards God' (III/2, 121). Therefore, on the basis of the christological criteria, these anthropological discussions were 'necessarily critical' and ultimately unsatisfactory (III/2, 121). But, as we have seen, rather than rejecting these alternative approaches, he appreciates them as presenting 'a progressively more penetrating analysis of the picture in which man can see and understand himself' (III/2, 121–22). Once again, then, Barth's 'No' is subsumed within a larger 'Yes'.[81] Though unable to reveal true humanity, he can nonetheless appreciate their accomplishments in their own frames of reference.

As we move into the next chapter and then into our own engagement with interdisciplinary dialogue in the second part of this study, we must, therefore, keep in mind (1) the foundational importance of Barth's christological criteria for ascertaining the true form and basic content of any properly theological anthropology; (2) the vital importance of alternate perspectives for developing a well-rounded understanding of the human person; (3) the close relationship between theology and these non-theological perspectives; and (4) the process by which Barth's christological anthropology analyzes, criticizes, and, when necessary, critically appropriates these insights. Holding together these four points, we will be able both to appreciate and more properly evaluate what Barth is doing as he addresses the question of human ontology.

---

[81] See Hunsinger 2000d: 280.

4

CHRIST, SPIRIT, AND COVENANT: A MODEL FOR HUMAN ONTOLOGY[1]

I. Wholeness, Duality, and Order: The Terms of Barth's Concrete Ontology

Having now established the method and form of Barth's christocentric anthropology as well as its openness to dialogue with non-theological perspectives, we are finally in a position to engage Barth's understanding of the body–soul relationship itself. As one of the three main foci in the constructive development of Barth's theological anthropology (relationality, ontology, and temporality), he clearly believes that ontology has decisive importance for understanding the human person.[2] He therefore treats this issue at great length in §46 as he presents an account of human ontology that is grounded in Christology, pneumatology, and the covenantal relationship between God and human persons.[3]

---

[1] Portions of this chapter will be published in a modified form in a forthcoming article; see Cortez 2008.

[2] It is true that Barth delays his treatment of human ontology until halfway through III/2. But he develops his account at this point not because it is only a secondary concern, but because he believes that it is only after having laid a properly christological foundation for theological anthropology that the question of human ontology can be adequately addressed. By proceeding in this way, Barth thinks that he gains an 'advantage over the older dogmatics' that failed to ground their discussions christologically (III/2, 325). This, he argues, will help him 'avoid a certain one-sidedness, exaggeration and vulnerability' (III/2, 325). Far from being of minimal importance, then, Barth identifies ontology as one of fundamental importance for theological anthropology and an issue he engages extensively (*contra* Price 2002: 247).

[3] Basing his ontology on these theological convictions, Barth thus differs from those contemporary theologians who have moved away from substance dualism as a response either to modern scientific developments, the perception that Greek philosophy has

As always, Barth is committed in this section to grounding his theological formulations in Scripture.[4] Indeed, Barth thinks the only way to reach 'a Christian understanding' of humanity that remains unencumbered by alien perspectives is through 'an adequately biblical and exegetical ground' (III/2, 326). He is well aware, though, that the biblical accounts do not specifically and unambiguously address many of the issues that arise in the course of such a discussion (III/2, 325–26).[5] Thus, although Barth strives to ground his ontological argument in the biblical text, he recognizes from the beginning that the material is rather limited and, consequently, his arguments are often driven more by theological commitments than exegetical arguments.[6]

But exactly what kind of ontology does Barth offer? According to Barth, the ontological constitution of human persons is best understood as a properly

---

unduly influenced theology at this point, or the conceptual problems associated with substance dualism (Grenz 1994: 158–60). As we saw in the last chapter, Barth's theology is open to correspondences with scientific disciplines (cf. Price 2002; and McLean 1986: 138), but Barth certainly would not have responded favorably to Price's suggestion that theology should alter its language about human ontology simply because of modern scientific developments (2002: 251–52). Likewise, Barth was well aware of Greek philosophical influences on theological anthropology at this point (III/2, 380–82), but rejected such philosophical influences as grounds for dismissing any particular theological formulations, since *all* theology is influenced by some philosophy (I/2, 728–29). Finally, we will see that Barth was familiar with the conceptual problems associated with substance dualism but they comprise neither the foundation of his argument nor even his most substantial objection.

[4] Barth's commitment to Scripture as the exegetical basis of theology can be traced to the earliest stages of his theological development (Watson 2000: 57–58). Indeed, Barth argues that commitment to Scripture is what distinguishes a properly Christian theology (I/1, 48). Though his exegesis has, at times, been subjected to pointed critique (e.g. Crawford 1972; Frey 1978: 209; and Barr 1994), several recent studies have affirmed his attentiveness to the biblical text and his careful and imaginative interpretations (e.g. Hunsinger 2000a: 210–25; Torrance 1990: 76–77; Watson 2000: 57–71; Ford 1979a: 55–87; and Cunningham 1995).

[5] Cf. also Berkouwer 1962: 31; Kümmel 1963: 38, 93–94; Jewett 1971: 1–4; and Green 2004c: 194. There is even significant disagreement about the proper background against which to understand the biblical texts. Joel Green, for example, has forcefully argued in a series of recent papers that the biblical milieu was not exclusively dualistic and, therefore, that we cannot simply assume a dualistic background for the anthropological language of the Bible (1998, 2002a, 2004a). N. T. Wright, on the other hand, contends that the proper background for understanding the biblical texts is the anthropological dualism of large strands of second temple Judaism (2003).

[6] This is certainly not to negate the significance of Barth's commitment to exegesis or his extensive use of exegetical argumentation throughout this paragraph. As Watson correctly warns, interpreters who minimize the significance of exegesis in the *Church Dogmatics* 'will radically misinterpret that project' (2000: 57). Rather than minimizing Barth's exegesis, then, this simply acknowledges, as Barth did, that the biblical texts do not answer many of the questions that must be raised in a discussion of human ontology and, therefore, the argument must move in a different direction.

ordered and unified duality of body and soul that is created, preserved, and regenerated by the Holy Spirit and so constituted as God's covenantal partner. Thus, as body *and* soul, the human person is 'wholly and simultaneously both, in ineffaceable difference, inseparable unity, and indestructible order' (III/2, 325). Barth thus builds his understanding of human ontology on two sets of terms: *body, soul, spirit* and *wholeness, duality, order*.

The very nature of this language, though, immediately raises 'a whole complex of problems' (III/2, 326) which renders its use problematic. The fact that Barth openly associates body–soul language with wide ranging word-pairs like spirit–substantial organism, rational–sensuous, inner–outer, invisible–visible, inapprehensible–apprehensible, intelligible–empirical, and heavenly–earthly indicates the broad associations this language has and the complex issues surrounding its application.[7] Fully aware, then, of the problems associated with body–soul language, Barth chooses this manner of speaking, not because of its terminological clarity, but because it serves to raise the primary problems that an account of human being must address and because it has the advantage of retaining the predominant biblical terms for human nature.

So, then, how should we understand Barth's ontology? From one perspective, Barth's ontology is clearly monistic. As we will see, he rejects any notion that the human person comprises two distinct substances, but affirms instead the holistic union of body and soul in one person. Barth's view, then, can be properly described as 'concrete monism' (III/2, 393). On the very next page, however, he asserts that his view could also be understood as 'the concrete and Christian dualism of soul and body' (III/2, 394). What kind of ontology does Barth think he is offering that can be adequately described, in some way, as both dualist *and* monist?

Barth's interpreters seem to be divided over this very issue.[8] Many interpreters affirm Barth's accent on the wholeness of the human person as it stands in contrast to the substance dualism of much traditional Christian theology.[9]

---

[7] It is worth noting at this point that the various word-pairs Barth identifies as being legitimate ways of characterizing human ontology strongly suggests that he would have been open to mind–body or even mind–brain as serving this same purpose, though admittedly with slightly different emphases. Indeed, as Frede points out, historically speaking 'to talk about the soul is to talk about the mind conceived in a certain way' (1992: 93).

[8] Spezio rightly comments that the differences among Barth's interpreters can be attributed both to misinterpretations and to Barth's own lack of clarity (2004: 587). Barth's occasional lack of clarity, however, is often due to his commitment to follow the object of his investigation wherever it might lead rather than bind himself to some arbitrarily determined idea of conceptual coherence (III/2, 583) – a concept that Spezio himself notes earlier in his article but fails to connect to Barth's methodology.

[9] For example, Anderson 1982: 210–11; Hoekema 1986: 216–17; Berkouwer 1962: 93–94; Price 2002: 20–21, 248; and McLean 1981: 46.

But these interpreters fail to acknowledge, or possibly fail to realize, that holistic language of this nature does not resolve the body–soul question. They appear to think that identifying Barth as a 'holist' is sufficient to distinguish him from other ontological approaches (e.g. reductive monism or substance dualism).[10] But, holistic language merely provides a different, though possibly superior, language for discussing the body–soul question rather than an actual answer to the problem of their particular relation.[11] Other interpreters, however, take a different approach. Noting Barth's use of the traditional body–soul language and his equally strong emphasis on the duality inherent in human nature, they conclude that his ontology at least implicitly affirms some form of dualism.[12]

As we take a closer look at Barth's ontology, we will see that the reason this question can be so difficult is because it is the wrong question. Or, rather, the question approaches the issue from the wrong direction. Focusing on the 'problem' of human nature, Barth's interpreters expect to see a 'solution' that can provide an adequate theory of the body–soul relation. Barth's focus, however, as we saw in Chapter 2, is on understanding the implications that (1) the person and work of Jesus Christ as the true human and (2) the covenantal relationship in which all humans have been summoned to participate

---

[10] The limitations of such holistic language for discriminating among approaches can be seen in the fact that it is used by both dualists (e.g. Cooper 2000; and Moreland 1995: 102) and physicalists (e.g. Green 2002b: 3–22; and Gregersen 2000: 153–88).

[11] Hirst ([1959] 2004: 105) and Kim (1998a: 8–10) both correctly argue that their emphasis on 'unity' and 'supervenience' respectively may provide superior languages for articulating the problem but do not actually provide solutions. Macquarrie similarly argues that 'personal' language does not resolve the body–soul problem but that it is less obviously biased toward idealism, materialism, or reductionism and, therefore, is a superior language for speaking of human persons (1982: 50). Noting, as Price does, that Barth views the body–soul relation in dynamic rather than substantialist terms may be another example of a different 'language' that, while somewhat useful, still does not address the more theoretical issues involved (Price 2002: 248).

[12] Paul Newman thus argues that in spite of Barth's statements and qualifications to the contrary, 'the oblique insinuation of dualism' persists because of his emphasis on the necessity of soul language (1981: 423). Similarly, Willis argues, 'it appears virtually impossible to employ this terminology without importing a note of dualism (classical, Cartesian, or other) into the discussion, however severely one warns against this possibility' (1971: 236). Taking issue with Barth's emphasis on the primacy of the soul in the human person, Moltmann asserts that Barth 'only slightly modifies the answers given by Plato and Descartes' (1985: 252). Even interpreters who do not posit an implicit dualism seem to think that there are dualistic impulses in Barth's anthropology. Price, who is fully aware of Barth's emphasis on unity and his rejection of dualistic approaches to humanity, argues that there are strong similarities between Barth and the interactionist dualist Sir John Eccles (2002: 254–55). Similarly, immediately after noting Barth's rejection of substance dualism, Berkouwer states that Barth 'rejects just as strongly *any* monistic anthropology' (1962: 94, emphasis added). Such a statement would seem to imply some level of openness to a *non*-monistic anthropology of some kind.

have for understanding human nature. In other words, given the reality of the incarnation, the atonement, and the covenantal relationship between God and all human persons, what must we believe about the ontology of the human person? In the course of our study, we will see that this methodology leads Barth to develop a particular picture of human nature – a pneumatologically grounded unity, duality, and order – that has implications for developing a theoretical account of the body–soul relationship but does not itself constitute such a theory.

Understanding the precise nature of this pre-theoretical presentation and the theological commitments upon which it is established will require two things. First, we will need to understand how Barth answers three questions: (1) *What* are the basic aspects or components of the human person's ontological constitution? (2) *How* is this ontological constitution maintained? And (3) *why* is the human person constituted in this way? As we have seen, though, Barth's theological presuppositions and methodological commitments require that these three questions in turn be subordinated to an even more fundamental question – *who* is the true human and thus the one who manifests true human ontology? Having answered these questions, we will also need to understand the theoretical implications of his ontology. We will see that Barth's anthropological ontology can be understood as a *model* of human nature generated by his christological *paradigm*, which has implications for generating more precise *theories* of the body–soul relationship.[13]

II. The What, How, and Why of Barth's Concrete Ontology

a. The Significance of the 'Who?' Question for Human Ontology

Although we have seen that Barth is sensitive to the phenomena of human existence, he denies that any 'purely' phenomenological depiction of humanity is adequate for establishing a firm foundation upon which to develop an understanding of human ontology (III/2, 419–22).[14] In keeping with his well-known dislike of abstractions in theology,[15] then, Barth maintains that

---

[13] That Barth does not develop a theoretical account does not mean that he would have been opposed to such a project. Elsewhere, Barth demonstrates his openness to philosophical constructions so long as they do not serve as a substitute for faith (e.g. III/3, 23).
[14] This is in contrast, then, with some contemporary theologians who explicitly adopt a more phenomenological approach (e.g. Macquarrie 1982 and Pannenberg 1985).
[15] See Hunsinger 1991: 51–52.

theological anthropology must focus on the 'concrete reality' of Jesus Christ (III/2, 393).[16] Thus, although §46 is focused on addressing important questions about *what* human beings are, *how* they come to be what they are, and *why* God has created them in this way, he asserts that these questions simply cannot be answered in abstraction from the '*who*' upon whom their answers are firmly established (III/2, 421). Acknowledging the primacy of the *who* question, according to Barth, is particularly important at this point. Barth is well aware that the realm of human ontology has been explored by many non-theological disciplines and, without a firm christological foundation, 'one can very easily go astray' (III/2, 325) among these other approaches.[17]

> Here too . . . . [w]e find our bearings and our instruction as we look to the constitution of the humanity of Jesus. With the clarity and certainty that we gain here, we can then set out the propositions in which the Christian understanding of the constitution of all men generally may be expressed and comprehended. (III/2, 327)

Failing to proceed christologically at this point 'would be intolerable, would have the most fatal consequences, and would give free entrance to the most varied ambiguities and errors' (III/2, 326). The precise nature of these intolerable consequences, ambiguities, and errors will become clear through the course of this chapter as nearly all of Barth's criticisms of alternate ontological perspectives stem from their inability or unwillingness to view man from this christologically determined vantage point.

b. *What* Are We? Wholeness, Duality, and Order in Human Nature

Beginning from the secure vantage point provided by the *who* of Jesus Christ, then, Barth argues that we must view the human person as having a nature that is *whole*, *dual*, and *ordered*. Using these three perspectives, Barth seeks to depict the relationship of *body*, *soul*, and *spirit* in the human person in

---

[16] Barth's insistence on understanding human ontology from a broad, christological perspective is thus antithetical to modern reductionistic approaches and consistent with Barth's overall emphasis on understanding parts only in terms of their comprehensive wholes (see McLean 1981: 13).

[17] This comment raises the question of Barth's relationship to these earlier approaches. While questions regarding the philosophical and theological background of Barth's ontology are interesting and worth exploring (though see McCormack's criticism of such studies for positing merely parallel relationships without establishing any solid connections [2002: 236–39]), they are ultimately of limited value in determining the validity and adequacy of his ideas. This study will, therefore, address such issues only in a very limited fashion.

CHRIST, SPIRIT, AND COVENANT

a manner that is faithful to the person and work of Jesus Christ and the covenantal relationship to which all human persons have been summoned in him.

1. 'One Whole Man': The Holistic Starting Point

The narratival presentation of Jesus Christ in the Bible, according to Barth, reveals that any suggestion of a discontinuous duality implied in his adoption of body–soul language is simply inadequate when applied to the person and work of Jesus (III/2, 327).[18] Instead, the Bible describes him from every direction as a whole person:

> Far from existing as the union of two parts or two 'substances', He is one whole man, embodied soul and besouled body: the one in the other and never merely beside it; the one never without the other but only with it, and in it present, active and significant; the one with all its attributes always to be taken as seriously as the other. (III/2, 327)

For Barth, the biblical emphasis on this holistic depiction of Jesus is so clear and strong that there can be no other starting point for developing an anthropological ontology (III/2, 371).[19]

Looking first at Jesus' life in general, Barth sees a person in whom there is no conflict or tension between the inner and outer dimensions of his existence (III/2, 338).[20] Although the Bible makes clear that Jesus' life was characterized

---

[18] Throughout this section, Barth's argument focuses primarily on the total impression generated by the biblical narratives rather than exegetical examinations of particular texts. Barth's argument, then, does not revolve around identifying particular (proof) texts that might support his point; instead it builds on the way the Bible portrays Jesus as a person through its various narratives. Several people have noted Barth's narratival emphasis on 'the overall shape and pattern of the text' (Mangina 2004: 43) and its similarity to contemporary narrative theology (e.g. Kelsey 1975: 44, 48). This can be a useful comparison if we recognize, as Bloesch rightly argues, Barth's 'firm insistence on the historical basis of the Christian faith' in distinction from any form of narrative theology that divorces the world of the text from its historical location (1992: 30; cf. also Mangina 2004: 43; and Broz 1988, esp. 23–24).

[19] Cf. Moltmann 1985: 244.

[20] Such a description of Jesus' life unfortunately neglects the real tensions that are occasionally seen in Jesus' life – that is, Gethsemane (Mt. 26.37 ff.). With respect to this scene Barth only comments that it demonstrates the reality of Jesus' inner life without noting its implications for depicting his body–soul relation exclusively in peaceful terms (III/2, 328). Barth may have been better served by using his emphasis on Jesus' solidarity with human persons in taking up human 'flesh' with its contradictions and tensions (III/2, 335–40; cf. IV/1, 171–75, 216) to argue that inner tension and conflict is a real aspect of our present earthly state even though the biblical emphasis on the unity of the whole person points in the direction of a redeemed life where harmony between these two aspects of the person is the goal (cf. Moltmann 1985: 352–53; and Sherlock 1996: 219–20).

81

by vital interior and exterior dimensions, he argues that the Bible always has the whole person of Christ in view and that passages focusing on one dimension or the other are quite rare (III/2, 328–30). The Bible thus leads the reader to view Jesus as 'the unity of two realms or aspects' and, therefore, as 'a real man' (III/2, 328). Both are essential, but their unity is the focus of the biblical portrayal.

Barth finds a similar emphasis in the biblical account of Jesus' work, particularly his atoning work.[21] Looking at the many biblical passages that talk about Jesus offering *himself* (ἑαυτός; e.g. Gal. 1.4; 2.20; Eph. 5.2, 25), his soul (ψυχή, e.g. Mt. 10.28; Jn. 10.11, 15; 15.13), or his body (σῶμα; e.g. Lk. 22.19; Heb. 10.10; Rom. 7.4), Barth concludes that the atonement was the unified action of a whole person (III/2, 328–40).[22] Indeed, all of Jesus' deeds demonstrate the unity of his work and, thus, the unity of his person. For Barth, then, only a holistic presentation of human ontology presents an adequate understanding of Jesus' work.

Finally, Barth finds this holistic emphasis even in the death and resurrection narratives. From beginning to end, the Gospels portray Jesus as a single, whole individual. Although there is 'a transformation' that takes place between Jesus' death and resurrection there is no change in his body–soul relation such that there is 'division' or 'subtraction' (III/2, 327). Rather, 'As the same whole man, soul and body, He rises as He died, and sits at the right hand of God, and will come again' (III/2, 327). Thus, against all docetic interpretations of the resurrection the Bible portrays the resurrected Christ as a whole body–soul entity who exists in continuous identity with the pre-resurrection Jesus.[23]

In every aspect of Jesus' life, ministry, and death, then, Barth finds the Bible describing him as a holistic union of body and soul; a holism that permeates everything that he says, does, and is.

> And He is one whole man in His relation to others, in what He does for them, what He gives them, what He asks of them, what He is for them and for the whole cosmos. He does not fulfil His office and His work from His miraculous annunciation to His fulfilment in such a way that we can separate His outer form from His inner or His inner form from His outer. Everything is the revelation of an inner, invisible, spiritual plane of life. But it is almost more striking and characteristic that everything has an outer, visible, bodily form. (III/2, 327)

An anthropological ontology that begins from the perspective of this concrete reality must, therefore, take the whole person as its point of departure.

---

[21] This is thus consistent with Barth's overall emphasis on the inseparable unity of Christ's person and work (IV/1, 122–28).
[22] Cf. IV/1, 225.
[23] Cf. III/2, 441–54.

2. Two Distinct Moments: The Duality of the Human Person

This does not mean, however, that such a holistic perspective exhausts the reality of human nature. According to Barth, the christological picture presents the wholeness of the human person so clearly that one might easily miss the important distinctions that must be drawn. Despite his holistic emphasis, Barth consistently maintains a duality within the human person.[24] Body and soul, though integrally united and interdependent, are neither identical nor reducible to one another. They are the 'two moments' of the one human person and are always distinguishable aspects of human nature (III/2, 399).[25] Consequently, we can only keep ourselves from 'prejudice, abstraction and one-sidedness' by realizing that, although Jesus presents the human person as 'wholly and simultaneously' both soul and body, there is still an 'inner differentiation' (III/2, 372.).[26] For Barth, then, body and soul are distinguishable determinations of human persons that are neither identical nor reducible. There can be no effective accounting of the human person without an equal emphasis on both soul and body. As soon as any attempt is made to address the nature of the human person, 'we are confronted by the remarkable fact that . . . we have to do with a whole, but with a whole in which there is antithesis, and therefore with a duality' (III/2, 367).

It will help at this point to define more clearly how Barth uses the terms *body* and *soul*. First, he understands a person's *body* to be her 'material body' (III/2, 350), which as such is 'visible, outward, earthly' (III/2, 367). The body, therefore, is 'sensuous', 'empirical', and available to study in ways that the soul is not (III/2, 326).[27] For Barth, then, the body represents the objective aspect of human nature and can be defined as:

> a spatio-material system of relations. . . . It is spatial, i.e., it is essential to it to be at its own specific point in space. It is material, i.e., it is essential to it to be distinct from other bodies in virtue of its own specific

---

[24] Drawing on Trinitarian language, Moltmann offers a similar perspective by affirming 'that body and soul interact 'perichoretically' and that the relationship is thus 'marked by differentiation and unity' (1985: 258–62).

[25] Willis misses Barth on this point when he argues with respect to Barth's portrayal of the body–soul relationship in Jesus that this distinction ultimately has no 'binding, absolute meaning' (1971: 209). It would be more accurate to say that, for Barth, the *tension* between them has no absolute meaning but the *distinction* is integral to understanding human nature.

[26] Price rightly points out that Barth's anthropology is thus quite consistent with the early Church councils, which maintained that both a human body and a human soul were necessary for true human existence (2002: 248).

[27] Barth's view of body and soul as being dissimilarly available to empirical analysis is also a prominent aspect of contemporary philosophy of mind where the empirical

material mode or compositions. It is a system of relations, i.e., it is free in its inner relation, but forming a specific composition. (III/2, 377)

Barth further associates body with the *being* of a creature as that which determines the 'manner' and 'nature' of its existence (III/2, 367). Although all earthly entities are material bodies of this sort, they are not all *merely* material bodies. Some material bodies can become 'besouled' and thus transcend their mere materiality as 'organic bodies' – material entities that have *soul* and are therefore alive.[28] An organic body is, therefore, understood as 'an object in relation to a subject', that is, the soul (III/2, 377).[29]

Soul, on the other hand, is understood primarily as the subjective life of a material organism:

> Soul is life, self-contained life, the independent life of a corporeal being. Life in general means capacity for action, self-movement, self-activity, self-determination. Independent life is present where this self-movement, self-activity, and self-determination are not only the continuation and partial appearance of a general life-process, but where there is a specific living subject. (III/2, 374)[30]

Soul is that which allows a material body to become a living body and to actualize the existence that is proper to it. It is the self-directed and self-determined activity of an independent living being,[31] that is, the subject of

---

status of a person's conscious state often demarcates a border between various views of the mind–body relation (e.g. van Gulick 2004).

[28] Some might be inclined to dismiss Barth's ontology at this point as a form of *vitalism* – that is, positing some 'unknowable factor' to explain the emergence of organic life (Bechtel and Richardson 1998). McGinn thus eschews any theistic account of the mind–body relation by associating it with vitalism and even alchemy (1991: 7, 17). Though widely discredited, some contemporary thinkers have pointed out that the term actually covers a very broad range of positions and that its more sophisticated versions are not so easily dismissed (e.g. Polkinghorne 1994; and Moreland 1995). Regardless, that theistic views cannot be dismissed as a naïve appeal to vitalism should become clear in the latter half of this study.

[29] Although Barth does use subject–object language in describing the body, his understanding is markedly different from the modern notion of the 'disengaged' subject acting instrumentally through its objectified body (C. Taylor 1989: 185–88). Given the inseparability of the two, Barth's rhetoric is intended to emphasize the leadership of the person's inner life in opposition to any form of biological determinism.

[30] By associating the soul with the principle of movement and independent life, Barth is, therefore, unwilling to attribute souls to plants (III/2, 374). Thus, although he does discuss the three 'levels' of living beings (plants, animals, and humans) in a very Aristotelian manner (III/2, 374; cf. *De Anima* 413 ff.), he differs in not affirming the souls of plants and in refusing the speculate on the nature of the animal soul (III/2, 374–77).

a particular life.[32] Soul is therefore associated with a variety of terms that all denote a human person's interiority – for example, 'inner', 'rational', 'invisible', 'intelligible', 'inapprehensible', and 'heavenly' (III/2, 326). The independent life of a material organism, the soul is 'the subject and form of specific apprehensions, thoughts, sensations, feelings, purposes and endeavours' (III/2, 353).

For Barth, then, the human person is characterized by a distinct duality: the objective and subjective moments of human existence. The first moment, the soul, involves the human being's subjective and conscious life. The body, the second moment, denotes that which executes the decisions of the soul, displays the attitudes developed by the soul, and represents outwardly the interiority of the subjective self. The soul, then, *is* the independent life whereas the body is that which 'lives the independent life' (III/2, 398).

Having established *body* and *soul* as indicating the duality of human existence, we must reaffirm the wholeness and unity that was so important to Barth. From the above definitions we can see that body and soul seem truly inseparable in Barth's anthropology. The very notions of soul and (organic) body are, for Barth, incoherent independent of one another. You can no more have life apart from that which is made alive than you can have an organic body without its subjective life. Understood in terms of such distinctions as inner–outer, movement–space, and action–means, body and soul can be

---

[31] In a similar manner, Pannenberg argues that the soul is 'that which makes us human in our bodily reality' while the body is 'the concrete form in which our humanity, the soul, finds appropriate expression' (1991: 2.184).

[32] This manner of speaking about the body–soul relation is somewhat similar to Aristotle's hylomorphism – that is, the soul as the form of the body (cf. Nussbaum and Rorty 1992 and Shields 2005). Indeed, Barth's description of the person as 'form and life of a substantial organism' (III/2, 325) is an explicit adoption of Aristotelian language (Moltmann 1985: 252). Other similarities include accepting the idea of animal souls (III/2, 377; cf. *De Anima* 413 ff.), using 'logos' with respect to the ordering of human nature (III/2, 335–36; cf. *De Anima* 403a), and associating soul with life (*De Anima* 434a) and movement (*De Anima* 415b). Indeed, both ontologies can be described as an attempt to mediate certain forms of materialism and dualism (Price 2002: 161, Burnyeat 1992: 15). Despite these similarities, Moltmann is incorrect in viewing Barth's ontology simply as a form of Aristotelianism (1985: 254). Indeed, Barth explicitly rejects Aristotle's ontology as theologically inadequate (III/2, 380). Barth's intense interest in the distinction between body and soul and the difficulty of maintaining their unity in the human person constitutes a substantial difference from Aristotle's hylomorphism in which their unity could almost be taken for granted (see *De Anima* 412b). Even the apparent verbal similarities are not as clear as they first appear given that Barth's christological use of 'logos' certainly differs from Aristotle's. While it may be useful, then, to note some parallels in their anthropological ontologies, we should be very careful about insisting on a closer relationship without recognizing the very real differences.

distinguished but not divided without destroying the entity in question.[33] In addition to this conceptual argument, Barth contends that every human action and experience also demonstrates this unity. The human person never experiences her self 'as a dual but only as a single subject, as soul identical with his body and as body identical with his soul' (III/2, 426). Every action of the human subject, even the apparently simple act of knowing,[34] is impossible apart from the inseparable operation of both body and soul.[35]

For Barth, then, the human person is an inseparable union of body and soul.[36] This union, though, cannot be understood in terms of 'identity', 'interchangeability', or 'the union of two parts' (III/2, 372). Instead, 'Soul and body are not two factors which merely co-exist, accompany, supplement, sympathise and co-operate with one another, but whose intentions, achievements and sufferings have different origins, ends and meanings. The one man is the soul of his body and therefore both soul and body' (III/2, 426). Rather than such language with its implicit substance dualism, Barth affirms the two moments of the human person in inseparable unity and irreducible differentiation: 'Soul would not be soul, if it were not bodily; and body would not be body, if it were not besouled. We are not free to make abstractions here, either on one side or the other' (III/2, 350). Barth thus contends that a human being is a duality of body and soul existing in differentiated unity.

3. One Proper Order: The 'Rationality' of Body and Soul

According to Barth, though, noting the unity and duality of the human person is inadequate; we must also consider the 'indestructible order' that

---

[33] Paul Jewett and Marguerite Shuster argue that this approach reduces the soul to a mere 'concept of thought' and counters that it should be viewed instead as having 'objective reality, though not the reality of a material object' (1996: 41–42). Similarly, Mangina refers to the body–soul difference as one among many necessary 'conceptual distinctions' (2004: 199). For Barth, however, the soul is not a merely conceptual reality. Although it cannot be considered independently of the body, it is, as we have seen, neither identical with nor reducible to the body and therefore has its own objective reality though never in isolation from the body.

[34] Thus, although Barth associates personal identity primarily with the soul, he recognizes that the body, as a 'participant . . . in my subjectivity' (III/2, 378), is integrally involved (for a similar perspective see Macquarrie 1982: 48). In this sense, Barth can associate the 'I' of the person with the body as well as the soul (III/2, 374, 377, 426).

[35] Barth thus views the soul as completely incapable of performing any action apart from a material body. Rather than viewing the soul as in bondage to the body, Barth contends that the soul would actually be in bondage (i.e. unable to act) apart from its embodiment (III/2, 351–52).

[36] Whether there is any sense in which the body and soul could be viewed as separable in any sense in Barth's anthropological ontology is a question that we will take up later in the chapter.

obtains in the body–soul relation. Again, looking first to the person of Jesus Christ, Barth argues that 'the oneness and wholeness of this human life is fashioned, structured and determined from within' (III/2, 332). From such examples as Jesus fasting in the desert (Mt. 4.1–2), his agony in Gethsemane (Matt. 26.39), and Jesus' affirmation of Mary's contemplation over Martha's bodily activity (Lk. 10.38–42), Barth argues that the biblical narratives demonstrate the priority of the soul as the director of personal life over the body as that which is directed. Rather than a 'chaos' in which there is no order to the body–soul relationship, Jesus' nature is a 'cosmos' – a 'formed and ordered totality' in which there is 'a higher and a lower, a first and a second, a dominating and a dominated' (III/2, 339). The order among the two moments, then, is that the soul leads, commands, and controls while the body follows, obeys, and is controlled.[37] Barth insists that the biblical narratives clearly portray Jesus as one who performed all of his deeds, particularly the atonement, knowingly, freely, and actively.[38] Affirming the priority of Jesus' subjective life over any biological determinants is, therefore, of 'decisive importance . . . in the anthropology of Jesus' (III/2, 418). Any view of the human person, on Barth's account, that gave primacy to the body in the activity of the person, would, therefore, undermine the biblical account of Jesus' person and work.

Four things must be kept in mind, however, with respect to this anthropological cosmology in Jesus. First, the unity of the two moments is not dissolved by the hierarchy. Despite the essential ordering of the body–soul relationship, there can be no thought of a division or separation between the two moments of Jesus' human existence. There is no 'original separation' or 'hidden conflict' in the order of the two moments, but simply the proper functioning of a single human person (III/2, 338). Second, there can be no valuing of the soul at the expense of the body – both alike are vital aspects of a human life.[39] The dignity of these two moments is not precluded by the

---

[37] The idea that there is a 'leading' element in the human was expressed by ancient Stoic and Epicurean philosophers by the term *hegemonikon* (Sedley 2005), which subsequently found its way into Christian theology (Lampe 1961: 599–601; cf. also Calvin, *Institutes*, 1.15.8; Verghese 1972: 121, Macquarrie 1982: 14, and Pannenberg 1991: 1.201). Though Barth, does not seem to have used the term, the concepts are basically parallel.

[38] See esp. Barth's summary of the doctrine of reconciliation (IV/1, 79–156).

[39] As Pannenberg notes, it is entirely possible for this hierarchical order to become a tyranny of the soul over the body (1991: 1.201). Moltmann thinks that Barth's ontology commits precisely this error and criticizes it on several points. First, he thinks that Barth's position involves a 'domination' of the soul over the body (1985: 253). He argues that this corresponds to a pattern of domination in Barth's doctrine of creation that follows a similar pattern in his doctrine of God (1985: 253–254). In a related criticism, he also contends, 'Barth never mentions a right to resistance on the part of the misused body, nor does he concede to the feelings any right to a say in the decisions of

hierarchy, but is actually established by that order as each is provided its unique status and dignity through its relation to the other. Additionally, this hierarchical unity is not maintained in Jesus by any external principle. Jesus not only *has* life but actually *is* life in himself (cf. Jn 6.35–51; 11.25; 14.6). Consequently, he is his own 'principle', 'ground', and 'intention' (III/2, 332). Finally, Jesus' existence in the differentiated unity of body and soul is not an accidental existence: 'Structured and determined from within', the unity, duality, and order of the body–soul relation in Christ is 'necessary and of lasting significance' (III/2, 332).

the reasonable soul' (1985: 254). His concern here seems to be that Barth has missed the integral relationship between the two whereby 'it is impossible to assign any fundamental primacies' (1985: 260). He contends that we should speak instead of flexible 'centricities' (1985: 261) that change over time rather than hierarchical orders. Finally, he criticizes Barth for so emphasizing order and hierarchy that he fails to 'even suggest that a harmony between the body and its dominating soul is something to be desired' (1985: 254).

Some of Moltmann's comments point in very helpful directions. He rightly notes that Barth's adoption of hierarchical language may have unintentionally undermined the very unity he was striving to maintain. It may be worth asking whether one needs to speak of the body as a 'lower' reality (III/2, 332) to maintain Barth's emphases on freedom, subjectivity, agency, and other vital aspects of human personhood. A greater emphasis on language affirming 'community, partnership, and mutual influence' may be worth pursuing (cf. Moltmann 1985: 257).

On other points, though, Moltmann's criticisms are less helpful. First, despite Barth's hierarchical language, his understanding of the body–soul relationship simply should not be characterized in terms of 'domination', despite the fact that he occasionally used such language himself (e.g. III/2, 339). The very concept implies a sharp distinction between the two moments that simply does not exist in Barth's ontology. We should also recognize with Pannenberg that the possibility of abuse does not necessarily preclude the validity of viewing the relationship in terms of leading and following (1991: 1.201). Even more strongly, we should note McLean's argument that Barth's actual intention, despite all of this 'somewhat conventional and seemingly linear' hierarchical language, is to radically redefine it in terms of the model of Jesus as Lord and Servant: 'For Barth servanthood and lordship are functions of one another' (1986: 112–13).

Second, Moltmann's arguments seem driven primarily by a pre-determined rejection of any form of sovereignty (see his remarks on the Father–Son and God–creation relationships; 1985: 254–55). McFague (1987; 1993) and Kaufman (1993) have similarly argued for a connection between domineering portraits of God and hierarchical views of human ontology. But, again Pannenberg rightly notes that sovereignty cannot be dismissed so easily without minimizing important biblical texts (1991: 1.201).

Finally, many of Moltmann's comments manifest a misunderstanding regarding the very nature of Barth's project. He repeatedly associates Barth's ontology with Platonic and Cartesian ideas while minimizing the various ways in which Barth distances himself from and even attacks those very conceptions (1985: 252–53). It may well be that Moltmann is led astray here by Barth's adoption of rather traditional language and concepts and has, as a result, missed the primary thrust of Barth's argument (similarly Newman 1981: 423).

This hierarchical relation is likewise manifest in human nature generally. Barth thus defines the human person as 'a rational being' (III/2, 419). Barth is not here referring to humanity's intellectual capacities but rather to the 'meaningful order' of human nature such that 'it is proper to his nature to be in rational order of the two moments of soul and body' (III/2, 419). Thus, in such key human activities, as perceiving, thinking, willing, desiring, and acting, we are faced with an ordered unity that transcends the notions of 'simple distribution ... or ... cooperation' (III/2, 400), but always involves 'the primacy of the soul' (III/2, 418).[40] Unlike Jesus, however, this rational ordering of the two moments in human persons generally is not obvious, but is, instead, hidden in the tensions and contradictions of human life.

4. One Undivided Existence?: On the Separability of Body and Soul[41]

One last question that remains to be answered regarding Barth's depiction of this psychophysical relation is whether the body and soul could have any form of independent existence after the death of the person.[42] From one perspective, it seems clear that Barth would reject any such intermediate existence. Indeed, Barth consistently affirms that physical death entails the end of the human person. Thus, at death the human person enters into a state of 'non-being' (III/2, 595–95). Death is, therefore, 'the limit of our existence

---

[40] Frey thus describes this ordered duality as 'hierarchical interactionism [*hierarchischen Interaktionismus*]' (1978: 208). Though this label is useful in demonstrating the ordered interdependence of Barth's ontology, the use of the term *interactionism* is weakened by its association with certain forms of dualism.

[41] We will not attempt in this section even to survey let alone resolve all of the issues involved in the debate regarding whether we should believe in an intermediate state. Our task, instead, will be to consider whether an intermediate state is compatible with Barth's christological framework. The debate on how to read the biblical data regarding human ontology and the intermediate state continues, with some arguing for a more dualistic emphasis (esp. Cooper 1982, 2000; cf. also Osei-Bonsu 1987; Chamblin 1993; Moreland and Rae 2000) and others contending for a monistic approach (esp. Green 1998, 2002a, 2002b, 2004c; cf. Robinson 1952; Kümmel 1963; Wolff 1974; van Inwagen 1995; Betz 2000; Heckel 2000; Stone 2004). Given the sharp discontinuity between these two approaches to the text, Green correctly argues, 'In short, simple appeal to "what the Bible teaches" will not resolve those anthropological questions arising from discussion of body and soul, mind and brain. It is worth asking, though, whether a reading of the narrative of Scripture as whole accounts best for a view of the human person characterized by dualism or by monism' (Green 2005: 21). Thus, Hoekema argues that although the Bible teaches that there will be an intermediate state, it does not specify exactly how it will take place and that, therefore, it is difficult to draw ontological conclusions (1986).

[42] As Bromiley rightly points out, we must be careful against trying to reconstruct Barth's eschatology from his scattered comments, but must limit ourselves to more tentative conclusions (1979: 245).

in time' (III/4, 588) and 'the end of all human and creaturely life and creativity and work' (IV/2, 295). Although this is not 'a death without hope', which would be to fall prey to a fear of the 'negation of being' (IV/2, 476), which was overcome through the death and resurrection of Jesus (III/2, 595), it is still 'the end of man's existence' (III/2, 427).[43] Death, therefore, deprives the individual of 'all prospects for the future' (III/2, 589). Indeed, 'Whatever existence in time may mean, it cannot consist of a continuation of life in time' (III/2, 589).

Such statements would seem to suggest that an intermediate state is completely inconceivable on Barth's account. A closer look at some of his other language, however, suggests that at least three readings are possible on this point. First, one could view Barth as affirming that at death the human person enters into a supra-temporal reality such that she immediately experiences her 'future' resurrection.[44] From this perspective, then, Barth argues that when the person dies, she crosses the 'frontier' (IV/3.1, 310) of death and immediately enters into the eternal life of God 'in fellowship with him' (IV/1, 111).

While this is certainly possible, Barth can also be understood as allowing the possibility of a temporal gap between the death and resurrection of the person, but not one in which the person continues to exist. Thus, Barth can say that Jesus 'ceased to be' after his physical death and that his existence was thus 'terminated by death like that of every other man' (IV/3.1, 312). Since all human persons cease to 'be' after physical death, it would seem possible to suppose that they could remain in this state for some indefinite period of time before they experience any future life, should God graciously choose to reconstitute them as the souls of their bodies.[45]

Some of Barth's language, however, presses in a third, and entirely different, direction. Thus, despite his emphasis on the cessation of the person at death, Barth can still speak of a dead human individual as 'a bodiless soul and a soulless body' (III/2, 355). In death, 'the soul is alienated from the body and the body from the soul' (III/2, 425). Such language indicates that Barth is not completely opposed to speaking of the soul and body as separated from one another after death. Since the soul is only active and expressive in its union with the body, however, such a disembodied soul would be incapable of engaging in the 'activity' that is the hallmark of human life (III/2, 425). Instead, the 'ostensibly all-powerful soul becomes completely impotent' (III/2, 370). Being 'deprived of the freedom for true and meaningful action and movement', dead human persons 'exist in a state of utter weakness and

---

[43] Cf. IV/3.2, 924–28.
[44] For a similar eternalist conception of the resurrection see Gutenson 2004. Oscar Cullmann contends that Barth consistently affirmed such an immediate resurrection in his earlier theology, a more nuanced version of which he maintains in the *Church Dogmatics* as well (1958).
[45] III/2, 362, 364, 427–28; IV/3.2, 926–28.

helplessness' and are 'incapable of enjoying the good things of life' (III/2, 589). For Barth, then, it would seem that death is a 'radically sharp and serious *limitation* of all human being and action' (IV/3.1, 310; emphasis added). We must notice, though, that all of this language suggests that Barth is able to view the soul as continuing to exist after the death of the body, albeit only as 'the spent soul of a spent body' (III/2, 370), which is unable to engage in meaningful activity. It seems possible, then, that Barth's ontology is compatible with the conceivability of the body and soul having a limited existence independent of one another, albeit not in such a way that the person herself can be said to still exist.[46] If this third reading of Barth's theology is allowed, then clearly the body–soul relationship can be understood as one of integral interdependence while still affirming the possibility that they could exist independently.

On the other hand, what if this reading of Barth is incorrect? What if we conclude that Barth's strong language regarding the cessation of human existence at death disallows any possibility of such independent existence?[47] It would seem that if this reading is correct, Barth's ontological conclusions may be overstepping the parameters of his own christological methodology.

Since Barth insists that an adequate anthropological ontology must begin with christological reflection, decisions regarding the state of human ontology during any intermediate state would have to begin with the biblical portrayal of Christ during his entombment. But, there are remarkably few verses in the Bible that could be read as making any reference to the nature of Jesus' existence during this time (e.g. Eph. 4.9; 1 Pet. 3.19). And, if we follow Barth's own interpretations, even these verses tell us nothing about the three days of his entombment (Lauber 2004). Thus, on Barth's interpretation, the Bible is entirely silent on the nature of Christ's existence during this time. But, if this is the case, then the christological narratives provide no basis upon which to make a definitive statement regarding the conceivability of an intermediate state.[48] While the narrative emphasis on Jesus as a whole person in the Bible affirms psychophysical interdependence, it does not

---

[46] This truncated existence could be understood to entail some form of soul sleep. If so, the viability of this third reading would seem to be substantially weakened by the fact that although this was a position with which Barth was quite familiar (Barth 1995), he makes no use of the concept, and he explicitly interprets passages that describe death as 'sleep' as referring to the process of dying rather than the state of death (III/2, 778–79).

[47] For the purposes of this study, it will not be necessary for us to draw any definitive conclusions about which of these three readings is the correct way in which to understand Barth's ontology.

[48] Of course, if one differs from Barth on this point and understands these texts to affirm that Jesus was active during this time, Barth's christological methodology would require us to affirm some form of an intermediate state.

actually entail inseparability.[49] Rather, the christological picture merely affirms that any account of the human person must view embodied wholeness as the normal condition of the human person. Whether there is an *abnormal* situation in which this wholeness is not a part of the human condition is simply not in view.[50] To remain consistent with his overall methodology, then, it would seem that Barth's anthropological ontology would need to affirm, as it does, the body–soul wholeness of the human person before and after the resurrection while remaining silent, and potentially open, on the status of human ontology during any interim period.[51]

From this discussion, then, it would seem that two conclusions are available to us. On the one hand, we could conclude that Barth's ontology views the human *person* as a body–soul entity that ceases to exist at death, but that the soul might continue to exist in a limited form during any interim period between death and resurrection. On the other hand, we could view Barth's ontology as closed to any such an interim existence for the soul. If this is the case, however, we must question whether this aspect of his ontology is actually consistent with his christological methodology. Either way, it would seem that there is room for developing some concept of an intermediate state within the parameters of Barth's christological anthropology, even if he did not choose to develop this option himself.

c. The Pneumatological *How*: The Holy Spirit and Human Ontology

Our earlier discussion of the tensions and contradictions that arise between body and soul raises an important question at this point. If there can be

---

[49] Barth seems to miss this point when he argues that the death and resurrection narratives make no suggestion of a separation of body and soul, without similarly acknowledging that neither do they deny any such state of affairs (III/2, 327).

[50] Similarly, Barth's emphasis on the concrete experience of the human person in perception and action simply affirms unity as the normative state of human nature. While it may provide a strong bias in favor of inseparability, it actually establishes no sure argument for the non-existence of a variant state. Unless Barth wishes to affirm the impossibility of spiritual beings possessing the capacity for perception and action (something Barth would presumably be averse to affirming with respect to angels, demons, and the triune God), it would seem that he should at least be open to the possibility that human persons could engage in both perception and action as disembodied beings – albeit in an abnormal and (possibly) functionally reduced manner.

[51] This would also suggest that attempts to support a dualist ontology based on Jesus' death and resurrection are similarly flawed. Moreland and Rae argue that the biblical narratives suggest that between Jesus' death and resurrection 'he continued to exist as a God-man in the intermediate state independently of his earthly body' (2000: 35; cf. Taliaferro 1995). Their only support for this conclusion, however, is that Jesus remains human through this transition. But, whether substance dualism is the only way to account for continued humanity through death and resurrection is itself a highly contentious issue that we will address in the next chapter.

tensions and contradictions with respect to the body–soul relation, how is their unity maintained? With that question we have arrived at the third, and decisive, term in Barth's anthropological ontology, *spirit*.

The importance of the Spirit for understanding human nature is again determined christologically.[52] Any consideration of Jesus' life must acknowledge the 'unique relation' he shared with the Holy Spirit as the Messiah and the Son of God (III/2, 332). Indeed, Jesus owes his very existence to the Holy Spirit. As the 'new man' who reveals the 'true nature of man', Jesus thereby demonstrates the close connection between anthropology and pneumatology, especially as regards human ontology (III/2, 334).

This connection is played out with respect to humans in general on three different levels. First, the Spirit is involved in the *creation* of the human person. As we have seen, Barth contends that humanity must be understood in terms of its absolute dependence on God. This is true of humanity's ontological constitution as well. Since, according to Barth, a material being is merely 'a spatio-material system of relations', no merely material body inherently possesses independent life (III/2, 377).[53] If, then, a material being actually becomes a living being and therefore subject of a personal life it can only be because of 'an event over whose occurrence he has no control' (III/2, 353).[54] For Barth, this is the 'event' by which the human person, as a union of body and soul and, thus, as both subjective life and objective corporeality, is an expressly pneumatological event. Consequently, 'Man is as he has spirit' (III/2, 354).[55] The Spirit is 'the fundamental determination' (III/2, 363) of human nature as 'the principle which makes man into a subject' (III/2, 364).[56]

---

[52] Rosato asserts, 'Barth's sincere efforts towards a genuine theological anthropology first led him to pneumatology' and, in the process, to the conclusion that Jesus 'had also to be understood pneumatologically' (1981: 95–96). This rather speculative attempt to understand the genesis of Barth's ideas unfortunately neglects the extremely important order in which Barth actually presents his ideas and thus misunderstands the significance of his christocentrism.

[53] Some may, however, possess the capacity for such life even if they do not possess that life inherently (III/2, 377).

[54] This is, of course, true for all living beings. What distinguishes humans in the sphere of living creatures is not their pneumatological constitution but their covenantal relationship with God (III/2, 359).

[55] Barth's presentation of the relationship between body, soul, and Spirit thus follows what Hunsinger refers to as Barth's 'theological grammar' (2004b). Body and soul are understood using the pattern of 'dialectical inclusion' and 'unity-in-distinction' that are characteristic of Barth's Trinitarian grammar. The 'incarnational pattern', clearly evidenced here, involves 'two terms and a relationship' (2004b: 182). Both forms of grammar seem to be at work in this section, as Barth seeks to explain how the unity-in-distinction of body and soul are maintained through the Spirit.

[56] According to Ray Anderson, Barth 'stands quite alone here in his radical interpretation of the relation of spirit to soul and body' (1982: 211). Although Barth's interpretation could probably be considered a minority interpretation, it is certainly not without

That Barth views this pneumatological constitution as an 'event' leads to the second aspect of the Spirit's work, *preservation*. For humans in general, the Spirit is a 'transcendent determination' (III/2, 348);[57] human life as a body–soul union is not a fixed possession, but is something that must be continually established by God through the agency of the Spirit.[58] This pneumatological event 'must be continually repeated' for humans to remain human (III/2, 359).[59] Human nature in general must be distinguished from Jesus at this point.[60] Unlike other humans, Jesus 'does not merely live from the Spirit but in the Spirit' (III/2, 334). Jesus alone has a relation to the Spirit that is intrinsic and enduring: 'He is the man to whom the creative movement of God has come primarily, originally and therefore definitively. . . . He not only has the Spirit, but primarily and basically He is Spirit' (III/2, 334).

Finally, we must also recognize the Spirit's work of *regeneration*. Though God graciously maintains the ontological connection between himself and human persons, the intimate relation between God and his covenant-partner has been lost through human unfaithfulness.[61] Although the Spirit constitutes all human persons as body–soul unities in his work as creator and preserver, this unity is not experienced as such by human persons. On the contrary, humans in general live in the *flesh* (σαρκός), which Barth understands as

---

precedent among modern theologians (e.g. Pannenberg 1985: 522–23; Newman 1981; Moltmann 1985: 263; Torrance 1989: 113). Interestingly, given Barth's extensive familiarity with Kierkegaard's writings, he too posits the human person as a synthesis of body and soul realized by the spirit (Macquarrie 1982: 48).

[57] One of Barth's concerns at this point seems to be to protect against any idea that humanity has, whether inherently or contingently, some part of the 'divine essence' as an ongoing possession (III/2, 363). He explicitly excludes this possibility, however, by arguing that Scripture understands the Spirit as an 'activity' and not a 'being' and as something that can not be possessed (III/2, 363).

[58] Ray Anderson thinks it is rather 'doubtful' that anyone would follow Barth on this because such an overemphasis on the Spirit would 'evacuate the human person of a truly human mortal spirit' (1982: 212). He thus accuses Barth of espousing a 'form of Apollinarianism' and prefers to speak of spirit as an 'orientation' of the human person (soul) brought about by the Holy Spirit (1982: 212; cf. Come 1963: 152). Contrary to this interpretation, however, Barth does not understand the work of the Spirit to eliminate or even minimize the reality of human subjectivity and spirituality but merely to emphasize its radical dependency at all points. McLean, thus argues, 'in preservation (providence) there is a "natural man", maintained by God's active and free relationship to this context. This relationship is designated as Spirit. Man is not absorbed. God created him, maintains him, and is constantly relating to him, *indirectly*, through the context of his life' (1981: 45).

[59] Mangina points out that Barth's similar event-language with respect to the church (IV/1, 650–724) should not be understood to imply that its pneumatological constitution is non-continuous, but rather as an attempt to emphasize the divine source and mystery of the church's being (2004: 154). The same argument would seem to apply to Barth's anthropological ontology.

[60] See Chapter 2.

'the condition of man in contradiction, in disorder and in consequent sickness' (III/2, 336).[62] In the incarnation, Jesus took up this fleshly existence and transformed it into something that is 'quickening and living and meaningful' (III/2, 336). This renewed human reality, however, cannot become a reality for individuals until they become aware of it and begin to take responsibility for its expression in their lives.[63] Thus, although Barth sees the ontological union of body and soul as universally realized through the creative work of the Spirit, he views the experience and expression of this union as an ongoing task.[64]

Having identified these three works of the Spirit with respect to human ontology, the specific relation between the Holy Spirit and the human spirit remains to be considered. Barth argues quite forcefully that 'spirit' in the Bible, both Old and New Testaments, refers primarily to the spirit of God as 'the creative movement' of God toward his creation (III/2, 333),[65] and only derivatively of something properly characteristic of the human person.[66] Barth thus distinguishes sharply between the human soul and the divine spirit by which it is made alive.[67] There remains, nonetheless, a close relation

---

[61] III/2, 26–41, 139, 347; cf. IV/1, 139–45.

[62] Barth recognizes that 'flesh' can refer generally to human physicality but contends that it is most commonly used with reference to the human state in rebellion against God (III/2, 336).

[63] IV/2, 421–22, 443–44, 454, 477–78.

[64] Gorringe 2004: 47; cf. Macquarrie 1982: 55; and Sherlock 1996: 219.

[65] Although *spirit* as divine spirit and derivatively as the spirit of humans are Barth's primary categories for understanding *spirit* in the Bible, he does recognize that it also has application to the commission of God (e.g. prophets) and to immaterial beings (III/2, 357–58; cf. Sherlock 1996: 222). Unfortunately he does not clearly address how these alternate uses, particularly the last, should impact his emphasis on *spirit* as primarily referring to the Spirit of God.

[66] For Barth, then, there can be no trichotomous understanding of human persons as body, soul, and spirit since he does not regard 'spirit' as a component of human ontology (cf. III/2, 355).

[67] Surveying the biblical terms, he argues that *nephesh* (נֶפֶשׁ) in the Old Testament and ψυχή, in the New Testament can indicate either life in general, the life of a particular individual, or, by extension, the individual herself and both are to be distinguished from the divine spirit (רוּחַ or πνεῦμα) (III/2, 378–79). He addresses several 'problem' passages for this interpretation (e.g. 1 Thess. 5.23; Lk. 1.46 f.; and Heb. 4.12) arguing in each case that 'spirit' refers primarily to the divine spirit and only by extension to human persons (III/2, 355). Following Gen. 2.7, the human person is understood to be a material being (הָאָדָם עָפָר מִן־הָאֲדָמָה) who is constituted as a 'living being' (חַיָּה נֶפֶשׁ) by the 'breath of life' (נִשְׁמַת חַיִּים), which Barth identifies with the Holy Spirit (III/2, 333–34, 361, 379, 396). Despite Barth's strong emphasis on the subjective life of the person associated with the soul, he does not want us to miss the fact that Gen. 2.7 refers to the material body of the person *before* the pneumatological event as 'man' (הָאָדָם) and, therefore, the materialist perspective is a valid, though limited, approach to the human person (III/2, 374).

between them such that 'the Bible can speak in general of the spirit . . . of man', although '[i]n practice, this means nothing else but the soul living through the Spirit' (III/2, 334).[68] This means, however, that *spirit* may not be viewed as an aspect of human being. The Spirit of God, though integrally and intimately related to human being, must never be identified with some portion of it.

Since the Spirit is what constitutes the human person as soul of his body, the removal of the Spirit can only be the death of the person: 'As the spirit makes of man an embodied soul and a besouled body, so the absence of spirit makes of him a bodiless soul and a soulless body' (III/2, 354–55). Upon this removal, the body–soul union is dissolved such that the 'ostensibly all-powerful soul becomes completely impotent' and the organic body becomes 'a mere material body' (III/2, 370).[69] That this withdrawal and dissolution will take place is certain. Whether there is a future for the human person after this death relies completely on whether God graciously chooses to reconstitute the body–soul relationship and restore the existence of the person.[70]

d. Covenantally Constituted: The *Why* of Human Ontology

Barth offers the pneumatological constitution of the human person, however, not just as an explanation of the creation, preservation, and regeneration of the body–soul relation, but also as an explanation of *why* such an ontological constitution is so important. Humans must be understood as a pneumatologically grounded and rationally ordered relation of body and soul because, for Barth, the pneumatological event is primarily a covenantal event:

> Spirit in His fundamental significance is the element in virtue of which man is actively and passively introduced as a partner in the covenant

---

[68] This interchangeability is possible because 'the constitution of man as soul and body cannot be fully and exactly described without thinking first and foremost of the spirit as its proper basis' (III/2, 355). The reverse, however, does not hold and Barth argues that it is 'never true that the soul is spoken of where the Spirit is unambiguously meant. . . . There is in fact no case where the LXX translates *nephesh* by πνεῦμα (III/2, 373). Although Job 7.15 would seem to provide a possible exception to this rule, his basic point seems to hold.

[69] As Price rightly notes, 'in Barth's anthropology, a body without a soul is not a "dead person", it is simply a body' (2002: 252).

[70] III/2, 362, 364, 370, 427–28. Although Barth thus views having a body as a necessary part of the future resurrection of the person, he does not address the question of material continuity that plays such a prominent role in physicalist accounts of the resurrection (e.g. Baker 1995; Corcoran 2001b; Merricks 2001b; and Peters 2002). For Barth this is simply consistent with his method of affirming *that* something is a theological truth and being less concerned to establish precisely *how* it can be realized.

of grace, in which he is installed in his position as God's partner in the particular stages and decisions of the history of this covenant and in which he is equipped for his function as such. (III/2, 347)

The pneumatological event, by which human persons are constituted as body–soul entities, is, therefore, the event in which human capacity for covenantal relationship is grounded:

> Man has Spirit, and through the Spirit is the soul of his body. This means at least that, by reason of his creaturely being, he is capable of meeting God, of being a person for and in relation to Him, and of being one as God is one. He is capable of being aware of himself as different both from God and from the rest of the created world, yet also bound up with God and with the rest of the created world. He is capable of recognising himself and of being responsible for himself. He exists in the execution of this self-recognition and self-responsibility before his Creator. (III/2, 395)

For Barth, then, human persons would have no capacity for being God's covenantal co-partners apart from their pneumatologically grounded dual constitution.[71] Barth contends that a purely material or spiritual account of the human person is inadequate for dealing with this reality-defining relationship. A purely material being, in Barth's view, simply does not have the capacity for covenantal relationship (III/2, 353). Apart from the subjective life enabled in the pneumatological event, the human being would be indistinguishable from other merely material realities and unable to express and experience the covenantal partnership. Likewise, if human persons were purely spiritual, they would not have the capacity for outward expression and action necessary for any real relationship. Humans are, therefore, constituted as body–soul entities specifically *because* they have been created for covenantal relationship.[72]

Barth develops this argument further by looking at two specific sets of capacities that humanity must have in order to function as 'a subject to whom God can entrust and from whom He can expect this partnership in intercourse with him' (III/2, 396).[73] That God meets with and reveals himself to humanity implies first, that human beings are capable of perceiving

---

[71] As we discussed in Chapter 2, the covenantal basis of humanity is clouded but not lost as a result of human sin because it is firmly grounded in the election of Jesus.

[72] Thus, as Prenter states, the human person is 'gifted with his body–soul nature [*mit dieser seelisch-leiblichen "Natur" begabt*]' specifically so that he might be granted the necessary 'functions [*diese Funktione*]' (1950: 215).

[73] Cf., Prenter 1950: 215.

God, distinguishing themselves from God, and knowing him as God.[74] Barth understands this percipient capacity quite simply as the awareness and thought necessary for an individual 'to receive another as such into one's self-consciousness' (III/2, 399). Consequently, in all God's dealing with humanity, he appeals to this ability as he expects that humans have the percipient capacity for self-conscious receptivity of another in relation to himself. Barth's discussion of the human capacity for perception is too long to analyze adequately at this point.[75] It is important to realize, however, that the activities of perception, awareness and thought, for Barth signify the two moments of body and soul.[76] Although there can be no 'simple distributions of the two functions in the act of perception to soul and body' (III/2, 400), he associates the act of awareness primarily with the body and that of thinking with the soul. In each, though, the primacy of the soul obtains. Without this percipient capacity God's summons to and encounter with humans 'would obviously be impossible' (III/2, 399). And apart from the pneumatological event and the dual constitution of human persons, this percipient capacity would be absent.

The second conclusion Barth draws from this divine–human relation is that God summons humanity to decision and action. Humanity's covenantal co-partnership with God is never a mere 'fellowship of knowledge', but always also a 'fellowship of action' whereby human persons are summoned into a relationship of obedience and service' (III/2, 406). As with perception, Barth maintains that God's summons to action presupposes the created capacity for action: 'Man in his relation to God is claimed as one capable of such activity' (III/2, 407). Activity, for Barth, entails a person's capacity 'to set oneself freely in motion in relation to another' (III/2, 406). This implies not only that the human person is free to initiate such action in response to the divine summons but also to desire and will such action. Once again, Barth argues that 'a special relation' obtains between soul-willing and body-desiring even though there can be no 'partition' between these aspects of human existence (III/2, 408). With both of these arguments, Barth thus contends that insofar as the human person is the covenantal co-partner of God

---

[74] Barth argues that even humanity's ordinary perceptual experiences are derivative of his encounter with God. Thus, humanity's general capacity for perception is grounded in its particular capacity to know and love God (III/2, 402–03).

[75] Although Barth devotes a rather lengthy discussion to human perception, he is not interested in a theoretical analysis of human perceptivity, but on the capacities of a person in covenantal relationship (III/2, 402).

[76] Moltmann thinks that Barth's emphasis on perception indicates 'a reduction of the "human act of living" to thinking and willing' (1985: 254). This, however, completely misses Barth's heavy emphasis on activity and agency as primary categories of true humanity (III/2, 175–98, 406–16). Barth's approach is quite consistent with that of John Macmurray who thinks that we should speak of human persons more in terms of the 'I do' than the 'I think' (1957: 84; cf. Macquarrie 1982: 39–40).

and, therefore, insofar as the human person must have the capacities necessary for perceiving and acting, he must have this dual constitution as body and soul so that he might be 'qualified, prepared and equipped' for carrying out these functions (III/2, 396).

With both of these arguments, Barth concludes that the unity, duality, and rationality of human nature is established simply and firmly in the fact that the human person has been addressed by God and 'it is thus presupposed that he was created as such by God' (III/2, 422). So, Barth argues that God's address to humanity 'treats him as a being who can rule himself and serve himself' and thus presupposes that God has already created him as 'a rational being' who has the capacities of perception and action necessary for responding to that address (III/2, 424). That God has created a being with such capacities and therefore a being that can serve as his covenantal co-partner is, of course, an act of divine grace. So, humanity 'is determined by the one grace, that of his creation, for the other grace, that of the covenant' (III/2, 349). In this event of grace, as a body–soul being, 'it becomes possible for him to meet the divine person as person, to be a covenant-partner' (III/2, 353). In this way, Barth has developed what may rightly be called a *covenantal ontology*.[77]

III. Christology and Ontology: A Christological Framework for a Theoretical Ontology

We have now developed a much clearer understanding of *what* Barth understands human ontology to be (a rationally ordered unity of body and soul), *how* that ontological constitution is maintained (the creating, preserving, and regenerating work of the Spirit), and *why* this particular ontology is necessary (the divine–human covenantal relationship).[78] As mentioned earlier,

---

[77] Noting the importance of covenant in Barth's ontology, John Webster rightly asserts: 'Without that substantial anthropology and its corresponding emphasis on the realisation of selfhood through action, Barth's understanding of covenant, and his consistent stress on the moral character of human response to God, would be simply unthinkable' (2001c: 56).

[78] Failure to emphasize all three of these theological loci have led to some rather imbalanced pictures of Barth's ontological framework. Neglecting the christological basis of Barth's anthropological ontology, Berkouwer thinks that Barth operates almost exclusively on a covenantal–creation framework and then criticizes him for being inconsistent with his christological methodology (1962: 94). Rosato makes the opposite mistake and argues that Barth's theology is 'rooted in man's recreation, that is, in soteriology and eschatology' in contrast with theological anthropologies in general, which tend to focus on humanity's creation (1981: 95). Though soteriology and eschatology have a profound impact on Barth's anthropology, Rosato unnecessarily downplays the key role of creation, providence, and covenant in Barth's anthropology (though these can

though, the manner in which Barth answers these questions, emphasizing both unity and duality, has generated some disagreement among his interpreters as to whether he is better characterized in monistic or dualistic terms. We can now see, however, how Barth's approach to the issue of human ontology is markedly different. Although he is well aware of the difficulties associated with human ontology, he does not begin with an ostensible *problem* but with a *person*. Beginning with Jesus, he argues for a particular way of viewing the human person with which any theoretical depiction must cohere.[79] Price, thus, correctly argues that Barth does not 'attempt a theoretical rejoinder to the mind–body problem' (Price 2002: 257). Despite making this observation, however, Price goes on to argue that Barth avoids the mind–body problem and merely shrouds the answer in the mystery of God's being. But that too misconstrues the nature of Barth's task. He is not attempting to avoid the mind–body problem or locate its insolubility in the divine being; rather, he is trying to locate the discussion within a theological framework that provides a firm foundation for human nature. Thus, he does not avoid the problem but actually attempts to clear the way for a valid, *theological* consideration of the issues.[80] To understand how Barth's anthropological ontology applies to the mind–body discussion, we will, therefore, have to lay out more clearly its specific implications.

a. The Ontological Criteria of Barth's Christological Ontology

While Barth's anthropology may have other implications for understanding the mind–body relation, it seems clear that the following are the most significant:

(1) Selfhood. Any attempt to understand the ontological implications of Barth's christological anthropology must begin with the fact that it clearly requires a 'rather robust sense of human selfhood' (Webster 2001c: 56).

---

not, of course, be separated from soteriology and eschatology). Similarly, Gorringe argues that 'failure to take Spirit into account is what leads us into either a monistic monism or a monistic spiritualism', without acknowledging the christological and covenantal aspects of Barth's framework as well (1999: 202). A full appreciation of Barth's anthropological ontology, therefore, requires a recognition of the vital roles that Christology, pneumatology, *and* covenant–creation play in its development.

[79] In his study of biblical anthropology, Kümmel similarly argues that Jesus 'developed no one *theory* of man, but that a very definite picture of man stood behind His gospel preaching' (1963: 36).

[80] Such theological considerations are often dismissed as a God-of-the-gaps solution to the mind–brain relationship (e.g. Flanagan 1984: 64; Polkinghorne 1994: 19). Barth does not posit the theological grounding of human ontology as an answer to an otherwise insoluble problem but rather as the presupposition to a proper understanding of human reality.

Barth's particular view of what it means to be a human self, though, differs markedly from many contemporary portraits.

According to E. J. Lowe, *self* can be defined broadly as 'a subject of consciousness, a being capable of thought and experience and able to engage in deliberative action. More crucially, a self must have a capacity for *self*-consciousness. . . . a self is a being that is able to entertain first-person thoughts' (1995: 817). This definition usefully captures the importance of the self as *subject* that plays such an important role for Barth (III/2, 371). Though Barth never clearly defines the term *subject*, it involves, at least, acknowledging the human person as an independent individual who can be identified with certain actions and experiences.[81]

The usefulness of Lowe's definition for describing Barth's anthropology, however, is limited for at least three reasons. First, Barth is not interested in understanding selfhood primarily in terms of capacities. Though we have seen that Barth is perfectly willing to argue *from* relationship *to* capacity (e.g. from the reality of the covenantal relationship to the capacity for perception and action), he resists the reverse approach (e.g. from the capacity for thought to selfhood). He thus refuses to speculate on the possibility that other creatures, with notably differing sets of capacities, might also experience inner lives as the souls of their bodies (III/2, 374–435). Second, although Lowe mentions 'deliberative action' at the end of his definition, the overt emphasis falls on the interiority of the human person.[82] While Barth's theology of the self certainly affirms the importance of such interiority, it calls for a much broader perspective.[83] Finally, Lowe's definition places too much emphasis on the individual. Barth's approach, on the other hand, prioritizes

---

[81] Esp. III/2, 335, 352, 371, 374.

[82] Such a focus on interiority has long been a prominent aspect of modern views of the self (cf. C. Taylor 1989: 111; and Grenz 2001: 59). Lowe's definition, however, does make a useful distinction between the self and the conscious experiences of which it is the subject (1995: 817). Failing to make such a distinction results in the 'punctual' self of which Charles Taylor has been so critical – the transient self constituted only by its ephemeral self-awareness (C. Taylor 1989: 49–50; this view is often associated with Hume's criticisms of selfhood [1911: 1.238–39]).

[83] Barth's understanding of human selfhood manifests an awareness of its external as well as its internal dimensions and, therefore, presents a sharp criticism of the autonomous, rational, self-constituting self of post-Enlightenment modernism (Fisher 1998: 192, Mangina 2001: 14, and Kerr 2002: 27). This resistance to any modernistic overemphasis on interiority, despite his occasionally strong language regarding the priority of the soul, means that Barth resists psychologism in his anthropological ontology as much as in his soteriology (cf. Anderson 2002). Additionally, though Barth's approach bears some resemblance to postmodern de-centered views of the self (cf. Schrag 1997 and Woolhead 1999), Webster rightly argues that his theological matrix is 'antipathetic to allowing reflexive subjectivity to function as a basic anthropological datum' (2001c: 56).

the relational constitution of humanity.[84] Although most of §46 focuses on the ontological constitution of the human individual, it is clearly grounded in her determinative relation with God.[85] We must also not lose sight of the important discussions in the previous paragraphs on the constitutive nature of intra-human relationships. For Barth, then, a properly formulated concept of selfhood must address the human person as a *subject* constituted by particular *relationships*.[86] As the remaining elements of Barth's ontology are unfolded it will become apparent that these two facets are not the sum of his notion of selfhood, but they do comprise its primary aspects.

(2) **Consciousness.** Though closely related to selfhood,[87] we can also affirm that Barth's anthropological ontology requires a real and vital subjective consciousness.[88] *Consciousness* can be used in a number of different ways,[89] but is used most often with respect to the 'phenomenal awareness' (i.e. experiences or subjective feels) of a given subject.[90] That conscious experience so understood is a requisite element of Barth's anthropological ontology seems

---

[84] In addition to the God–human relationship so clearly evidenced throughout this discussion, Barth also places a priority on human relationships for maintaining a healthy body–soul balance (IV/2, 443–44).

[85] As Freyer points out the kind of subjectivity that Barth has in mind is not the 'subjectivity [*Subjektivität*]' of the human person understood in abstraction from God, but the human person who is a subject specifically because he has been drawn into covenantal relation through call of God' (1991: 195). Since Barth views this determinative relationship as a *historical* reality (see Chapter 2), Barth's view of selfhood may well share some similarities with those who view selfhood as grounded in particular narratives (e.g. Ricoeur 1992; Dennett 1992; and Hutto 1997).

[86] A more complete discussion of human selfhood as it applies to Barth's theological anthropology lies well beyond the scope of this chapter. Adopting an admittedly broad view of the self that focuses on the relational constitution of the human subject, therefore, should not be interpreted as denying the many other useful ways of understanding selfhood (some general studies of selfhood include C. Taylor 1989; Carrithers et al. 1985; Marsella et al. 1985; and Grenz 2001, esp. 58–140). Rather, it simply seeks to affirm two important elements of Barth's theological anthropology while, at the same time, drawing on one prominent strand of contemporary theology (cf. Macmurray 1961; McFadyen 1990: 100–101; Zizioulas 1985; Teske 2000; and Grenz 2001).

[87] The other aspects of Barth's ontological framework laid out below can all be viewed as further elaborations of Barth's broad view of selfhood.

[88] Though Barth's view of the self cannot be limited to personal consciousness, it nonetheless remains an important part of his overall ontology.

[89] Most agree that 'consciousness', as commonly used, is a rather ambiguous term with a variety of distinct uses (e.g. Block 1995a; Rosenthal 1986; van Gulick 2004; and Lormand 1998). M. Antony, however, helpfully points out that these uses can be viewed as different modalities of the more general, intuitive notion of phenomenal awareness (2001).

[90] From this perspective, consciousness can be understood as the 'what's-it-like' (i.e. qualia) of a phenomenal experience made famous by T. Nagel's 'What Is It Like to Be a Bat?' (1974; cf. Crane 2000 and Tye 2003).

without question.[91] Barth clearly affirms that the human person must be regarded as a self-conscious entity capable of knowing itself and its experiences through an 'inner experience' of itself (III/2, 375). Additionally, these self-conscious experiences must be understood to have a certain 'feel' for the human subject – that is, there must be something that it is like to have undergone that particular experience.[92] Barth's depiction of the vital 'inner life' of Jesus (III/2, 329) and of humans in general would be incomprehensible without some notion that there is a distinctive phenomenal quality to such experiences. The same holds for Barth's understanding of perceptual awareness. Barth argues that the very idea of a covenantal relationship requires the capacity for a self-conscious experience whereby the human becomes aware of some other being (III/2, 399–401). Any attempt to construe that awareness in such a manner as to eliminate, or even unduly minimize, the qualitative experience of the encounter would seem antithetical to Barth's covenantal ontology (III/2, 397). Among the many issues often associated with human consciousness, then, it would seem that Barth's ontology is, at least, committed to the importance of self-consciousness, first-person perspectives, and phenomenal experiences.[93]

(3) **Continuous Personal Identity.** Given Barth's emphasis on the human person as an individual subject, it is unsurprising that his ontology also addresses the question of identity in both its synchronic (identity at a given time) and diachronic (identity through time) forms.[94] Although he associates synchronic identity more closely with a person's conscious life, he maintains that it necessarily involves the body as well; the human person is an identifiable subject only as an embodied soul.[95] Barth is also fully aware that the human person is a fully temporal reality; indeed, he considers it one of the

---

[91] Barth specifically affirms that the human person as soul and body is 'conscious' (III/2, 398).

[92] Though some contemporary philosophers would disagree with Barth on this point (Shoemaker and Hywel 1975; Garcia-Carpintero 2003; and Dennett 1991), many argue strenuously in favor of such qualia (Searle 1992; Block 1994; Chalmers 1996; and de Leon 2001).

[93] This does not mean that Barth's ontology commits him to a 'strongly realist' notion of consciousness – that is, that it has an independent existence similar to a magnetic field – but only to the notion that human life is characterized by a certain set of properties that we categorize with the concept of consciousness (see van Gulick 2004). Whether Barth's ontology is similarly committed to other issues commonly addressed in philosophical studies of consciousness (e.g. the irreducibility of first-person to third-person perspectives, the ineffability of qualia, and the 'explanatory gap' between neurobiology and consciousness), will be considered in the next two chapters (for a good summary of these issues see Lycan 2005).

[94] On the synchronic–diachronic distinction see Olson 2003b: 353.

[95] III/2, 353, 375, 378.

defining aspects of the human person and a constituent element of the soul.[96] Together, though, these issues, identity and temporality, raise the problem of diachronic identity.

For Barth, however, the continuous identity of the human person is quite clear. Looking to the person of Christ, he notes that Jesus is the 'same whole man, soul and body' both before and after his resurrection (III/2, 327). Continuous identity through death and resurrection thus applies also to humans in general as they await their promised resurrection.[97] Continuous identity would also seem to be required by the self-responsibility and accountability necessitated by his covenantal framework.[98] Indeed, the very nature of a covenant would seem to presuppose the relatively stable identities of the individuals involved. Barth's view of the continuity of human identity, then, is more properly grounded on the covenantal faithfulness of God than speculative arguments regarding her psychological and/or somatic continuity.[99]

(4) Agency. Agency can be loosely defined as the capacity of some particular being for developing 'intentions' that are causally related to the production of actions.[100] Understood in this way, Barth's ontology entails human agency. Barth's presentation of the atonement as the freely chosen and intended act of Jesus suggests a necessary and strong view of personal agency; so too his emphasis on self-responsibility (III/2, 396–97) and the human person as a volitional being (III/2, 406–9). Indeed, his entire account of human nature as a rationally ordered being envisions the soul as the agent that directs the intentional actions of the person.[101] Thus, for Barth, the very nature of

---

[96] Barth includes 'movement in time' as part of his definition of soul (III/2, 373) and devotes §46 to temporality as the third key aspect of human persons.

[97] III/2, 353, 360–62, 364, 370–71; III/4, 338; IV/1, 111–13. Although Barth's language at times would seem to suggest that human existence is limited to this life alone (e.g. III/4, 588–91), he clearly states that humans enter into the eternal life of God 'in fellowship with him' (IV/1, 111). Although this is life 'in' God, 'the creaturliness and identity of man will certainly not be destroyed' (IV/1, 113).

[98] Philosophers have long recognized the close relationship between continuous personal identity and concern for the future (see Kind 2004).

[99] Thus Barth argues, 'even in death God watches over him' and remains faithful to the human person (III/2, 371; for a similar argument see Anderson 1998). Similarly, Barth argues in CD IV.2 that the continuous personal identity of the human person is maintained only by her covenantal participation in the eschatological eternity of Jesus (III/2, 315–16).

[100] Cf. Searle 1983: 83–98; Kapitan 1991; and Knobe 2005. Tim Bayne and Neil Levy suggest a more encompassing view of agency that involves mental causation, authorship, effort, freedom, and decision-making (2005). While we will see that many of these are also important aspects of Barth's ontology, Philip Clayton rightly warns against the tendency of some philosophers to bias the ontological discussion from the beginning by presupposing too robust a notion of personal agency (2005). Consequently, our discussion will proceed with the more limited notion of agency indicated above.

human life involves the agential 'capacity for action, self-movement, self-activity, self-determination' (III/2, 374).

(5) Mental Causation. Closely related to agency, Barth's ontology seems firmly committed to the stance that a person's mental life has causal powers and can exercise causal influence on extra-mental realities. For Barth's account of the soul's agency to have any real meaning, this inner reality must have causal powers. Indeed, in language very similar to that being used in contemporary philosophy, Barth argues for the 'downward' causal influence of the soul (III/2, 339) as it controls the body (III/2, 368). Barth thus explicitly rejects any 'epiphenomenal' understanding of causation (III/2, 382).

(6) Freedom. We have already briefly noted the importance of human freedom in Barth's anthropology in general. He continues to develop this notion in his depiction of human ontology. Related to, though distinct from, his account of mental causation, Barth continues his emphasis on the divinely constituted freedom of the human person. Barth's view of Jesus as the obedient son and atoning sacrifice in particular mandates a strong view of human freedom (IV/1, 157–10). And, again, Barth's understanding of the rational order of human as necessary for maintaining covenantal relationality entails that human persons are determined for freedom by the self-determination of God and not merely by cultural or biological influences.[102] Indeed, for Barth, 'The soul is itself the freedom of man' (III/2, 418).

(7) Embodiment. Barth's understanding of Christology and the concrete reality of human existence as well as the embodied nature of human agency and personal identity, all suggest that any adequate anthropology must include an emphasis on personal embodiment as part of human existence. Along with Barth's emphasis on the resurrection, these things also suggest that embodiment is an important part of the future reality of human beings as well. An adequate anthropology must, therefore, include at least the hope of resurrected embodiment as part of its picture.[103]

(8) Contingent Personhood. As we have seen, Barth's pneumatological framework requires that any adequate anthropology will understand humans to be persons only contingently as they are constituted as soul–body entities through the work of the Holy Spirit. Barth, therefore, strongly opposes any

---

[101] Such an approach would seem to commit Barth to some form of agent causation, although certainly not one that affirmed the completely indeterminate nature of human action (see Chapter 2). Although agent causation is widely considered to be problematic because of its indeterminacy and interruption of the causal chain, some philosophers are reviving the argument by associating causation with agential substances (e.g. Harre 2001; and Lowe 2003). Others dismiss the objection as stemming from an inadequate materialistic framework (see Chapter 6).

[102] See esp. III/4, 565–685; see also Webster 1995 and 1998; Busch 2004: 116–21; and Mangina 2004: 99, 151–52.

[103] See Chapter 6.

move to understand some portion of the human person to be inherently immortal.[104] Human persons exist only and continuously as they are maintained as such by the Spirit for God's glory.[105]

From this brief survey we can see that the theological framework of Barth's anthropological ontology commits him to viewing the human person in a way that requires: (1) a strong concept of selfhood emphasizing humans as subjects constituted by particular relationships, (2) an inner life comprising self-conscious experiences, (3) an understanding of continuous personal identity that involves both the body and the soul but is ultimately dependent on divine faithfulness, (4) an appreciation of humans as capable of initiating intentional actions, (5) someview of mentality that allows a causal relationship with extra-mental realities, (6) an awareness of humanity's determination *and* freedom, (7) a strong appreciation for the role of the body in every facet of human experience, and (8) a recognition that all aspects of human life and nature are contingent realities.

It is worth noticing at this point that Barth makes very little reference in this paragraph to the christological criteria that he established in §44. This does not mean, however, that these criteria are not operative in this discussion. Though he does not mention them explicitly, it seems clear they continue to play a foundational role in his argument. Indeed, Barth's understanding of subjectivity, selfhood, agency, and freedom seem to be inherent aspects of criteria 5 and 6 (participation in redemptive history and obedient service). Similarly, his argument for the contingency of human personhood is almost a direct continuation of his first three criteria (the primacy of God, the christological constitution of human persons, and the fact that human persons exist for the glory of God). The only aspect of Barth's ontological framework that does not seem to be clearly grounded in his early christological criteria is his emphasis on the absolute inseparability of soul and body and the corresponding rejection of any form of conscious existence between death and resurrection.

b. The Framing of a Theoretical Ontology

The question remains, however, whether these ontological positions commit Barth to some particular theory of human nature. On the one hand, Barth's depiction of human identity, agency and embodiment would seem to suggest some form of physicalism. On the other hand his strong emphasis on selfhood, agency, and mental causation are often associated with various forms of dualism. This tension can be seen in the fact that Barth rejects certain forms of both physicalism and dualism.

---

[104] For example, III/2, 380, 392–93.
[105] Similarly Pannenberg 1991: 2.198.

Thus, he critiques 'monistic materialism' (III/2, 382) for reducing the human person to mere corporeality and denying the real existence of the inner life of human persons. Anything that is not 'corporeal, spatial, physical and material', on this view, must be rejected as illusory and 'epiphenomenal' (III/2, 382). The human person is rendered 'subjectless' (III/2, 382–92).[106] Such a reductive account of the human person stands in stark contrast to the ontological requirements of Barth's anthropology. As we will see in the next chapter, though, while this may have been an accurate description of physicalistic theories in the middle of the twentieth century,[107] it accounts for only a small portion of such theories today. The term *physicalism* now encompasses a broad range of theories, many of which view the human person as a purely material being (i.e. only one substance) but as one with a real and significant mental life.[108] Barth's explicit rejection of 'monistic materialism', therefore, does not necessarily indicate a stance with respect to these more recent physicalistic proposals.

But he also denies the validity of any theory that construes the duality of the human person in terms of two substances. According to Barth, dualism understands the human person as comprising two substances that are 'self-contained and qualitatively different in relation to the other' (III/2, 380). These two substances are seen to be so different that they are only tentatively united, resulting in an ultimate identification of the human person with the soul alone (III/2, 380–81).[109] Even those theories that seek to mediate the relationship between the two substances (e.g. interactionism and parallelism), Barth argues, fall far short of the holistic unity of the person required by Christology and covenantal relationship (III/2, 428–36). Based on this definition, dualism is clearly inconsistent with the framework of Barth's ontology. But again, this is a rather limited view of dualism as espoused by theologians and philosophers today. A number of proposals are now understood to fall under the broad label *dualism*, many of which do not fit the definition offered by Barth and may escape at least some of his objections.[110] In fact, one of Barth's key concerns about dualism, that it views the soul as inherently immortal and is, therefore, incompatible with

---

[106] Similarly, he rejects 'monistic spiritualism' (III/2, 390) for the reverse denial of material reality in favor of the soul that thus renders him 'objectless' (III/2, 390–92). Such idealistic accounts of human nature, though, will not be considered in this project.

[107] Whether this is in fact an accurate depiction of the philosophy of mind at that time lies beyond the scope of this project.

[108] For nice overviews see Stoljar 2001b; and Melnyk 2003.

[109] Barth thinks that even though substance dualists often affirm the essential unity of the human person, their dualistic conception necessarily entails that any ostensible unity be problematic and ultimately ephemeral (III/2, 380–81).

[110] For example, Taliaferro 1994; Hasker 1999; Moreland and Rae 2000; and Goetz 2005.

the contingency requirement in Barth's ontology (III/2, 380), is not an element of most contemporary forms of dualism.[111]

Neither of these two sets of arguments, however, clarifies the precise nature of Barth's own ontology. While Barth uses them to explain more clearly what a properly theological view of human ontology is *not*, they do not establish a precise theory as to what it *is*. It may be more helpful then, to view Barth's argument in terms of the relationship between paradigms, models, and theories in theological formulation. From this perspective we can understand *paradigm* to denote the grid through which we perceive some aspect of reality, *model* as a conceptual construction by which we seek to understand and apply the paradigmatic framework to a particular aspect of reality, and *theory* as an attempt to explicate more precisely the reality depicted by some particular model.[112] Using this language, the incarnation clearly functions paradigmatically in Barth's theology as he strives to understand all of reality through its influence. In turn, Barth posits his unity-duality-order model of the body–soul relation as the most accurate depiction of the human person in light of this incarnational perspective. As with most models, though, this ontological model does not seek to address all of the pertinent theoretical issues so much as to provide a useful way of viewing and speaking about the phenomenon in question.[113] From this perspective, Barth's model of human ontology can be understood as a way of *conceptualizing* the human person that seeks to integrate two important perspectives (inner and outer), and a way of *speaking* about human nature with an emphasis on holistic language. Although such an account does not provide a specific theory of human nature, it can serve to *limit* the range of legitimate options for such a theory.[114] Webster makes a similar argument with respect to the relationship between Barth's theology and cosmological theories: 'it may be that what Barth provides is the *framework* – if not the actual execution – of a dogmatic cosmology' (2000a: 111; emphasis added).

---

[111] See Chapter 6.

[112] This understanding of paradigms as frameworks through which we view reality is widely accepted (see Kuhn 1970; Barbour 1974; and Clark 2003). On the relationship between paradigms, models, and theories, though not necessarily using this terminology, see Barbour 1974; Dulles 1974; Godlove 1984; and Clark 2003. For a discussion of how this language can be used to understand the function of theological formulations see Cortez 2005.

[113] See Barbour 1974.

[114] Barth's distinction between 'doctrine' and 'theory' (I/2, 761–62) suggests that he would have been open to using this kind of language and would have argued that theological formulations should focus on developing biblically valid paradigms and models. This does not mean, however, that he would have been opposed to theoretical constructions – indeed he saw such theories as indispensable aspects of any world view (see his comments on the legitimacy of developing a theoretical philosophy of history; III/3, 21–26).

Barth's approach, then, is best understood as providing the paradigmatic framework within which an anthropological ontology must function, without providing the actual execution of such an ontology.

IV. Conclusion

Barth thus develops an anthropological ontology that can be properly construed as christological, pneumatological and covenantal. As he argues,

> We have not deduced this from an abstract consideration and assessment of man. We have not given it a basis in scientific or cultural studies, but in theology. The starting-point was that man stands before God, who is his Creator. We brought out the presuppositions which result in respect of his creatureliness. We asked concerning that which is thereby credited to man and expected from him. We tried to understand man's special nature in the light of the fact that at all events it had to be so constituted as to comprise within itself the ability corresponding to his special relationship with God. (III/2, 416–17)

On this ground, Barth presents a holistic model of human nature that offers a useful way of conceptualizing and speaking about the human person that values both the objective and subjective dimensions of human life.

In the next two chapters, we will also consider whether, in addition to presenting a useful language, this ontological model also provides a helpful framework for engaging the more precise theories of human nature generated in contemporary philosophy of mind. As we saw in the previous chapter, however, this will involve more than simply noting whether a particular theory supports the ontological criteria mentioned above. Barth's methodological commitments will require us to consider whether it is both consistent with Barth's incarnational Christology *and* coherent within its own framework. Both of these factors must come into play in determining the usefulness of an ontological theory for adequately explaining the nature of the human person.

5

PHYSICALISM, BUT NOT REDUCTIONISM: CHRISTOLOGICAL ADEQUACY AND NONREDUCTIVE FORMS OF PHYSICALISM

I. *The Prospect of a Christologically Adequate Physicalist Ontology*

Now that we have developed a basic understanding of Barth's christological vision of human ontology, we are well positioned to move into a consideration of specific theories of the mind–body relationship. Our task in the next two chapters will be to understand the implications that Barth's christocentric orientation of theological anthropology has for understanding and evaluating contemporary theories of human ontology. Our goal, then, is not to try and resolve the mind–body debate, or even to conduct a thorough analysis of any specific proposal, but to view some of the more commonly espoused positions through a christological lens.

With that in mind, we turn our attention in this chapter to a group of theories that understands the human person in a decidedly physicalist sense. That is, we will consider various theories that understand human persons to be completely physical beings (i.e. comprising no additional non-physical or spiritual substance) whose 'inner' dimensions (e.g. beliefs, desires, intentions, feelings, etc.) must be understood in terms of their physical bases.

In the course of this chapter, we will see that there are a number of different ways to construe a physicalist ontology. At the far end of the physicalist spectrum *eliminative materialism* views human persons as strictly physical beings; language concerning 'mental' realities[1] results from erroneous ways of thinking about the human person (i.e. the so-called 'folk psychology') and should simply be eliminated (e.g. Churchland 1981). Somewhat less radical, *reductive* or *conservative physicalism* argues that mental properties are identical with physical properties but that they, and the corresponding 'folk psychology', should not simply be eliminated. This position thus espouses the reducibility of mental properties to physical properties (e.g. Kim 1993c), but in such a way that our language and concepts concerning the mental are retained.

For a variety of reasons that should become clear through the course of the chapter, it seems highly unlikely that either eliminative or reductive physicalism could be developed in a way that would prove adequate to a christological anthropology.[2] Our focus, then, will be on a third group of theories that we will refer to broadly as *nonreductive physicalism* (NRP).[3] NRP seeks to find a means of articulating a commitment to the physicalist paradigm, thus rejecting dualism, while eschewing the eliminative and reductive implications of the other physicalist approaches. Having become the most influential mind–body theory in the last part of the twentieth century, various forms of NRP continue to dominate among philosophers of mind despite a recent rise in more reductive approaches (cf. Kim 1998b).

This chapter will thus seek to analyze the prospects of developing a nonreductive physicalist mind–body theory within the ontological framework established by a christological anthropology. To do this, we will first need to define the basic tenets of NRP and examine its key philosophical commitments. Having done this, we will see that the christological adequacy of NRP can be challenged in three areas: mental causation, phenomenal consciousness, and the continuity of personal identity. The second half of the chapter, then, will survey each of these areas to determine the nature of the problem and the various solutions nonreductive physicalists have proposed. The extent to which NRP is successful in meeting these three challenges will largely determine the extent to which it can be considered a viable option for a christologically adequate anthropological ontology.

II. What Is Nonreductive Physicalism?

Depending on how one defines NRP, it can encompass a rather broad range of theories and ideas. In this study, we will use the term to denote any

---

[1] In this chapter, we will use a variety of terms to refer to mental realities (e.g. entities, events, properties, etc.), without making any concerted effort to distinguish sharply between them. When a particular discussion requires a more particular use of one of these terms, that will be made clear.

[2] Barth made his own opinion of the christological inadequacy of such theories quite clear (III/2, 382–94).

[3] As will become clear later in the chapter, we will be using 'nonreductive physicalism' in a broad sense to describe any theory affirming the basic tenets of NRP.

mind–body theory that affirms: (1) *epistemological nonreduction*, (2) *materialist monism*, (3) the *causal efficacy* of mental properties, and (4) the *asymmetric dependence* of mental properties on physical properties.

Before addressing these in detail, though, it will be important to understand a key concept used in most NRP ontologies. According to many philosophers, the various entities in the universe and the sciences that study them are best understood hierarchically (cf. Campbell 1974; Wimsatt 1976, 1994). According to Kim,

> The Cartesian model of a bifurcated world has been replaced by that of a layered world, a hierarchically stratified structure of 'levels' or 'orders' of entities and their characteristic properties. It is generally thought that there is a bottom level, one consisting of whatever microphysics is going to tell us are the most basic physical particles out of which all matter is composed (electrons, neutrons, quarks, or whatever). And these objects, whatever they are, are characterized by certain fundamental physical properties and relations (mass, spin, charm, or whatever). As we ascend to higher levels, we find structures that are made up of entities belonging to the lower levels, and, moreover, the entities at any given level are thought to be characterized by a set of properties distinctive of that level. (1993b: 190)[4]

The picture thus presented is of a 'world stratified into levels, from lower to higher, from the basic to the constructed and evolved, from the simple to the more complex' (Kim 1999: 19).[5]

This hierarchy factors into the mind–body discussion precisely at the point where we try to determine the relationships that obtain among the various levels. Unlike eliminative materialism, which denies the reality of higher-level processes and properties, both reductive and nonreductive thinkers affirm their reality, but disagree on the best way to explain them. Reductive thinkers view the hierarchy as 'the stepwise explanation of the phenomena of the one level in terms of those of the next lower level, until finally the bottom rung of the ladder is reached, that is, the level of fundamental physics, where only a few basic laws of nature are needed' (Schouten 2001: 680). According to the reductive approach, then, 'A property or event is explained

---

[4] Stoeger explains this by reference to 'constitutive relationships' (2002). That is, the higher levels are constituted by *both* the lower-level particulars *and* the relationships that obtain among them.

[5] Despite the widespread use of this hierarchical model, Kim points out a number of important questions that do not seem to be adequately addressed by those adopting this approach – e.g. the difficulty of individuating the levels, defending the use of one simple hierarchy to encompass all reality, and the oversimplification involved in such a linear framework (1998: 20; cf. Murphy 1996; and Sharpe and Walgate 2003).

when we can show how suitable arrangements or sequences of lower-level properties or events (which do not themselves involve or presuppose the target phenomena) would constitute just such a property or event' (Carruthers 2001a: 65). The nonreductive approach, on the other hand, insists that even though higher-level properties are dependent on lower-level properties, each level complements the others such that none can be reductively explained, in terms of the others (e.g. Murphy 1996).[6] These higher-level properties and processes are dependent upon but always distinct in some way from their lower-level constituents.[7] This disagreement on the relationship of higher- and lower-level properties pervades the entire physicalist mind–body discussion.

a. The First Principle of Nonreductive Physicalism: Epistemological Nonreduction

Although *epistemological reduction* can be explained in a number of different ways,[8] the underlying premise is that higher-level features can be exhaustively explained using the terms and theories proper to lower-level disciplines.[9]

---

[6] The near-simultaneous rejection of several 'reductive' theories in the early part of the twentieth century (e.g. logical positivism, behaviorism, type-physicalism) led to a growing dissatisfaction with reduction in general (Kim 1998a; and Budenholzer 2003).

[7] Indeed, much of the discussion surrounding NRP can be construed as an attempt to understand and evaluate the coherence of maintaining the distinctiveness of higher-level properties within a properly physicalist ontology.

[8] Understanding the nature of reduction and the antireductionist response, however, is complicated by the fact that, as Meyering rightly notes, 'the notion of reduction itself is hardly a unitary concept any longer' (2001: 761). The term is thus used with reference to several different kinds of reduction (ontological, epistemological, logical, semantic, methodological, causal, etc.; cf. Peacocke 1986; Murphy 1998b; and Bielfeldt 2000) and without any clear agreement about the methodology for performing a proper reduction (cf. Peacocke 1976; Brooks 1994; Block and Stalnaker 1999; Chalmers and Jackson 2001; Budenholzer 2003; and Jones 2003). Additionally, we must note the differences between 'classical reductionism', which affirmed the direct correlation of higher-level theories and concepts with those of lower levels, and 'new wave reductionism', which allows for a much fuzzier correlation while still maintaining their ultimate reducibility (cf. McCauley and Bechtel 2001).

[9] Cf. Kim 1993c; 1998b; Melnyk 1995; and Crick 1994. The form of epistemological reduction cited most commonly is the model of intertheoretic reduction developed by Ernst Nagel (1961; though cf. Kim 1993c; and Melnyk 1995). According to this approach, the intertheoretic reduction of one theory, T_1, to another, T_2, is possible just in case all the laws of T_1 can be fully deduced from the laws of T_2. This is accomplished by virtue of biconditional 'bridge' laws or principles which connect the laws and terms of T_1 with the laws and terms of T_2. Once this 'bridge' has been formed, it should be a relatively simple matter to express the truths and laws of T_1 in the language of T_2 (cf. Heil 2004b; and Kim 1993c). This approach to reduction, however, is commonly criticized for setting impossibly high standards in that it 'requires that each mental

As examples of successful reductions of higher-level phenomena, philosophers commonly point to the reduction of chemistry to physics and heat to motion (Melnyk 1995; Kim 1998a);[10] often holding out the hope of the eventual reduction of biological, psychological, and sociological phenomena to the fundamental sciences as well (e.g. Churchland 1981).

It is important to realize two things about this form of epistemological reduction. First, even a successful intertheoretic reduction does not entail the *elimination* of the reduced theory (Smart 1959; Lewis 1966). It may still prove heuristically and conceptually useful to continue using the higher-level theory because of its greater clarity and simplicity (Heil 2004b: 362). As Kim comments, 'impugning the reality of what is being reduced would make all of our observable world unreal' (1993c: 102). Thus, unlike eliminative reductivist views that reject the continued use of such 'folk' theories, a conservative reductionism maintains their continued validity. Second, a reductive epistemology only requires an *ultimate* or *in principle* reduction.[11] As Wacome states,

> Reductionism's promises about the reducibility of one science to another are always related to what is possible in principle; no one seriously maintained that we might in practice dispense with the concepts, generalizations, and, if there are any, laws of the higher-level sciences on the grounds of their reducibility to physics. (2004: 328)

Consequently, even eliminative materialists tend to argue only for the *eventual* elimination of higher-level concepts *when* suitable lower-level ones become available.

Despite these two caveats, NRP firmly rejects epistemological reduction. According to van Gulick, NRP 'argues that we must not confuse the plausible claim of ontological physicalism with the implausible claim that the physical sciences provide us with conceptual and representational resources adequate for describing and explaining everything within the physical world' (1992: 158).[12] NRP thus holds that at least some higher-level theories and concepts are incommensurable with those of the lower levels.[13]

According to Meyering (2000, 2002), nonreductivists commonly level five primary arguments against epistemological reduction.[14] First, nonreductivists

---

property be provided with a nomologically coextensive physical property, across all species and structure types', thus making it easy prey for the kinds of critical arguments we will be surveying in this section (Kim 1998b: 26). For a more positive evaluation, see Marras 2002.

[10] Even these textbook examples of reduction are not without their critics (Wacome 2004).

[11] Even if the reduction is only 'in the mind of God', it still qualifies as an 'in principle' reduction (Bonevac 1995).

[12] Cf. also Kirk 1996, 2000.

maintain that higher-level explanations are often necessary due to a lack of precise knowledge regarding lower-level entities.[15] Second, as we will see in the next section, nonreductive thinkers argue that mental and physical types are not identical to one another and, therefore, there is no way of mapping precise nomological relationships between them.[16] Third, higher-level theories often provide an explanatory account of the causally relevant properties of seemingly unrelated physical events that is unavailable on a physical description alone. Fourth, the possibility of *multiple supervenience* – that is, the fact that particular physical properties can realize multiple higher-level properties depending on the circumstances involved – indicates that appeal to lower-level explanations alone is inadequate for describing the *pertinent* causal factors.[17] Finally, the downward causal influence of higher-level properties, a basic commitment of NRP and something we will address in more detail later, entails epistemological nonreduction. Although some of these arguments are weaker than others, they nonetheless present clearly the NRP case for epistemological nonreduction.

b. The Second Principle of Nonreductive Physicalism: Physical Monism

Philosophers commonly describe NRP as being ontologically monistic or reductionistic.[18] From one perspective, this is certainly true and noncontroversial. A basic tenet of all physicalist ontologies is that 'everything is physical'.

---

[13] Peacocke 1986; van Gulick 1992; Murphy 1998b; Meyering 2001; Arbib 2002; and Rosenberg and Kaplan 2005. Of course, this nonreductive argument does not require the dismissal of *all* forms of reduction. NRP proponents are quick to affirm that reduction is necessary at times and that it has usefully served to eliminate unsuccessful philosophical ideas like phlogiston (Sharpe and Walgate 2003). What they deny is that *all* higher-level phenomena are so reducible.

[14] Wacome lists a number of less effective but popular antireductionist arguments (2004).

[15] This argument is, of course, inadequate for establishing a robust epistemological nonreduction since it is consistent with complete reductionism, though it concedes that we do not always have such reductive theories available to us (Meyering 2000).

[16] As we will see in the next section, arguments of this type are also insufficient to ground a fully nonreductive epistemology since they fail to preclude the possibility of an *in principle* reduction in a theory that is able to encompass the entire disjunctive set of physical realizers of a particular mental kind.

[17] As an example, Meyering (2001) argues that a given realizer state (e.g. atomic constituents of an aluminum ladder) have various dispositional properties (e.g. thermal conductivity and electrical conductivity) that are selectively activated depending on the circumstances (e.g. lightning strike or bright sunny day). A higher-level explanation thus plays a distinctive role in explaining the cause of a particular event (e.g. being electrocuted or burned) by taking into account the overall context in a way that cannot be done by a mere description of the physical realizer.

[18] For example, Kim 1993b; Murphy 1998a; and Brown 2004.

Although this can be understood broadly to preclude the existence of *any* non-physical beings, we will understand it more narrowly to refer to the principle that all human are physical beings.[19] That is, NRP is monistic in that it rejects any appeal to non-physical substances as an explanation of human ontology.

From another perspective, though, that of understanding the precise relationship between human persons, their mental features, and their physical features, the ontology of NRP becomes slightly more complicated. We will thus see that nonreductive physicalists differ with respect to the precise nature of the relationship between physical and mental items.

1. Defining Physicalism without Losing the Physical

At this point, however, an important question arises. What exactly is physicalism? Or, even more basically, what does it mean to be *physical*? Unfortunately, there does not seem to be any widely established definition of 'physical' to which we can appeal. As a result, the term has tended to be used in a rather imprecise manner, leading to significant confusion as to what constitutes a proper physicalist theory of the mind–body relation (E. Lowe 1993).[20] Indeed, Horgan argues that defining physicalism is itself an inherently philosophical question and suggests that theories of the mind–brain relationship can be understood as ways of explicating particular notions of what it means to be physical (1993a).[21]

General definitions of physicalism tend to fall into two different categories.[22] From one perspective, physical things are identified based on their conformity to certain paradigmatic physical characteristics. Usually this comprises an appeal to the spatio-temporal nature of physical things.[23] Montero points out, however, that such a spatio-temporal approach struggles to provide an adequate account of things like neutrinos and photons that most would

---

[19] Vallicella (1998) distinguishes *global physicalism*, which posits that everything that exists is essentially physical (e.g. Crane 1994; Post 1995; Melnyk 1997, 2003; Shagrir 1999; and Bennett 2004), and *local physicalism*, a more limited thesis contending that human persons are essentially physical (Strawson 1994; Murphy 1998b; van Inwagen 2002; and Brown 2004). Of course, these two definitions are not exclusive and many thinkers use both (e.g. Kim 1993b). But, as the former is clearly incompatible with Christian theism and as the latter is more pertinent to the matter at hand, the term *physicalism* will be used throughout this chapter with respect to *local physicalism*.

[20] Fink (2006) points out that similar problems plague attempts to define *natural*.

[21] Montero goes so far as to argue that failure to solve 'the body problem' (i.e. defining the nature of the body and the physical) is a pervasive problem that has inhibited contemporary philosophy's ability to resolve the mind–body debate (1999; cf. Sussman 1981).

[22] Stoljar labels these two approaches the 'object-based' and 'theory-based' conceptions of the physical (2001c).

[23] For example, Kim 1993b: 193; and Honderich 2001; cf. also van Inwagen 1990.

consider to be physical in nature (1999: 184). Similarly, McGinn argues that such definitions are weakened by our limited understanding of the nature of space and time; a limitation that can easily render such definitions vacuous (2003: 155).

Recognizing the difficulties of establishing a satisfying, abstract definition of the physical, many philosophers opt for a more pragmatic approach. These thinkers follow the common practice of defining physicalism in terms of those things that are studied by the physical sciences.[24] But this approach likewise runs into trouble. What do we mean by science? If we mean science as it is currently understood, then physicalism is almost certainly false, given the historical track-record of scientific theories (Melnyk 2003). But, if we mean some form of ultimate science, a theory that will eventually be able to account for everything within some scientific framework (e.g. Kirk 2000), then physicalism again flirts with vacuousness since there is no reason to think that even such disparate things as minds, atoms, and fairy godmothers could not be accommodated within such a grand theory.

Based on these difficulties, McGinn (2003) argues that we should stop using a vague term like 'physicalism'.[25] Although there is some validity in such a proposal, it may prove more useful to continue using it while recognizing its inherent limitations. In this study, then, we will adopt a rather general definition of 'physical' as that which refers to those entities and processes that are studied by the physical sciences, either as those sciences are currently understood, or in some future form that will not be radically different from their present state.

Having explored the difficulties of defining physical *things*, we must consider two further issues. First, any definition of physicalism must make room for physical *properties* as well. Thus, van Inwagen proposes that we define *physicalism* in terms of 'an individual thing made entirely of those things whose nature physics investigates' and a *physical property* to be 'a property that can be possessed by a physical thing and *only* by a physical thing' (2002: 167). Although determining precisely which properties thus qualify as physical properties can be as difficult as defining physicalism itself (Burge 1993), such a distinction will be necessary for understanding the relevant discussions. Second, physicalism must also account for physical *processes*. Thus, physicalism seems necessarily committed to the premise that all causal

---

[24] Cf. Melnyk 1997; and Ellis 2000. Thus, Melnyk proffers a definition consisting of the following two assertions: '(1) There is some science, S, distinct from the totality of all the sciences, such that every entity (property) is either itself mentioned as such in the laws and theories of S or is ultimately constituted (realized) by entities (properties) mentioned as such in the laws and theories of S' and '(2) S is current physics' (1997: 633).

[25] Radder goes even further, arguing that these difficulties indicate fundamental problems with physical monism as a tenable metaphysic (2001).

processes are *in some sense* fundamentally dependent on the causal processes studied by the physical sciences. Indeed, many philosophers contend that the causal completeness of the physical universe (i.e. the principle that all physical events have sufficient physical causes) is a defining factor of any true physicalism (Horgan 1993b; and Kim 1993c).[26] And indeed, nonreductive physicalists agree.[27]

With these principles in mind, *physicalism* will be used in this chapter to identify the theory that (a) human persons are either themselves physical entities or are exhaustively composed of physical entities; (b) that all the properties of human persons are either themselves physical properties or are properly related (whatever that proper relation turns out to be) to physical properties; and (c) that all causal processes are either physical processes or are causally dependent on physical processes (cf. Melnyk 1997).[28]

2. What Does It Mean to Say that the Mental is Physical?

Although all physicalist theories are thus committed to the general form of physicalism outlined above, they differ substantially when it comes to understanding the relationship between physical properties and processes and other things like mental properties and human persons. Given the commitment to physical monism, we might expect that physicalists would simply identify things like mental properties and human persons with physical things. Indeed, early physicalists like U. T. Place, Herbert Feigl, and J. J. C. Smart understood the premise that 'everything *is* physical' to mean that mental features are *type-identical* with physical features (Place 1956; Feigl 1958; and Smart 1959).[29] On this view, a mental type (e.g. pain) simply *is* a physical type (e.g. a particular neural state).[30] Thus, affirming a very clear relationship between the physical and the apparently non-physical, the type-identity theory became the orthodox view in philosophy of mind (Kim 1999).

Such an ontologically reductionistic view of higher-level realities, though, did not remain unchallenged for long, and by the late sixties and early seventies the type-identity theory had been abandoned by most philosophers.

---

[26] The 'causal completeness' principle is sometimes referred to as 'causal closure', though some prefer to reserve the latter term for a stronger thesis that combines causal completion with the denial of overdetermination (cf. Lowe 2000; and Robb and Heil 2005).

[27] For example, McLaughlin 1989; Bontly 2001; Murphy 2002a; and Meyering 2002.

[28] Thus, although dualists are often criticized for their inability to provide a clear definition of the soul, we can see that similar problems arise for the physicalists ability to define the nature of the physical; both are inherently difficult tasks that rely heavily on philosophical analysis and we should, therefore, be careful about asserting a *de facto* scientific superiority for physicalistic approaches over dualistic ones (see E. Lowe 1993).

[29] For more on the nature of the distinction between type- and token-identity see Horgan 1981; Foster 1994; Latham 2003; and Wetzel 2005.

The reason for this rejection was the growing conviction that the kind of identity relationship required by type-identity was too strong. In a series of essays, Hilary Putnam convincingly argued that it was quite conceivable that mental properties could be realized in a variety of different ways.[31] In other words, a mental state like pain could be realized in a human by a C-fibre firing,[32] in a mollusk by a D-fibre firing, or in a Martian by some other mechanism entirely. Pain could then be seen to be *multiply realizable*. But, if mental states can be realized by multiple physical states, it would appear that there can be no strict identity relationship between them.[33] The multiple realization argument, as this argument has come to be known, seemed to establish clearly the impossibility of type-identifying mental properties with physical properties.[34]

---

[30] Most of these early identity theorists argued that they were positing an identity relationship that was both 'strict', that is, an identity relationship that an object has only with itself, (Place 1956; and Smart 1959), and 'contingent', that is, the mental kinds associated with physical kinds could have been entirely different in some nomologically different possible world, (Smart 1959; and Lewis 1966). Kripke, however, famously responded by arguing that strict identity relationships are necessary and non-contingent (1971). Although his arguments have not convinced everyone, most philosophers have followed Kripke on this point.

[31] See Putnam 1975 for a collection of his papers published during this time. For an overview of arguments related to multiple realizability see Bickle 2002.

[32] 'C-fibre' should be understood to refer to whatever complex physical state is involved in realizing the relevant pain state.

[33] Gene Witmer summarizes the multiple realizability argument against identity as follows (2004):
  1. There exists at least one mental property M such that there is a set of distinct physical properties $\{P_1 \vee P_2 \vee \ldots P_n\}$, no one of which realizes M on every occasion, while each realizes it on some occasion.
  2. If M is identical with any physical property, it is identical with one of $\{P_1 \vee P_2 \vee \ldots P_n\}$.
  3. M can't be identical with any of $\{P_1 \vee P_2 \vee \ldots P_n\}$ because there is no member of it with which it is coextensive.
  4. There is no physical property with which M is coextensive, and hence none with which it is identical.

[34] As Block points out, multiple realizability has not been without its critics (1978). According to Kim multiple realizability defeats global type-reduction but has nothing to say about local type-reduction (1993c: 180–81, 273–75). In other words, there is nothing in multiple realizability that precludes one from arguing that even though pain could be multiply realized across species, pain could be singly realized within a given species (assuming that we allow for the inevitable variations among particular members of that species). But, Kim argues, species-specific or local reduction of this kind is all that we need to establish reductionism. Horgan agrees and contends that local reduction of this kind is incompatible with NRP (1993b).

Even more significantly, Kim argues, against Fodor (1974) and Putnam (1975), that *disjunctive* physical types can be type-identified with mental types and that denying this possibility calls into question the nomological consistency of mental kinds (cf. van

In place of type-identity, many philosophers have argued for a weaker identity theory known as *token-identity*. Rather than establishing an identity relationship between mental and physical *kinds*, token-identity merely posits the identity of mental and physical *particulars*. In other words, according to token-physicalism, a particular mental event or token (e.g. the pain experienced on some occasion by a particular individual) is identical with a particular physical event or token (e.g. a C-fibre firing on some occasion in a particular individual), but that there is no identity relationship between these two *kinds* of events (i.e. a C-fibre firing is not required for the instantiation of pain states in general). This approach became quite popular with philosophers looking for a way to maintain their physicalist commitments without the perceived drawbacks of the type-identity theory.

There is a third option, however. Some physicalists reject both type- and token-physicalism by asserting that higher-level entities and properties are *constituted by but not identical to* the lower-level entities and properties that constitute them.[35] For example, macro-entities like statues, dollar bills, and persons are constituted by but distinct from their copper, paper, and biological constituents. That this should not be understood as an identity relationship, according to constitution theorists, is established by the fact that such macro-entities have different properties than their constituent elements (Baker 1997). According to one famous example, then, a statue and the bronze that constitutes it can be distinguished by the fact that the lump of bronze possesses properties (e.g. malleability) not possessed by the statue (i.e. if the bronze were melted down, the statue would cease to exist but the bronze would not). Given the property of the indiscernibility of identicals, constitution theorists argue, the differences in properties entails the non-identity of

---

Inwagen 2002; Block 2002; Sawyer 2003). Putnam and Fodor both argued that multiple realizability could not be defeated by positing a disjunctive physical type that would include all the possible realizers of a given mental type. Such 'wildly disjunctive' physical types are not nomologically related to one another and thus not proper members of a set. In response, Kim has argued that if this is true and if mental tokens stand in nomologically consistent causal relationship with their physical tokens, then mental kinds likewise are 'wildly disjunctive' and nonnomic (1993c: 316–25).

Kim's arguments have not been universally accepted (see Melnyk 2003; and Horgan 1993a). Antony (2003) helpfully points out, however, that much of this is extraneous to the question of nonreduction. As we will discuss a little later, both token- and type-identity run into problems with respect to causal reduction. The main issue for nonreductivists, then, is not whether mental kinds can be identified with physical kinds, but whether mental properties stand over-and-above their physical realizers (whether types or tokens) sufficiently to facilitate causal nonreduction.

[35] Cf. Pereboom and Kornblith 1991; Corcoran 1998; 2001b; 2005; and Baker 1997, 2001. Some prefer to restrict nonreductive physicalism to token-identity theories (e.g. Marras 1994). Since constitution theorists maintain the four basic commitments outlined in this chapter, we will consider them to be nonreductive physicalists.

the statue and the lump of bronze constituting it. On this view, then, mental properties should be viewed as constituted by but not identical to the physical properties that constitute them.

From the preceding discussions, it seems reasonable to conclude that any physicalist ontology that seeks to affirm a nonreductive understanding of mental items will be inclined to reject type-identity in favor of either token-identity or constitution theory. In this study, then, we will understand the *physicalism* component of NRP to refer to some form of either of these two approaches.

c. The Third Principle of Nonreductive Physicalism: Causal Efficacy of the Mental

The third principle to which NRP is committed is the causal efficacy of the mental.[36] Since the complex issues surrounding the question of mental causation will be the focus of the next section, it will only be mentioned briefly here to complete our discussion of NRP's basic commitments.

When saying that NRP is committed to mental causation, two opposite ideas must be kept in mind. First, as we have already noted, NRP holds a simultaneous commitment to the causal completeness of the physical and the existence of mental realities. NPR must, therefore, reject any theory inconsistent with these two fundamental commitments. And second, by affirming the causal efficacy of mental properties, NRP rejects any form of epiphenomenalism – that is, any theory that posits that mental properties are real but causally irrelevant.[37]

As we will see in the next section, NRP's commitment to mental causation within a physicalist framework committed to the causal completion of the physical universe is highly contentious and marks one of the most significant objections to NRP as a coherent mind–body theory.

---

[36] Except when necessary for addressing particular arguments, we will not concern ourselves with the question of whether mental causation is best understood in terms of mental states, properties, or events. This chapter will largely focus on mental causation in terms of the causal efficacy of mental properties but it seems unlikely that any of the arguments would be significantly affected if mental states or events were in view.

[37] Many have pointed out that epiphenomenalism, understood as affirming real but causally irrelevant mental properties, is incoherent in that there seems to be no reason to affirm the existence of causally impotent properties (cf. Kim 1993b; and McLaughlin 1993). A less effective argument used by some is to contend that epiphenomenal properties make no sense in an evolutionary scheme because there is no way to explain why such 'empty' properties would have been selected (e.g. Midgley 2000; and Elder 2001). It would seem entirely possible, though, to view such epiphenomenal properties as merely resultant aspects of biological selection rather than as specifically selected themselves.

d. The Fourth Principle of Nonreductive Physicalism: Asymmetric Psychophysical Dependence

The epistemological and ontological irreducibility of mental features to physical features, however, is an inadequate basis upon which to develop a mind–body theory. As Kim points out, NRP needs to complement this negative thesis with a positive account of a nonreductive understanding the mind–body relationship (1993b: 194). Nonreductivists often seek to do this utilizing some set of terms that indicates an irreducible *asymmetric dependence* of the mental on the physical.[38] In this way the physical is accorded epistemological and ontological primacy, but not ultimacy.

1. The Realization Relationship

The first of these terms, *realization,* was originally introduced by functionalist thinkers to refer to the physical realization of functional states (cf. Kim 1998a).[39] Kim defines realization as:

> When P is said to "realize" M in system s, P must specify a microstructural property of s that provides a causal mechanism for the implementation of M in s. (Kim 1993b: 197)

On this definition we can see that the realization thesis is intended to affirm the asymmetrical dependency of M on P in s.[40]

The usefulness of realization-language for nonreductive thinkers, though, is limited for three reasons. First, realization-language has come to be associated primarily with functionalism (Kim 1993c, 1998a). Though many nonreductive physicalists use functionalist ideas in developing their theories,[41] NRP is not committed to functionalism, nor is functionalism necessarily consistent with NRP as we have defined it here (see Pereboom 2002; Block 2004).[42] Second, many have argued that realization-language actually generates such a strong psychophysical dependency relation that it may actually

---

[38] Kim suggests that dependence and determination are the two key ideas of the nonreductive theory (1993b: 194). For now we will not address whether asymmetrical psychophysical dependence entails some form of psychophysical determination, leaving that question for our later discussion of mental causation.

[39] Functionalism, often referred to as the 'reigning presumption' (Dennett 2001) in contemporary philosophy of mind (cf. Kim 1998a; Honderich 2001), is the view that mental states are functional states which should be defined in terms of their causal inputs, outputs, and relations to other functional states (see Lewis 1966; Armstrong 1968; Putnam 1967; Fodor 1981, 1983; and Shoemaker and Hywel 1975, 1981).

[40] For a broader analysis of *realization* and its role in mind–body theories, see Shoemaker and Hywel 2003.

[41] For example, van Gulick 1992; and Meyering 2002.

be incompatible NRP's basic commitments, especially its commitment to mental causation.[43] And third, as Kim suggests, the concept of realization has been used in ways 'that are neither uniform nor clear', thus reducing its usefulness (1998a: 72; cf. Kim 2003: 166). Possibly for reasons like these, realization-language, though used by nonreductive physicalists, tends not to be the primary way in which they express themselves.

2. The Supervenience Relationship

The term *supervenience* rose to popularity in the 1980s as a result of its perceived ability to affirm three important tenets of NRP:[44] (a) the *covariance* of mental and physical properties; (b) the *dependence* of mental properties on physical properties; and (c) the *nonreducibility* of mental properties to physical properties (Savellos and Yalcin 1995; Kim 1993c). It was thus thought by many that supervenience was the ideal term for espousing NRP. It came under heavy criticism, however, and, though still used extensively by nonreductive physicalists, no longer bears the explanatory weight that it once did.

The core idea of supervenience, according to Kim, is that 'mental properties or states of something are dependent on its physical, or bodily, properties, in the sense that once its physical properties are fixed, its mental properties are thereby fixed' (1998a: 7). More explicitly, we can say that supervenience entails that higher-level properties or states (A-facts) supervene on lower-level properties or states (B facts) if and only if (1) A-facts are real (i.e. they are not merely conceptual); (2) A and B facts are distinct (i.e. they are not simply different ways of referring to the same properties or states); and

---

[42] Functionalism is often developed as a nonreductive mind–body theory itself. We will not be addressing it in this chapter, however, because it does not seem to be clearly committed to physical monism or the causal efficacy of mental properties. Although it is usually formulated in ways that indicate a commitment to both principles, many have pointed out that functionalism is at least theoretically compatible with dualistic ontologies (e.g. Putnam 1967), while others have argued that it is best construed as a fully reductive theory (e.g. Honderich 1994; and Kim 1993c), with the possible implication that mental properties are causally inefficacious (Block 1990). Additionally, Block points out that functionalism can be used in support of or against the phenomenological realism that we will see is a necessary part of the nonreductive program (2002; cf. Block 1978 for more general arguments against functionalism). Thus, although nonreductive physicalists often use functionalistic ideas in developing their systems, we will consider them distinct approaches and not deal with functionalism as a form of NRP.

[43] Cf. Kim 1993b, 1993c: 363–67; Melnyk 1995; Bielfeldt 2001; and Bontly 2001.

[44] The term rose to prominence in philosophy through its use by the British emergentists and moral philosophers like R. M. Hare in the first part of the twentieth century (Kim 1993c; and Horgan 1993a), but did not become significant in philosophy of mind until the 1980s when it was introduced by Donald Davidson (1980: 214).

(3) there is some objective dependency relationship between *A* and *B* facts such that *A*-facts cannot change without a corresponding change with respect to *B*-facts.[45]

For two reasons, though, supervenience-language is now widely regarded as being inadequate *by itself* to articulate a nonreductive position. First, attempts to clarify the supervenience relationship beyond the general definition offered above have produced such a wealth of different definitions as to limit its practical usefulness.[46] Second, despite the fact that supervenience-language was originally introduced as a way of affirming the asymmetrical dependency of the psychophysical relationship, it is now widely accepted that it fails to do so.[47] The concern is that supervenience merely establishes the necessary *covariation* of *A* and *B* facts without establishing either *how* or *why* this covariation takes place.[48] But covariation by itself is insufficient to ground a properly physical mind–body theory. Kim rightly argues that mind–body covariation is a theory that could be supported by reductive

---

[45] Cf. Horgan 1993a; Lynch and Glasgow 2003; and Wilson 1999. Although supervenience can be understood as dealing exclusively with facts intrinsic to the subvenient bases, several thinkers have argued convincingly that supervenient properties require a broader base that includes extrinsic factors like relations and relational properties (Baker 1993; and Horgan 1993a).

[46] Philosophers commonly distinguish different supervenience concepts based on their scope and strength (Lynch and Glasgow 2003). As to scope, we can distinguish between *global*, *local*, and *regional* supervenience depending on whether the supervenience relationship in view is directed at entire worlds, specific regions, or particular individuals. Some thinkers have argued for an additional distinction between strong and weak forms of global supervenience (e.g. McLaughlin 1995 and Stalnaker 1996), but Bennett convincingly demonstrates that the strong form is not interestingly different from strong supervenience and that weaker forms are insufficient to establish a significant dependency relationship (2004). These distinctions will, therefore, not come into our discussion.

With respect to strength, supervenience is commonly divided into strong and weak forms (Haugeland 1982; Kim 1993c, 1994; Horgan 1982, 1993a, 1995; McLaughlin 1995; Savellos and Yalcin 1995; Stalnaker 1996; and Bielfeldt 2000). Surveying the extensive literature on this distinction would take us too far afield. The basic distinction between them is that weak supervenience holds that A-facts only supervene on B-facts with nomological necessity whereas strong supervenience maintains that the relationship holds with metaphysical necessity. They thus differ with respect to whether or not the relationship holds in nomologically different worlds (on these modal issues see Chalmers 1996; Schouten 2001; Lynch and Glasgow 2003).

Noting the tremendous number of different theories of supervenience and their correspondingly diverse applications, Kim nonetheless argues that the term still usefully expresses its 'core idea', that is, 'No difference of one kind without a difference of another kind', even though we must now recognize the many different ways in which this core idea can be expressed (1993c: 155).

[47] Horgan 1993a; Kim 1993c; Goetz 1994; Wilson 1999; Schouten 2001; and Melnyk 2003.

physicalists, nonreductive physicalists, epiphenomenalists, and even some dualists (1998b: 12).

Kim is probably correct to view supervenience not as 'a metaphysically deep, explanatory relation', but as 'a phenomenological relation about patterns of property covariation' (Kim 1998a: 10).[49] Thus, supervenience can play a useful role in articulating an important NRP commitment, the asymmetrical dependency relationship between mental and physical properties, but is not by itself a sufficient principle of a physicalist ontology.[50]

3. The Emergence Relationship

A third term often used in NRP, *emergence*, needs to be carefully distinguished from its use in other contexts.[51] As we will see in the next chapter, emergent dualism uses emergence-language to affirm the emergence of non-physical substances. This, however, is clearly inconsistent with NRP's commitment to physical monism. But NRP must also be distinguished from a form of emergent monism that espouses emergent causal powers in a manner that is inconsistent with NRP's commitment to the causal completeness of the physical universe.[52] Searle (1992) suggests that we should distinguish between emergent theories that espouse autonomous emergent causal powers that violate the causal completeness principle (emergent$_2$) and those that do not (emergent$_1$).[53] As we will see later in the chapter, NRP is strongly committed

---

[48] Thus, Kim correctly argues that even strong supervenience does not entail asymmetrical dependence (1993c: 67). The failure of supervenience to ground dependence can be clearly seen in the general definitions of supervenience that have been offered. For example Davidson describes his position on supervenience as: 'a predicate *p* is supervenient on a set of predicates *S* if and only if *p* does not distinguish any entities that cannot be distinguished by *S*' (1993: 4). Similarly, Lynch and Glasgow define supervenience as entailing that 'the *B*-facts supervene on the *A*-facts if and only if there are not two possible situations that are identical in *A*-facts, but different in *B*-facts' (2003). Despite the fact that supervenience is often taken as almost synonymous with the dependence of *A*-facts on *B*-facts, neither of these definitions even suggests such a dependence relation.

[49] Kim thus argues that much of the literature on supervenience is misdirected since it focuses primarily on the question of reduction when the real issue is whether or not supervenience can serve as a mind–body theory at all (1998a).

[50] Horgan 1993a; Kim 1998b; Hansen 2000; and Melnyk 2003.

[51] For good studies of the concept of emergence and its historical development see van Cleve 1990; Stephan 1992; McLaughlin 1992; and Clayton 2005.

[52] For example, Crane 1995, 2001; Clayton 2000, 2004, 2005; and O'Connor 2001, 2003. Brüntrup argues that emergent monism can be understood as consistent with the causal closure principle if it is understood as a form of dual-aspect theory (1998). While this may be true, it seems clear that at least some (if not most) forms of emergent monism operate largely outside the framework established by causal completeness.

[53] McGinn draws a similar distinction between properties that are '*conservatively emergent*' and those that are '*radical* or *brute*' (2003: 154).

to the causal efficacy of mental properties, but it seeks to explicate this causal efficacy within the framework of physical causal completeness.[54]

With these two distinctions in mind, emergent-language still has a role to play in articulating NRP.[55] Specifically, since emergence-language is widely viewed as the opposite of reduction-language, nonreductive physicalists have found emergence to be a useful concept for articulating its commitment to epistemological and causal nonreduction.[56] Emergence is thus used to express the conviction that higher-level realities come 'to exhibit novel properties that in some sense transcend the properties of their constituent parts, and behave in ways that cannot be predicted on the basis of the laws governing simpler systems' (Kim 1991:3).

Thus, emergence-language can serve a useful role in developing NRP so long as it is kept distinct from other proposals that use such language in ways that would undermine NRP's commitment to the asymmetrical dependence of the mental on the physical.

4. The Constitution Relationship

We have already discussed briefly the fourth term that is often used to articulate a nonreductive understanding of the psychophysical relationship. According to the *constitution* theory, higher-level features are asymmetrically dependent on lower-level features in that they are constituted by them. Using the example of the statue again, constitution theory holds that the statue is distinct from the bronze that constitutes it but that the statue depends on the bronze, which thus has a certain ontological primacy.

NRP has thus tended to rely on four different terms in an effort to express its commitment to the primacy of the physical and the asymmetrical dependency of the mental on the physical, while still maintaining that the mental is not in any way reducible to the physical. We have seen that the four terms express various aspects of the basic commitments held by nonreductive physicalists, but that each has significant limitations. As Kim notes,

> We have learned from work on causation and causal modal logic the hard lesson that the idea of causal dependence or determination is not so easily or directly obtained from straightforward modal notions alone. . . . Ideas of dependence and determination, whether causal,

---

[54] Kim has argued that nonreductive materialism is merely a contemporary version of emergent-theory and that the two are roughly synonymous (1999). Differences between them regarding the nature and status of mental causal powers, though, would seem to be sufficient to establish that they are distinct theories (cf. Pereboom 2002).
[55] See especially the useful set of essays in Beckermann, Flohr, and Kim 1992.
[56] For example, Peacocke 1986, 1990; Searle 1992; Polkinghorne 1994; Murphy 1998c, 2005; and Brown 2004; cf. Newman 2001.

supervenient, or of other sorts, stubbornly resist capture in simpler and more transparent terms. (1993c: 67)

These four terms, then, should be viewed as helpful but limited attempts to express basic commitments held by any NRP theory.

III. Christology and Coherence: The Viability of Nonreductive Forms of Physicalism

As we saw in the previous chapter, viewing the human person from the vantage point provided by the person and work of Jesus Christ has important implications for understanding human ontology. Specifically, we saw how Barth's christological ontology can be understood as providing an ontological framework within which any christologically adequate anthropological theory must operate. At first glance, NRP appears to fare rather well with respect to this framework. Its physicalist approach allows NRP to affirm the importance of embodiment, while its nonreductive stance accords well with the commitment to the subjective and mental aspects of human life. NRP seems well positioned, then, to provide an account of human ontology that addresses the full range of concerns posited by Barth's christological framework.

The evaluative task is not so easy, however, when we look a little more closely and consider some of the many criticisms that have been raised regarding the nonreductive position. Specifically, many feel that the attempt to mediate between irreducible mental properties and fundamentally physical realities results in some level of incoherence. Tim Crane speaks for many when he asks, 'If the mind is not physical, then how can it have effects in the physical world; but if it is physical, how can we explain consciousness?' (Crane 2003: 234). In this section, then, we will evaluate NRP more closely on three specific issues, regarding which it has been subject to some criticism: (1) mental causation, (2) consciousness, and (3) the continuity of personal identity through death and resurrection. As we have seen, all three are required for a christologically valid ontology. Each is its own field of study with an impressively large body of literature. We will, therefore, not attempt to do more than simply survey some of the key arguments as we seek to establish whether or not NRP has coherent and christologically adequate responses to these concerns.[57]

---

[57] Consequently, none of the following sections will attempt to engage all of the arguments and responses that have been offered. Rather, each section will selectively adopt several important arguments and note the ways in which NRP proponents have responded as a way of testing its coherence and adequacy.

a. Descartes' Revenge: The Problem of Mental Causation

As we will see in the next chapter, the problem of mental causation constitutes one of the primary objections to dualist ontologies. It might seem somewhat surprising, then, to discover that it is no less problematic for physicalists.[58] Unlike the dualist problem of accounting for the causal interaction of two disparate substances, NRP bears the burden of establishing the causal relevance of mental properties in a physical universe (Kim 1998b; Robb and Heil 2005). This becomes critical when we realize that some account of such causal relevance seems necessary for grounding personal agency, moral responsibility, and rational mental processes.[59]

Most thinkers recognize that there are actually several problems for a physicalist account of mental causation.[60] They can be divided broadly into two categories. In the first fall those arguments that question whether the nature of mental properties themselves rules out their causally efficacy (the suitability argument). In the second we can place those arguments to the effect that even if mental properties are suited as causes, there is no room for them in the causal structure of the physical universe (the exclusion argument). Although the causal suitability of mental properties has been called into question by a number of important arguments,[61] they are highly contentious.

---

[58] Kim refers to this intriguing situation as 'Descartes's Revenge' (1998b: 38). For a good survey of different ways of understanding causation see Tooley 2003.

[59] Hornsby 1993; Kim 1998b; Midgley 2000; Harre 2001; Torrance 2003; and Lowe 2003.

[60] Robb and Heil note that the physicalist problem of mental causation can actually be divided into four separate issues: property dualism, anomalous monism, exclusion, and externalism (2005). Since all four arguments are closely related and since the problem of exclusion has received the most attention, we will focus our discussion on that issue and address the other problems as necessary.

[61] The primary objections to the causal suitability of mental properties have been advanced in two ways. From one direction, Donald Davidson's *anomalous monism* theory contended that there are no strict laws governing the relationship between mental and physical events and, therefore, no strict causal relationships (1980, 1993). Mental properties are causally *relevant* in that they are individuating properties of causally efficacious physical events (1993). Davidson's argument has been widely criticized for providing at least tacit support for epiphenomenalism (Kim 1993a; McLaughlin 1993; and Sosa 1993) and is no longer widely followed (though cf. LePore and Loewer 1989).

A second set of objections stems from the *externalist* conception of mental states. According to this theory, most, if not all, mental states have extrinsic (i.e. relational properties) that are essential to them (see Burge 1979; Putnam 1981; Heil 1987; Brown 2002; and Lau 2004). For example, a belief that Paris is the capital of France is at least partly determined by extrinsic geo-political criteria. But, the argument goes, if the extrinsic properties of mental states include such distant and causally irrelevant relations, how can they have any immediate causal relevance themselves? (see Hansen 2000). The issues involved here are complex and turn on whether externalism about mental properties is true and, if so, whether extrinsic properties are a problem for causation (cf. Yablo 2003).

Most philosophers thus affirm that there is no reason to believe mental properties to be intrinsically inadequate as causal properties. We will, therefore, focus our attention on the second category. Specifically, we will concentrate on the influential form of the argument developed by Jaegwon Kim (cf. esp. 1993b, 1998b, 2003).

1. The Exclusion Argument[62]

Kim contends that NRP fails to establish a coherent account of mental causation because it cannot do so without either violating the causal completeness of the physical or appealing to overdetermination. Since, he argues, neither option is available to the proponent of NRP, it fails with respect to mental realism. He thus concludes that a reductive account of mental causation is the only coherent one available for a physicalist.

The first step in Kim's argument is to contend that NRP is committed to the principle of downward causation – that is, that mental events and/or properties are causally efficacious with respect to physical events and/or properties. Given that NRP proponents have consistently affirmed their commitment to this position (see below), it would not seem to require much argument. A brief summary of Kim's argument, however, will help clarify the nature of his overall point.

Kim argues that NRP's commitment to the causal efficacy of the mental requires, at least, that some mental event (M) can cause some other mental event (M^*). And, given the physical primacy thesis, M^* is instantiated in a subvenient physical base (P^*). But, if M^* comes about because it is instantiated in P^*, what role does M play in bringing it about? According to Kim, '*To cause a supervenient property to be instantiated, you must cause its base property (or one of its base properties) to be instantiated*' (1998b: 42). In other words, for M to cause M^* it must do so in virtue of causing P^*. So, Kim concludes, any form of mental-to-mental causation requires some form of mental-to-physical causation.

The second step in Kim's argument, though, is to contend that mental-to-physical causation is incoherent within a nonreductive framework given the causal completeness of the physical (CCP): 'for each and every physical event that has a cause at some time t necessarily has a physical cause at t' (Kim 1993c: 280). Or, as Horgan describes it:

> Metaphysical naturalism includes the view that physics is causally and explanatorily complete, within its own domain: i.e., every fact or

---

[62] Kim prefers to label this the 'supervenience argument' (1998a). But, as Kim himself points out, the exclusion problem is a problem for any theory that posits mind–body dependence, not just those that espouse supervenience (2003: 155). The prominence of the idea of overdetermination in the following argument has led some to contend that

phenomenon describable in the language of physics is fully explainable (to the extent that it is explainable at all) entirely on the basis of facts and laws of physics itself. There are no causal 'gaps', in the nexus of physically describable events and processes, that get 'filled in' by causes that are not themselves physically describable; and there are no explanatory gaps. (1993b: 301)

Any physical event must therefore have a physical cause. But this raises the question of the extent to which M can be seen to cause M^* in virtue of its causing P^*.

Remember that M is itself instantiated in its own subvenient base P. The question then becomes, what is the causal relationship of M and P to P^*? Whether causal relations are formulated in terms of nomological sufficiency (e.g. the cause of an effect is that which is nomologically sufficient for its instantiation) or counterfactuals (e.g. the cause of an effect is that without which the effect would not, or might not, have taken place),[63] it would seem that P qualifies as a cause of P^* – that is, it is nomologically sufficient for P^* as the instantiator of M and as that without which P^* might not have come about (assuming no other concurrent subvenient base). This conclusion is in turn supported by CCP which requires that P^* have some physical cause, P.

But, if P qualifies as a cause of P^*, how do we understand the proposition that both P and M are causes of P^*? Kim lays out the following options (1993c: 250–52):

1. They are actually the same event (i.e. $P = M$)
2. M is reducible to P ($M > P$)
3. M and P constitute two parts of a single, sufficient cause ($M + P$)[64]
4. M and P are two segments in a causal chain ($P \rightarrow M$)
5. M and P are distinct and are both sufficient causes of P^* ($P \ldots M$)

Immediately, though, we can see that CCP raises problems with (3), (4), and (5) since each of them appeals to a non-physical element as an essential causal aspect of a physical event. Kim raises some additional objections as well. He rejects (3) because P seems to be causally sufficient for M^* *by itself* and, therefore, the combination of M and P seems to add little to the overall

---

it is better understood as the 'overdetermination problem' (e.g. Hansen 2000). While there is some validity to this observation, we will follow the more commonly used label in this section.

[63] For a good overview of some of the difficulties involved in establishing the proper understanding of causation see Field 2005.

[64] As an alternative to (3), Kim also lists the possibility that M could be understood as a proper part of P.

causal effect. Kim also argues against (4) because most thinkers agree that the relationship between a supervenient property and its subvenient realizer should not be construed as a causal relationship (see also Bennett 2003; though cf. Searle 1992). The only options that remain are (1) the elimination of M, (2) the reduction of M to P, and (5) and the causal overdetermination of P^*, leaving the nonreductive physicalists in the difficult position of having to accept the elimination or reduction of mental properties, deny causal completion, or affirm the highly unintuitive position that all events involving mental causes are systematically overdetermined.[65]

Hansen helpfully summarizes the main steps in Kim's argument as follows:

1. Suppose that a mental property instantiation M causes P^*.
2. M has a physical supervenience base P.
3. On the standard accounts of causation, P qualifies as a cause of P^*.
4. Mental properties are not reducible to physical properties.
5. M and P are distinct (simultaneous) sufficient causes of P^*.
6. Overdetermination is unintelligible.

Conclusion: Mental-to-physical causation is unintelligible given nonreductive physicalism. (2000: 470)

According to Kim, then, the best way to account for mental causation is to recognize mental causes as epiphenomenal 'parasites' that are causally efficacious inasmuch as they are strongly supervenient on physical causes. Any other solution allows the ostensible mental causes to become 'causal danglers' that serve no purpose and 'are an acute embarrassment to the physicalist view of the world' (1993c: 100).[66]

2. Responding to the Exclusion Argument

Unsurprisingly, nonreductive thinkers reject Kim's arguments against the causal efficacy of mental properties, though they have tended to do so in several different ways.

---

[65] Cf. Sturgeon 1998; Elder 2001; Witmer 2003; Bennett 2003; Ehring 2003; and Kim 2003.
[66] Since a reductive approach can simply type-identify mental properties with physical properties, reductivists have no problem with affirming that mental properties are causally efficacious (Kim 1993c). Thus, contrary to what some thinkers have argued (e.g. E. Lowe 1993), mind–body reduction does not constitute a problem for mental causation. Of course, the price that they pay for this solution is a form of epiphenomenalism where mental properties are causally efficacious only insofar as they are identical to physical properties and, consequently, play no independent role in causal explanations (Rockwell 2004).

Option #1: Undermining the Basis of the Exclusion Argument. One way of responding to this argument is to undermine its strength in some way. One common approach is to criticize Kim's argument as having unacceptable consequences for our entire understanding of reality. These thinkers contend that the exclusion argument generalizes into a problem for the causal efficacy of *all* higher-level properties and processes. In other words, if mental causes can only play an epiphenomenal role piggy-backing on the microcausal powers of its subvenient constituents, then *all* higher-level entities and properties, and possibly even some lower-level properties and processes, are similarly constrained.[67] Thus, van Gulick contends, 'If the proponent of the Exclusion Argument takes such a hard line, he will have to concede that none of the properties of the special sciences are causally potent' (1993b: 249).[68] However, although the generalization argument thus indicates that Kim's argument has significant implications with which most thinkers are uncomfortable, and may provide some epistemic warrant for questioning the cogency of Kim's argument, it does not constitute an actual defeater for Kim's argument (Kim 2003: 165). To formulate an adequate response, NRP must provide a positive argument for the coherence of its own position.

Another strategy for undermining Kim's argument is to suggest that it proceeds on an invalid understanding of the relationship between explanations and causality (e.g. Baker 1993; Burge 1993). These thinkers contend that our causal framework should follow from our epistemic processes. Since we can provide successful explanations of the world in terms of higher-level properties, we should recognize these as causally legitimate. According to this argument, to contend, as Kim does, that causality should determine our explanatory framework gets it entirely backwards. However, Kim rightly argues that this approach misses the heart of the problem (1998b).[69] Kim's argument does not call into question the efficacy of our mental properties in a manner that would violate our epistemic explanatory practices as this approach contends. Rather, Kim fully agrees that we should assume the

---

[67] For example, Pereboom and Kornblith 1991; van Gulick 1993b; Burge 1993; Hansen 2000; Bontly 2002; and Schröder 2002.

[68] Kim, however, denies that his arguments against mental causation can be generalized in this manner (1997; 1998b). His basic contention is that his mental causation argument does not generalize because mental causation is an intra-level relation while the special sciences deal with inter-level relations. He also argues for a broader understanding of 'physical' that would incorporate the processes and entities studied in the special sciences and preclude the possibility that they involve non-physical causes. As Hansen points out, however, the distinction between intra- and inter-level relations is not as clear as he supposes them to be and his redefinition of 'physical' has significant implications for his mental causation argument (2000; cf. also Bontly 2002). Thus, although we will not be considering the generalization argument in detail here, there seems to be a continuing concern to the cogency of Kim's argument.

[69] Cf. also Leiter and Miller 1998.

PHYSICALISM, BUT NOT REDUCTIONISM

causal efficacy of the mental but, at the same time, seek a meta theory that can provide an adequate explanation for this state o Kim's argument is a challenge for NRP to offer its own explana defend its coherence.[70]

A third response that could be offered is explicitly theological. This argument points out that any theological system that allows divine causal action in the physical universe already requires some form of non-physical causation (cf. Bielfeldt 2001). If God can act in the physical universe, then at least some physical events cannot be reduced to merely physical explanations. Even without entering into a discussion of divine causality and its implications for physicalism, it seems that this response is inadequate. At the least, we should be very careful about positing an analogy between supernatural–natural causation and mind–body causation.[71] More to the point, however, is that this response does not seem to be available to the physicalist who remains committed to the principle of causal completeness.

Option #2: Systemic Influence. A second way of responding to Kim's argument is to affirm the validity of his basic premises, but to develop nonreductive explanations of mental causation that avoid Kim's reductive conclusions. A variety of different ways have been offered to account for mental causation within a physical framework. We shall consider three.

One common approach has been to appeal to the properties of complex physical systems (cf. Jackson and Pettit 1990). From this perspective, higher-level properties can be seen as causally efficacious in that the way in which the constituent elements of a system are organized must be included in any causal account. It is, therefore, impossible to account for the behavior of the system in terms of its constituent elements alone. Thus, van Gulick argues:

> The events and objects picked out by the special sciences are admittedly composites of physical constituents. But the causal powers of such an object are not determined solely by the physical properties of

---

[70] Ned Block has another way of undermining the validity of the exclusion argument based on a *reductio ad absurdum*. According to Block, if the causal powers of higher level properties all 'drain away' to the causal powers of their determinate bases and if, as may be suggested by contemporary quantum physics, 'there is no bottom level of physics', then it would seem that there can be no causal powers of any kind in the universe (2003: 138). Kim, however, rightly points out that this argument (1) fails to recognize that the exclusion argument (reasonably?) presupposes the existence of just such a physical 'bottom level' and (2) implies the nonreducibility of even physical entities (e.g. molecules, atoms, etc.) about whose reducibility philosophers are generally agreed (2003).

[71] This argument does suggest, though, that the implications of principles like CCP need to be carefully considered before they are adopted wholesale into a christologically adequate ontology.

its constituents and the laws of physics, but also by the organization of those constituents within the composite. And it is just such patterns of organization that are picked out by the predicates of the special sciences. (1993b: 250)

The causal influence of the higher-level properties of complex systems is typically depicted in terms of their ability to activate selectively the causal powers of lower-level systems (van Gulick 1992, 1993b; Meyering 2000, 2002). In any given situation the micro-particulars of complex systems are understood to have a range of causal powers. But, understanding which of those causal powers gets activated in any particular situation requires that the 'circumstances' (Murphy 1998b),[72] 'environment' (Peacocke 1986),[73] or 'initial boundary conditions' (van Gulick 1993b) of the system as a whole be taken into account.[74]

The same argument is then applied to higher-level mental properties. Though they do not operate with the same kind of 'direct' causality associated with micro-physical causality, they are causally efficacious in that they play a 'structuring' (Dretske 1993), 'facilitating' (E. Lowe 1993), or 'sustaining' (Audi 1993) role in the 'selective activation' (van Gulick 1993b)[75] of physical causal powers.[76] In other words, mental states can be thought of as providing the relevant background information for causal explanations involving conscious beings. From this perspective, then, mental causes are not in competition with physical causes. Rather, they play a different role in the total causal process.

We thus seem to have an account of mental causation in nonreductive terms that does not violate the basic principles of physicalism. However, several concerns could be offered to such an account. First, one might well

---

[72] See also van Gulick 1993b; and Murphy 1998c, 1999a, 1999b, 2002a, 2002c.

[73] See also Searle 1992.

[74] On this point, some nonreductive physicalists appeal to the notion of *multiple supervenience* – that is, the idea that not only can higher-level properties be instantiated by multiple physical bases (i.e. multiple realization), but particular physical bases can instantiate multiple higher-level properties depending on the broader circumstances (Meyering 2000, 2002; and Murphy 1999b; cf. also Yablo 1992).

[75] See also Murphy 1998c, 2002c, 2005.

[76] Though all of these thinkers present their ideas in slightly different ways, the basic idea of mental properties as background states that enable the selective activation of physical properties is common to all of them. Jackson and Pettit have offered a similar argument in which they concede that mental properties are not causally efficacious but assert that they are causally relevant in that they 'program for' or 'ensure' the presence of the causally efficacious property (1990). It is hard to see, though, that this is any improvement on Davidson's problematic 'anomalous monism' (see note 41). Thus, Kim rightly argues that causal relevance without causal efficacy is an empty concept (1998b: 75).

wonder if this approach properly construes the reductive program. Their emphasis on the complexity of total systems could almost lead one to believe the reductionists entirely eschewed such reasoning (Cullen 2001; Wacome 2004). But this is not the case. Reductionists are entirely aware that any valid causal explanation must account for both the relevant particulars and their extrinsic relationships. Indeed, Kim states, 'Clearly then *macroproperties can, and in general do, have their own causal powers, powers that go beyond the causal powers of their microconstituents*' (1998b: 85, Author's emphasis). The reductive argument is not that higher-level properties are causally irrelevant but that their causal relevance is established by their reducibility. Thus, it is up to the nonreductive physicalist to establish that their systems–explanations are sufficiently distinct from reductive systems–explanations as to constitute a significant advance with respect to systemic causal explanations.[77]

Second, as nonreductive physicalists are well aware, one could argue that these broader contextual considerations are themselves reductively determined (cf. Bielfeldt 2000). That is, NRP seems to entail that these broad macro-systems are themselves asymmetrically dependent on their microphysical bases. If that is the case, any systemic influence these mental properties have is simply a larger part of the whole microphysical causal process.

And third, even if we hold that higher-level properties have sufficient autonomy to be causally effective, the nonreductive argument still requires some mechanism by which they can causally effect lower-level properties (Horgan 1993b). But if this is the case, the system–explanation simply shifts the focus from mental–physical causation to system–physical causation. At the very least it would seem that such influence would require the transmission of some kind of information.[78] But information transfer in any sense currently available to us requires some form of causal interaction and fails to avoid the problem (Bielfeldt 2001; Sharpe and Walgate 2003). Burge rejects the requirement for a physical causal mechanism stating that such a requirement simply presumes the kind of physicalistic model of causation that NRP seeks to overturn (1993). But, if this is true, then NRP owes us

---

[77] Murphy contends, however, that the reductionist cannot accommodate circumstances within his system (1998c). According to her, the multiple realizability argument and problem of disjunctive subvenient sets (see note 31) demonstrate the nonreducibility of at least some of the causally relevant circumstances. But, if the circumstances are irreducible and are causally relevant, then any causal explanation that appeals to circumstances will be irreducible. Though her argument is valid, it remains questionable in that (1) it is still an open question whether reductionism is actually defeated by the multiple realizability argument and (2) it odes not address the concerns raised by such an externalist understanding of mental properties.

[78] Peacocke 1986; and Polkinghorne 1994. The same objection can be raised to Murphy's argument for 'complex feedback loops' as an explanation of mental causation (cf. 1998c, 2002c, 2005).

an explanation of how systemic properties activate or otherwise influence physical properties in a way that is consistent with causal completion. Although appeals to explanatory practice and counterfactual analysis may provide epistemic warrant for *speaking* of systemic causes in this manner,[79] they do little to provide a coherent account of *how* this causal interaction takes place.[80]

Option #3: Causal Compatibilism. Another option for responding to Kim's argument is to contend that there is a sufficiently close relationship between the physical and the mental that they do not compete as causal factors.[81] Two arguments have been particularly influential.[82] Pereboom and Kornblith argue for a constitutional view of causal powers – that is, a mental token has its causal powers in virtue of the causal powers of the micro-physical particulars that constitute it (1991). Pereboom thus rejects Kim's argument that psychophysical realization entails that the causal powers of mental properties be identical to those of their physical bases (2002; cf. Kim 1993c: 326). According to Pereboom and Kornblith, this is sufficient to avoid overdetermination:

> Just as Kim claims that no competition between explanations arises in the case of reduction and identity, I propose that no competition arises in the case of mere constitution either. For if the token of a higher-level causal power is currently wholly constituted by a complex of micro-physical causal powers, there are two sets of causal powers at work that are constituted from precisely the same stuff (supposing that the most basic microphysical entities are constituted of themselves), and in this sense we might say that they *coincide constitutionally*. (1991)

Thus, rather than competing for causal primacy, different causal explanations pick out different sides of the constitutor–constituted relationship.

Yablo has made a similar argument based on the distinction between *determinate* and *determinable* properties (1992). According to Yablo, a determination relationship of this kind is established when some property necessarily

---

[79] For example, Burge 1993; Baker 1993; and van Gulick 1993b.

[80] Thus, it could be argued that NRP needs to spend more time working on the metaphysics of causation itself before addressing the metaphysics of mental causation.

[81] For example, Pereboom and Kornblith 1991; Yablo 1992, 2003; Pereboom 2002; and Witmer 2003. This kind of approach is often referred to as 'causal compatibilism' in that it construes mental and physical causes as being entirely compatible with one another. Another version of causal compatibilism that we will not be considering has been espoused by Terence Horgan based on a counterfactual analysis of causal relationships (1994, 1997).

[82] For a discussion of other options that have received attention in recent literature, see Ritchie 2005.

entails the instantiation of some other property but that one could have the latter without the former. So, for instance, he suggests, '*crimson* is a determinate of the determinable *red, red* is a determinate of *colored*, and so on' (1992: 252). Based on this principle, he identifies mental properties as determinables of physical determinates.

This becomes significant for the issue of mental causation when we consider the relationship between determinates and determinables with respect to causation. According to his argument, we cannot distinguish between determinables and determinates with respect to causal relevance.[83] Any form of the exclusion argument that would render the *violence* of an earthquake or the *suddenness* of a bolt breaking causally irrelevant, as though they could be construed as 'causal rivals' (Yablo 1992: 272–73), must be suspect (see also Yablo 2003). 'As a rule, determinates are tolerant, indeed supportive, of the causal aspirations of their determinables. Why should it be different, if the determinate is physical and the determinable mental?' (2003: 260).

However, even though determinates and determinables cannot compete with respect to causal *influence*, Yablo contends that they can compete for the role of *cause* (2003: 273–74). This is because we expect proper causes to be both *adequate* and *commensurate* to their effects. But Yablo presents a number of cases in which it appears that the determinable property is more causally commensurate, based on a counterfactual analysis, than the corresponding determinate property. Thus, we can 'attribute effects to mental causes ... when we believe ... that the effect is relatively insensitive to the finer details of *m*'s physical implementation' (2003: 278) – that is, when the mental causal explanation is more commensurate with the given effect.

These two approaches certainly offer a convincing way of construing mental causal powers in such a way that they can be viewed as having real causal influence but without identifying them with physical causal powers in any way. The way in which this is done, though, raises the question of whether they have avoided the problem by tightening the psychophysical relationship to the extent that it offers no real help in establishing the kind of mental efficacy required for establishing human agency and free will. Constitution theorists often note that 'constitution is as close as one can get to identity *without* identity' (Corcoran 2005: 159). But is this *too* close for real mental causation when Pereboom is willing to affirm that mental causal powers are 'nothing over and above' their physical constituents such that they can be described as being 'absorbed' or 'swallowed up' by physical causal powers? (2002: 6–7). A similar concern arises when we consider that Yablo can compare the psychophysical relation to the relationship between rectangles and their squareness, colors and their hues (1992). With such a tight relationship, it becomes difficult to see how mental causal explanations

---

[83] Leiter and Miller, however, point out that he does very little in his argument to establish this point, merely assuming it to be true (1998).

can be anything more than pragmatic conceptual necessities that offer no real help in establishing human agency.[84]

3. Mentality, Causality, and Moral Freedom: Continuing Difficulties for Nonreductive Physcialism

Having offered a rather quick survey of NRP responses to Kim's argument, what can we conclude about their christological adequacy? First, given NRP's commitment to the physicalist program, we can say that there does not seem to be any easy way to escape the basic premises of the argument (Option 1). An appropriate NRP response, therefore, will have to be along the lines pursued by the two alternate explanations offered above (Options 2 and 3).

With respect to those arguments, it does seem that they offer coherent accounts of mental causation within a physicalist framework while still retaining their commitment to epistemological nonreduction. Though a number of significant difficulties remain to be addressed, particularly with respect to systems–explanations, they are both worth exploring. To that extent they must be considered successful accounts of mental causation.

The problems arise when we consider the price that has been paid for these solutions. We have seen that both of them raise concerns with respect to their ability to account for free human agency. Although free will remains a contentious philosophical issue,[85] we have seen that some account of free human agency is required for a christologically adequate ontology. To lift these concerns, a systems–explanations must be able to establish that its appeal to circumstances does not necessitate environmental determination; but, it must do this without violating its own commitment to causal completion. Similarly, causal compatibilists need to be able to show that the tight psychophysical relationship entailed by their account of causality does not preclude free agency without opening up so much space between physical and mental causes that the overdetermination argument comes back into play (Ritchie 2005). Leiter and Miller have argued that these solutions only succeed to the extent that they import dualistic ideas into their physicalist systems (1998). Corcoran, similarly argues that such explanations can only

---

[84] Crane offers another objection to this line of argument; he contends that this approach infelicitously allows for mental causation only by denying that it is a cause 'in the same way' as physical causation (1995: 211–236). By thus rejecting 'the homogeneity of mental and physical causation', according to Crane, this approach robs mentality of any significant causal involvement. Although Witmer dismisses this argument as 'just fallacious' (2003: 210), his concern seems legitimate. Indeed, one wonders if any real advance has been made if mental causation can only be construed in such a 'parasitic' manner.

[85] Cf. van Inwagen 1983; Hasker 1999; Flanagan 2002; Dennett 2003; and O'Conner and Wong 2005.

succeed if they rely on a more robust notion of emergent causation (2005; cf. Clayton 2005). Both arguments suggest that these explanations, by themselves, fail to establish a robust sense of mental causation without appealing to notions that are incompatible with the NRP system.[86]

It would seem, then, that NRP offers some interesting but still incomplete answers to the question of mental causation. Until it shows itself able to address these concerns, it will be difficult for it to serve as the backbone of a christologically adequate ontology.

b. Experiencing Subjectivity: The Problem of Phenomenal Consciousness

Although the term 'consciousness' can be used in a variety of different ways, indeed it is often used to encompass the entire range of mental phenomena,[87] the aspect we will address in this section is that which is often referred to as 'phenomenal consciousness' (Block 1995a).[88] This aspect of consciousness focuses on those mental states that consist of 'inner, qualitative, subjective states' (Searle 1999) – that is, they have a particular 'feel'.[89] In other words, it refers to those, what it is like to undergo certain kinds of experiences (e.g. hit your thumb with a hammer, see a bright color, or smell burnt food).[90]

---

[86] Additionally, to the extent that NRP relies on functionalist accounts of human mentality, they run afoul of what Rupert calls 'the problem of metaphysically necessary effects' (2006). That is, since functionalism defines a mental property in terms of it being the kind of state that causes *e*, any functionalist account of mental causation appears to argue that the state of being that which causes *e*, causes *e*.

[87] Although consciousness can be used in this broader sense (e.g. Searle 1992), most agree that consciousness and mind should not be conflated since there seem to be certain intentional mental states (e.g. beliefs, desires, etc.) that continue to exist even when we are in completely unconscious states (Rosenthal 2002a).

[88] Block distinguishes between phenomenal consciousness, which is characterized by qualitative experiences, and access consciousness, which involves mental states that are available for conscious reflection (1995a). Though he also posits a third category, reflexive consciousness, involving mental states that reflect on one another, this distinction will not be necessary for our discussion (2001). Block's taxonomy has not been without criticism (e.g. Rosenthal 2002b), but it is widely used and usefully distinguishes the concepts addressed in this section.

[89] Although distinctions are possible between terms like subjectivity, phenomenal experiences, qualia, and raw feels (cf. van Gulick 2004), they will be used interchangeably in this section.

[90] Tye suggests that a list of mental states characterized by such phenomenal qualities should at least include perceptions, those associated with bodily states, emotions, and moods (2003). According to this understanding of consciousness, it ends when someone is in certain bodily states (e.g. a coma, dreamless sleep, etc.; cf. Searle 1999). This, of course, does not mean that all aspects of consciousness cease in such states but only those that have a phenomenal aspect.

These phenomenal aspects of human experience are commonly referred to as phenomenal properties or *qualia* (singular *quale*).[91]

Accounting for phenomenal properties, however, has long been regarded as one of the most significant problems for any physicalist ontology (cf. Chalmers 1995). How is it that 'brain processes, which are objective, third person biological, chemical and electrical processes produce subjective states of feeling and thinking?' (Searle 1999). It does not seem conceivable that there is anything that is like to be an atom or a chemical process, so how does it come about that organisms solely constituted by atoms and chemical processes are characterized by vital subjective lives? There thus seems to be an 'explanatory gap' between our subjective experiences and our ability to explain them (Levine 1983). According to Chalmers, then, the 'hard problem' in philosophy of mind is to explain how a physical universe can give rise to subjective qualities (1996).[92]

Given the importance of the subjective life of human persons for any adequate christological anthropology, an ontological theory must be able to provide some account of these subjective qualities. The task of this section, then, is to consider whether NRP is able to offer an understanding of human subjectivity that is both coherent within its physicalist framework and christologically adequate.

1. *Phenomenal Properties without Reductionism*

According to Block (2003) there are basically four approaches that a physicalist, broadly conceived, could take to the problem of phenomenal consciousness. The first two correspond roughly to what we have been calling the eliminative and reductive positions. An eliminativist argues that qualia, understood as irreducible experiential properties, simply do not exist.[93] Although we certainly have experiences, the properties of those experiences are fully physical properties and the 'folk psychology' that we use to describe

---

[91] Determining what phenomenal properties are properties *of* is itself a contentious issue. The traditional position is to view them as properties of subjects or mental states. Alternately, one could view them as properties of experiences that are then represented in mental states or as higher-order properties (i.e. properties of properties). For a good discussion see Chalmers 2004.

[92] Or, more specifically: 'The hard problem is one of explaining why the neural basis of a phenomenal quality is the neural basis of *that* phenomenal quality rather than another phenomenal quality or no phenomenal quality at all' (Block 2002: 394).

[93] Dennett 1979; Churchland 1983; and Rey 1997. Eliminativist positions like that espoused by Dennett and Churchland have often been misconstrued as a simple denial of consciousness in general (e.g. Searle 1997). Eliminativists, though, do not reject the idea that human persons have certain phenomenal experiences. What they deny is that qualia should be understood as ineffable and incorrigible subjective states that are accessible only through first-person introspections of experiential properties (cf. Sousa 1996; Byrne 1997; and Tye 2003).

them in non-physical terms should (ultimately) be eliminated in favor of more 'scientific' explanations (Churchland 1981). Reductionism, or *'phenomenal deflationism'* (Block 2003) by contrast, allows the existence of consciousness but analyzes it in non-phenomenal (e.g. behavioral, functional, representational, etc.) terms. Currently, the two most popular candidates for such a reductive account are representationalism[94] and higher-order thought (HOT) theories.[95] Both of these positions view consciousness in terms of the representation of experiential properties. Although they differ from one another in understanding the precise manner in which this representation takes place,[96] they generally agree that phenomenally conscious states are *identical* to the content and manner of the intentional representation of experiential properties. According to both of these perspectives, then, there is no 'hard problem' involving an irreducible explanatory gap since phenomenal properties are given non-phenomenal explanations (e.g. Papineau 1998).

Such non-phenomenological accounts of phenomenal consciousness, though, have left many unconvinced. The standard objection is to contend that no matter how carefully a non-phenomenal depiction of consciousness is formulated, it still fails to account for the nature of the experience – that is, the phenomenon itself. Two famous arguments along these lines have been presented by Thomas Nagel and Frank Jackson. Nagel proposes that we try to imagine what it is like to be a bat (1974). Though we may be able to imagine what it is like for a human to be a bat, he argues that we cannot conceive of what it is like for a bat to be a bat. This is because our ability to explain the nature of a particular form of existence is necessarily related to our possessing certain conceptual categories that are themselves dependent on having the relevant form of experience. Even if we were able to provide an exhaustive physical account of the bat's neurophysiological state, we would still be incapable of explaining its phenomenological states without already having the requisite concepts that can only be acquired through the relevant bat-experiences.

Jackson offers a similar argument positing the existence of Mary, a brilliant color scientist who has been imprisoned in a black and white room for her entire life (1982, 1986). Although unable to experience color, she performs extensive research and develops an exhaustive knowledge of the physical aspects of color and vision. In fact, she becomes the world's leading expert on the physics of color and understands *all* of the relevant physical facts. Upon being released from prison, she steps outside and discovers what it is like to *experience* red. Therefore, according to Jackson, despite knowing

---

[94] Lycan 1987; Tye 1995; Shoemaker and Hywel 1994; Dretske 1995; and Crane 2001.
[95] Lycan 1996; Rosenthal 2002a; and Carruthers 2001a, 2001b, 2005.
[96] They differ primarily in terms of whether consciousness should be understood as the first-order *representation* of experiential properties or higher-order *reflection* on such first-order states.

all of the relevant physical facts regarding the color red, she still lacked the knowledge of the corresponding experience. Both the Nagel and Jackson arguments, then, contend that consciousness cannot be reduced to physical facts.[97]

From thought experiments like these, nonreductive thinkers conclude that any attempt to provide a non-phenomenological explanation of phenomenal properties simply misses the point. As McLaughlin argues, 'There *is no* a priori sufficient condition for phenomenal consciousness that can be stated (noncircularly) in nonphenomenal terms. *Replacing* our concepts of consciousness with "deflationary" purely functional concepts that have such a priori sufficient conditions . . . would not change that. It would only change the subject' (McLaughlin 2003). Nonreductive thinkers have long contended that phenomenal properties resist any attempt to 'functionalize' them – that is, define them solely according to their causal role.[98] Nonreductive thinkers are thus concerned to maintain the phenomenological 'feel' of experiential properties and contend that no attempt to depict the structure or function of consciousness can adequately account for that experience.

Of course, reductive thinkers reject thought experiments like those offered by Nagel and Jackson[99] and contend that the nonreductivist sets the standard for explaining consciousness too high.[100] Thus Carruthers argues, 'We just need to have good reason to think that the explained properties are *constituted by* the explaining ones, in such a way that nothing *else* needed to be added to the world once the explaining properties were present, in order for the world to contain the target phenomenon' (2001b). But this simply reflects the divide between reductive and nonreductive thinkers. Reductivists contend that phenomenal properties can be exhaustively explained in terms of what they *do* while nonreductivists and dualists both insist that such an account misses important aspects of what they *are*.

2. Phenomenal Properties without Dualism

This does not mean, however, that NRP simply affirms a dualistic account of phenomenal properties. Although these two ontologies agree regarding

---

[97] For a good recent discussion of these arguments and recent attempts to block them by positing important differences between phenomenal and non-phenomenal concepts, see Stoljar 2005.

[98] Levine 1983; Pereboom and Kornblith 1991; Humphrey 2000; and Pereboom 2002. Even a reductive philosopher like Kim recognizes that qualia might resist attempts to functionalize them (2004). His concern, though, is that such non-functional qualia can only be epiphenomenal. Since we addressed this in the previous section, we will not go into it again here.

[99] Cf. Levine 1986; Loar 1990; Lycan 1995; and Tye 1995.

[100] Tye 1999; Carruthers 2001b; and Lycan 2001. For a very helpful discussion, see the collection of essays in Ludlow, Nagasawa, and Stoljar 2004.

the reality of phenomenal properties, they disagree substantially on the ontological implications of this position. Substance dualists contend that the only way to adequately account for such phenomenal properties is to recognize them as properties of non-physical substances.[101] Even some philosophers who do not affirm substance dualism argue that the conceptual irreducibility of phenomenal properties entails their ontological irreducibility.[102] According to these philosophers, then, we should recognize a basic duality in the fundamental structures of the universe. This could be construed in terms of (1) 'panpsychism', or the theory that all physical entities have intrinsic phenomenal properties, (2) 'protophenomenal properties', or the theory that all physical entities have properties that are disposed toward the production of phenomenal properties, or (3) 'neutral monism', that is, the idea that physical and mental properties are properties of some fundamental substance that is itself neither mental nor physical.[103] In any of these three ways, mental properties are understood to be fundamental properties of the universe in a form of 'naturalistic dualism' (Chalmers 1996).[104]

Nonreductive physicalists reject such dualistic approaches, though, by denying the principle that the conceptual irreducibility of phenomenal properties entails some form of fundamental dualism.[105] Indeed, as we discussed in our first section, one of the basic commitments of NRP is that you can have physical monism without epistemological reduction based on the rejection of psychophysical type- and, possibly even, token-identity. Although many nonreductive physicalists can be properly understood as 'property dualists' (i.e. they espouse both mental and physical properties), this is distinctly different from the form of *fundamental* property dualism espoused by such 'naturalistic dualists' (Chalmers 1996). Thus, Block and Stalnaker argue that, even though phenomenological properties are resistant to conceptual analyses of the sort often presumed necessary for nomological

---

[101] For example, Swinburne 1986; Foster 1991; and Moreland and Rae 2000.
[102] Cf. Nagel 1974; Chalmers 1996, 2002, 2003; and Chalmers and Jackson 2001.
[103] See Chalmers 1996, 2003; and Stubenberg 2005.
[104] It is not clear, though, that such a theory really provides a significant advance over earlier emergent theories. If the properties of the basic substrate (whatever that might be) are phenomenal properties, then panpsychism would seem to be committed to the idea that things like quarks and atoms have some form of phenomenal consciousness (Searle 1997; and McGinn 1999). If, as is more likely, these are *proto*phenomenal properties that are not themselves phenomenally conscious but can give rise to phenomenal properties, then it does not seem to have really solved the problem. For now we must give an account of how protophenomenal properties give rise to phenomenal properties (van Gulick 2004). It would thus seem that panpsychism must ultimately appeal to some form of emergence based on latent protophenomenal powers (Seager and Allen-Hermanson 2005) and thus surrender its status as a distinct theory of consciousness.
[105] For example, van Gulick 1992; and Wacome 2004.

reduction, this does not establish ontological dualism, nor does it even defeat epistemological reduction (1999).[106] For example, 'life', they argue, similarly resists conceptual analysis and yet we have no difficulty affirming that it does in fact have a neurophysiological basis. Indeed, many nonreductive thinkers have responded to the argument that subjective phenomenal properties are intrinsically incompatible with objective physical properties by arguing that subjectivity and objectivity are properties of *concepts* rather than properties of properties.[107] The irreducible subjectivity associated with qualia is, therefore, a result of how we think about them rather than how they are in themselves.

3. *Phenomenal Properties and Phenomenal Realism*

Most nonreductive physicalists, then, opt for Block's fourth position, *phenomenal realism*.[108] This approach rejects the ontological implications of the dualists as well as the reductivism of phenomenal deflationists. Thus, though conceding the epistemological force of the Explanatory Gap argument, they deny that it amounts to anything more than a denial of reductionism and a support for the 'plurality of theoretical frameworks' posited by the nonreductive approach (van Gulick 1992: 172).

A nonreductive view of consciousness would thus seem to be committed to three ideas. Ontologically, NRP should affirm the asymmetrical dependence of phenomenal features on physical features, whether in terms of supervenience (Block 2002), emergence (Searle 1992), or some other dependency relationship.[109] Epistemologically, NRP denies the possibility of fully explaining the essence of phenomenal properties in strictly non-phenomenological terms. Functionally, however, NRP can allow the possibility that non-phenomenological analyses of phenomenal properties may be useful for understanding the role of consciousness in human life so long as this functional role remains distinct from its phenomenological essence.[110] Indeed, several

---

[106] For a reply see Chalmers and Jackson 2001.
[107] Loar 1990; Searle 1992; van Gulick 1993a; and Block 2003.
[108] McGinn 1991; Searle 1992, 1997, 1999; Block 1995a, 1995b, 2002, 2005; Flanagan 1992, 2002; Loar 1997; and McLaughlin 2003.
[109] Chalmers has argued that zombie thought experiments establish that phenomenal features do *not* supervene on physical features (1996). Many nonreductive physicalists, though, have responded to this by calling into question the realizability of such conceivability arguments, Chalmers' understanding of identity relationships, and his characterization of possible worlds (Balog 1999; Block and Stalnaker 1999; Loar 1999, Yablo 1999; and Gertler 2002; for more on arguments from conceivability see van Cleve 1983; Stoljar 2001a; Barnes 2002; Gendler and O'Leary-Hawthorne 2002; and Marcus 2004). In general, it would seem that NRP must reject zombie arguments with their implication that microphysically indistinguishable creatures could have radically different phenomenological states.
[110] Block thus contends that access consciousness is functionalizable but not phenomenal consciousness. (2003).

philosophers inclined toward nonreductive thinking are actively exploring representational or HOT approaches to consciousness.[111] While such an approach may well be fruitful and certainly bears further consideration, nonreductive thinkers will continue to argue that they will ultimately be unsuccessful in uncovering the essence of what's-it-likeness.[112]

4. A Nonreductive Understanding of Phenomenal Consciousness

The question, then, is whether NRP and phenomenal realism offers a coherent and christologically adequate account of phenomenal consciousness. As to coherence, it would seem that NRP's understanding of phenomenal consciousness is fully consistent with its basic commitments. It acknowledges phenomenal properties to be fully subjective, internal aspects of human mental life while rejecting any move toward dualism. At the same time it affirms their physical basis without succumbing to reductionism. So long as it is successful in maintaining this balancing act, it would appear to be capable of articulating a view of consciousness that is sufficiently robust to support a christological ontology.

The key question, then, is whether or not this mental balancing act is successful. Both dualists and reductionists argue that it is not and that it either needs to affirm the fundamental irreducibility of phenomenal properties or acknowledge their ultimate functionalization. To a large degree, though, this argument comes down to a contest of basic intuitions. According to the dualist intuition, phenomenality is so distinct from physicality as to preclude any possibility of bridging the divide. The reductionist intuition, on the other hand, is that consciousness is simply a functionalizable state of a highly complex neurophysiological being. The nonreductive intuition is to maintain that both are partly right.[113] This clash of basic intuitions has so far

---

[111] For example, van Gulick 1992, 2000; and Shoemaker and Hywel 1994. Chalmers has recently argued that reduction is not a necessary aspect of representationalism and that a nonreductive formulation is perfectly feasible (2004). He contends that representationalism requires an account of both the intentional *content* and the *manner* of the representation. Nonreductive representationalism, then, could simply argue that conscious states *are* representational but that the manner of the representation is itself phenomenological. Whether such a nonreductive understanding of representationalism succeeds and whether a similar argument can be made for higher-order theories remains to be seen. But Chalmers offers a convincing case that such an avenue is worth exploring.

[112] A complete discussion of the ontology of phenomenal properties would need to address those projects exploring other cognitive (e.g. Dennett 1991), neural (e.g. Crick and Koch 1990; and Crick 1994), or quantum (e.g. Penrose 1989) bases. The literature on these projects is vast and will not concern us here (cf. van Gulick 2000).

[113] This clash of basic intuitions is revealed most clearly in the arguments surrounding what is *conceivable* about phenomenal properties. Such thought experiments seem most effective in revealing basic intuitions and the points at which they differ.

produced no widely accepted account of phenomenal consciousness other than the simple acknowledgement that consciousness remains a mystery.[114]

It would seem, then, that so long as NRP's account of consciousness is consistent with its basic principles, coherent within its own framework, and adequate to sustain a christological ontology, there is no outstanding reason to reject it, barring future philosophical or scientific developments.

c. I Am I, But Am I the Same 'I' that I Was Yesterday?: The Problem of Personal Identity

One final issue that has often been raised as a problem for any physicalist ontology deals with the continuity of personal identity. In a theological context, the question usually arises around the need to explain the continuity of personal identity both before and after that resurrection.[115] As we saw in Chapter 4, a christological anthropology requires that an adequate ontological theory be able to account for both embodiment and persistent identity.[116] For NRP to be considered an adequate ontological theory, then, it must have resources for addressing this issue.

The question has been repeatedly raised, however, whether any physicalist ontology can adequately account for the continuity of personal identity through such a radical experience as death and resurrection.[117] If the human person is a bodily organism and, therefore, cannot survive bodily death,

---

[114] Indeed, several philosophers have made 'mystery' the central aspect of their position regarding consciousness (e.g. McGinn 1989, 1991; Chalmers 1995; and Searle 1997). For such thinkers, the mystery of consciousness stems from (1) a limitation in our current knowledge that may be addressed by future scientific developments (Searle 1997), (2) a fundamental limitation in the structure of human knowledge (McGinn 1989), or (3) a fundamental limitation in the nature of physicalist explanation (Maxwell 2000). Some, like Daniel Stoljar (2005), have argued that the mystery stems from an anemic understanding of the physical universe, which refuses to accept the possibility that the physical is a far broader concept than we have been willing to accept up to this point.

[115] We will, therefore, be concerned in this section with diachronic identity (i.e. the identity of persons through time) as opposed to synchronic identity (i.e. the identity of persons at a given time).

[116] A number of philosophers have argued that we should not be overly concerned about identity questions and should simply focus on what establishes the greatest amount of continuity between yourself and any future persons (e.g. Nozick 1981; Parfit 1986, 1995; and Martin 1995). Given that the Christian view of the resurrection seems to require the *identity* of pre- and post-resurrection persons, we will not address these arguments and, instead, simply assume that the identity question is neither trivial nor empty (cf. Lewis 1983; and Sosa 1990).

[117] This problem is made even more difficult by the fact that the Christian doctrine of resurrection requires some significant *transformation* of the pre-mortem person; consequently, a viable theory cannot lean strongly on qualitative similarities (Davis 1986).

how could a post-resurrection bodily organism of any kind be numerically identical with a pre-resurrection bodily organism? As Flew asked, 'How is the reconstituted person on the last day to be identified as the original me, as opposed to a mere replica, an appropriately brilliant forgery' (1967: 140).[118] Similarly, Cooper thinks that physicalist ontologies raise the worry that we are really dealing with 'two distinct people rather than one and the same human being' (1988: 26). Any physicalist ontology must demonstrate itself capable of meeting this objection.

1. The Nature of Personal Identity

To understand the various proposals we need to begin with a few preliminary comments on the persistence of personal identity. First, as Olson rightly notes, the persistence question is a question about *numerical* rather than *qualitative* identity (2003b). Two things are qualitatively identical only when they are exactly indistinguishable. No person, then, is qualitatively identical with the person she was five years ago or will be five years from now. Numerical identity, on the other hand, cannot change. If two things are numerically identical, they simply *are* the same thing and cannot become two different things (Olson 2003b).[119] The question with which we are concerned, then, is properly understood as a question about the persistence of numerical identity through time.[120] We can, therefore, formulate the persistence question as follows: Under what circumstances is some person who exists at one time, *a*, numerically identical with something that exists at another time, *b*? (Olson 2003b).

But how do we go about answering such a question? What determines whether a person at one time is identical with something that exists at another time? It would seem that to answer such a question requires that we posit certain *criteria* by which personal identity can be established. Such criteria will also need to transcend the merely epistemic issues involved in recognizing continuous personal identity, but will need to be 'nontrivial metaphysical truths about conditions necessary for personal identity through time' (Quinn 1978).

---

[118] Flew's objection was primarily aimed at Hick's notorious 'replica' theory where the post-mortem person is simply a divinely created replica of the pre-mortem person (see Hick 1976). For a useful survey of the debate around Hick's theory see Loughlin 1985.

[119] Any talk about one thing 'becoming' another thing, then, must either be a metaphorical reference to qualitative change without loss of numerical identity, or it actually involves the cessation of the first thing and the beginning of some new thing.

[120] Whenever 'personal identity' is used in this discussion, then, 'numerical personal identity' is understood. For the sake of our discussion, we will simply assume that persistence of numerical identity is possible and will not address theories to the effect that human persons do not persist, as Hume famously argued (MacDonald 2003).

While it would seem reasonable to expect that physicalist ontologies would require physical criteria for establishing personal identity, this is not actually the case. A number of different criteria have been offered and each leads to a slightly different way of accounting for personal identity through resurrection.

Before moving on to discuss those criteria, though, we must also consider the nature of the resurrection itself as one of the factors contributing to this problem. First, we must acknowledge that the resurrection is an essentially mysterious event. Consequently, we cannot expect any theory to do more than posit hypothetical examples of how an identity theory *might* be constructed. Thus, difficulties raised regarding the *believability* of a particular identity theory must be set aside in the face of something as inscrutable as the resurrection. We will focus instead on questions of coherence and adequacy. Second, some of the proposals posit divine involvement as a solution to the problems raised. While it is generally recognized that one should avoid such *deus ex machina* devices, since the resurrection necessarily entails divine agency, we should assume that it is appropriate to invoke divine involvement to a certain extent (cf. Baker 1995).[121]

2. Understanding Personal Identity through a Physical Lens

The Biological-Continuity Criterion. As expected, many philosophers have argued that personal identity is closely connected to the human body.[122] But, 'body' according to these thinkers means more than a mere collection of physical parts, the persistent identity of which would be notoriously difficult to establish (cf. van Inwagen 1990, 2001).[123] Rather, these philosophers assert material continuity in virtue of their understanding of the human body as a

---

[121] Although the intermediate state often factors into the discussion at this point, Lynne Baker rightly argues that an intermediate state by itself does not raise any issues for physicalist ontologies that do not already arise with respect to resurrection in general (1995). We will, therefore, postpone our consideration of this issue until the next chapter.

[122] For example, Williams 1970, 1973; van Inwagen 1978, 1997; Corcoran 1998, 2001b, 2005; and Olson 2003a, 2003b.

[123] A number of philosophers have argued that a material (rather than biological) criterion of personal identity fails in the case of the resurrection because it is impossible for a material object to maintain its identity without spatio-temporal continuity (e.g. Flew 1967; Penelhum 1970). After surveying a number of these arguments, Mavrodes concludes that, if they are successful, they raise problems for any diachronic theory of human identity (1977). But this is precisely what reductive identity theorists argue in contending that identity is either a matter of identifying the 'closest continuer' of an individual (e.g. Nozick 1981) or simply a matter of convention (e.g. Penelhum 1970). Some have suggested brain-continuity as the proper criterion (Nagel 1986; and Unger 1990). Since this proposal seems to be merely a subset of either the body- or biological-continuity theories, we will not discuss it separately.

self-sustaining living organism.[124] According to the 'somatic view' (Olson 2003b), *a* and *b* are identical just in case *b* is simply a later temporal stage in a continuous biological organism of which a was an earlier stage (Corcoran 2001b).[125]

A problem arises for such an account, however, when we consider the resurrection. If continuous personal identity requires the continuity of a living organism, how can you have any continuous personal identity *after* death? One possibility would be to argue that the causal connections necessary to depict an organism as a continuous biological organism are able to cross temporal gaps such that *b* could be part of the same biological organism as *a* even though there was a time when the biological organism of which they are temporal stages did not exist. The possibility of such a temporally 'gappy' existence, however, has been rejected by most philosophers as being incoherent within a physicalist framework.[126]

The primary alternative to such an account is to suggest that although there can be no biological continuity beyond the death of the biological organism and although it seems that all biological organisms do in fact die, it is at least conceivable that God could intervene at the death of the person so as to miraculously continue her biological life despite the appearance of death. At least two different ways have been suggested for how God might accomplish this. According to van Inwagen, God could create a simulacrum in place of the person's corpse, which God whisks away to be miraculously preserved until the resurrection (1978).[127] Corcoran, on the other hand, suggests that a better, and less theologically disturbing, proposal would be to imagine that God copies a person's 'simples' (i.e. the basic microphysical components of the human body) such that one set becomes a corpse and

---

[124] By rejecting the possibility that the body as a materially composite entity could be the ground of personal identity, these thinkers all reject the classic 'reassembly' version of the resurrection (e.g. Corcoran 2001b). They also tend to reject the possibility of a human person having 'temporal gaps' in its existence (cf. van Inwagen 1990). Some, who reject the biological-continuity theory, however, have presented arguments suggesting that this traditional view should not be set aside so quickly (Baker 1995; and Davis 2001).

[125] Chisholm has argued that it is impossible for even living organisms to have any persistent identity since, according to him, nothing can have different parts at different times and yet retain identity (1976). Chisholm's view, though, is not only contrary to our strongest intuitions about living creatures, but also fails to stand up to the substantial arguments developed by van Inwagen for the identity of living beings (1990, 2001).

[126] See van Inwagen 1978, 1990; though cf. Davis 1986.

[127] The theory of van Inwagen is thus distinct from Hick's 'replica' theory (at least) in that Hick posits no real continuity between *a* and *b*, whereas van Inwagen's theory requires direct biological continuity. The continuity of the human person, then, is sustained in that the person's life is *suspended* rather than *disrupted* (van Inwagen 1992).

the second set continues the biological life of the person (1998, 2001b).[128] Either way, the basic premise remains the same. Despite the difficulties of establishing biological continuity, it is conceivably within God's power to intervene and sustain biological identity.

The Psychological-Continuity Criterion. For a long time, the most common way of establishing the persistence of human identity over time was through an appeal to some form of *psychological* continuity.[129] Using thought experiments like transferring a mind from one body to another or gradually replacing a human person's biological parts with entirely synthetic parts, these thinkers argue that the identity of the human person is most closely associated with her mental states and that even a total lack of spatio-temporal material continuity would not preclude continuity of identity. From this perspective *a* and *b* are identical just in case there is mental continuity between them that is appropriately connected.[130] On this view a theory of the resurrection could simply be constructed around the conceivability of God transferring the relevant mental states from one body to another.

Many philosophers have called the psychological-continuity criterion into question because of the problem of duplication (cf. Merricks 1999). In other words, if mental states are transferable and if identity coincides with mental continuity, what is to prevent the conceivability that a given set of mental states could be transferred into multiple physical organisms? We seem to have a situation in which multiple individuals would have equal claim to being the same person.[131] Shoemaker and Hywel respond to this objection by stipulating that identity is only sustained in cases where there is no such

---

[128] Corcoran also has to posit this as an answer to the objection that this allows the possibility that God could create multiple biological organisms who are all biologically continuous with the same person (e.g. Zimmerman 1999). Since such an account would render Corcoran's identity theory untenable, he must respond and does so by simply stating that God would not participate in such an action (2001b). Though this certainly seems reasonable, it is not clear that he has sufficiently addressed the problem that his solution raises for the Kripkean notion of strict identity (cf. Kripke 1971). Van Inwagen's solution, though problematic as well, at least avoids this problem.

[129] Lewis 1983; Shoemaker and Hywel 1984b; and Parfit 1986, 1995.

[130] Early forms of the *psychological* argument, often associated with John Locke, appealed to continuity of memory (Martin and Barresi 2003). This quickly ran into objections from thinkers like Thomas Reid who pointed out the problems that memory gaps and non-mental states raise for any such theory (Olson 2003b). Though some have tried to reformulate the memory criterion to handle such objections (e.g. Shoemaker and Hywel 1970), most now recognize that continuity of memory is insufficient to ground personal identity (cf. van Inwagen 1990: 183–88).

[131] Note that the same objection has been raised with respect to certain forms of the biological-continuity theory. It seems to be considered more of a problem for psychological-continuity because there is no way to establish the kind of causal relationship between mental states that is characteristic in a self-sustaining biological organism.

duplication (1984). The duplication of mental states necessarily results in the destruction of the original person and the creation of multiple new persons. Such a response, however, requires that we view strict identity relationships as both contingent and extrinsically dependent; neither of which are appealing positions for most philosophers. Reductive thinkers like Parfit and Lewis argue that the duplication argument simply establishes that our concern should not be with *identity* but with significant *continuity* (cf. Martin and Barresi 2003). The denial of identity, though, seems entirely inadequate to account for the Christian doctrine of the resurrection.

Van Inwagen goes even further and argues that the very nature of the psychological-continuity theory is inconsistent with a physicalist ontology. He constructs a *reductio* argument to show that mind-transfer thought experiments imply that a human person, which is identical to some physical thing, could suddenly become identical with some other physical thing by the mere transfer of information (2001: 144–61). But, according to van Inwagen, on any realistic view of identity this is simply absurd. Since many proponents of psychological-continuity are also constitution theorists,[132] one could try to block the argument by denying that human persons are ever identical to their physical bodies. As van Inwagen argues, though, for a mind–body theory to be a materialist theory, it must maintain that human persons are identical to *some* material thing (otherwise, what are they?).[133]

A Four-Dimensional Proposal. A third option that we will only discuss briefly relies on an alternate conception of time. According to *four-dimensionalism*, material objects are *temporally* as well as *spatially* extended.[134] From this perspective, then, *a* and *b* are understood to be temporal components of a single, temporally extended human person, *f*. That is, *a* refers to that temporal segment of *f* that is *f-at-a* and *b* refers to that temporal segment that is *f-at-b*. Thus, *a* and *b* are identical in that they are temporal parts of a temporally extended human person.

The view of the resurrection that arises from such a theory would seem to be rather straightforward. The pre-resurrection person, *a*, is identical with the post-resurrection person, *b*, inasmuch as they are temporal parts of the same human person irrespective of any 'intervening' temporal gaps.

Four-dimensionalism, though, is a highly contentious theory of human identity with significant metaphysical implications that has attracted much criticism.[135] Thus, it would seem that more work needs to be done before it is sufficiently well established to serve as a theory of resurrection identity.

---

[132] For example, Shoemaker and Hywel 1984b; and Parfit 1986, 1995.
[133] Lynne Rudder Baker notes, though, that this argument does not touch her version of the constitution theory because she contends that '*human person* is a material-object category' (2000: 144).
[134] Cf. Sider 1997, 2001; and Rea 2003.
[135] For example, van Inwagen 2001: 75–23; and Barker and Dowe 2003, 2005.

The No-Criterion Solution. A fourth possibility is to agree that personal identity persists, but argue that there are no *criteria* of identity (Merricks 1998, 1999, 2001a). Merricks asserts, 'Because criteria must be informative, criterion-based worries about temporal gaps are closely related to the suspicion that nothing could *explain* what makes a person in the distant future identical with a person who, long before, died, decayed, and disintegrated' (2001a: 186).[136] Similarly, Lynne Rudder Baker argues, 'I doubt that there are any noncircular, informative, plausible criteria of personal identity to be stated' (2000: 132). This does not mean that it is *never* possible to explain how *a* could be identical with *b*, it may in fact be possible to do this in many cases, but Merricks's anti-criterialism argument rejects the possibility that we could devise metaphysical criteria that would establish the identity of *a* and *b in every case*. Though we can affirm that identity persists, we will, on this argument, not always be able to explain it.

This approach also lends itself to two other ways of understanding identity. According to Baker, the lack of substantial criteria suggests that a more useful approach is to ground personal identity in the 'sameness of first-person perspective' over time (2000: 132–41). On this view, then, although there are no strong criteria of identity, it can be known intuitively through the self-representation of a coherent narrative.[137] Thus, *a* and *b* are identical just in case there is a coherent narrative connecting them.[138]

It would also seem that this would be the best place to categorize some attempts to develop a multiple-criteria model for understanding identity. Murphy posits such an approach when she argues that there is no one criterion of identity but it is instead grounded in some combination of material, psychological, narratival, moral, and relational issues (2002b). Although it might seem at first that this is actually an *all*-criteria solution, Murphy's argument would seem to be more consistent with the suggestion that *none* of these are necessary in every situation, but that some combination of them will prove to be sufficient to ground identity in any particular case.[139]

---

[136] Reichenbach seems to make a similar argument by contending that there are criteria by which we can be justified in identifying *b* with *a*; a judgment that apparently leaves us in the dark about whether *a* and *b* are actually identical (1978).

[137] Cf. MacIntyre 1989; Peters 2002; Schechtman 2003; Green 2004a; and Gutenson 2004.

[138] Capitalizing on this approach to understanding human identity, Madell argues that monism is fundamentally inadequate for grounding such identity as a result of its inability to account adequately for the kind of first-person subjectivity that this approach entails (1989). Since we have seen that NRP is not without resources for addressing the problem of phenomenal consciousness, this is not necessarily the decisive argument that it might first appear.

[139] Her approach would thus be distinct from a multiple-criteria approach that posited that all the criteria were necessary and that they were jointly sufficient (e.g. Davis 1986).

From this perspective, then, the continuity of personal identity through death and resurrection is possible, but there are no non-trivial criteria on which we can base it. At best we can suggest that the identity of the person is grounded either in a narratival self-representation or in some undeterminable but jointly sufficient set of criteria. The theory of the resurrection that results from such an account would seem to affirm the post-resurrection identity of the human person, but deny that there are any a priori criteria for its establishment.

3. Continuous Physical Persons: The Prospects of Nonreductive Solution to the Identity Problem

It would seem that each of these four ways of understanding the identity of human persons through death and resurrection at least presents itself in such a way as to be christologically adequate.[140] In addition, assuming that we reject the reductive solution espoused by Parfit and others, it would seem that all are consistent with a nonreductive view of the human person.

The real question comes when we consider the extent to which these various options can be coherently maintained within a physicalist framework. As we have seen, a number of significant arguments have been raised against the psychological-continuity theory that must be addressed before it can be considered a viable identity theory for nonreductive physicalists. The same concerns could be raised against narratival approaches to identity, since the continuity of a first-person narratival framework seems almost entirely dependent on a mental-continuity criterion. Without that or some other criterion of identity, would we not simply conclude that the individual is deluded about the coherence of her narratival framework? The same objection might also be raised against multiple-criteria arguments that include mental and narrative aspects, although the strength of the objection would be diminished somewhat in that a multiple-criteria approach is not dependent on these psychological factors alone.[141]

Although the other theories have their weaknesses and their detractors, it does seem that they present viable and coherent theories of personal identity through death and resurrection that maintains the commitments of physicalism.[142] Not everyone will find these various suggestions believable but, as we saw earlier, believability is not the most useful criterion in discussions regarding the resurrection.

---

[140] One final account of identity that could be drawn into this discussion is that of *relative identity* (cf. Geach 1967, 1968; and Harry 2002). This approach, though, has not found wide acceptance and we will not address it here.

[141] For a more sustained critique of the no-criteria solution see Zimmerman 1998.

[142] For other thinkers who argue that the various physicalist theories of personal identity through death and resurrection are coherent and viable see Quinn 1978, Baker 1995, and Davis 2001.

IV. Is There Hope for Nonreductive Forms of Physicalism: Problems and Prospects

We have seen that nonreductive materialism is a physicalist theory that views the mind as asymmetrically dependent on its microphysical base in such a way that it can neither be reduced to that base (reductivism) nor regarded as possessing autonomous causal powers (strong emergence). Whether it can be viewed as a christologically adequate ontology depends on how we evaluate its answers to the three questions raised in the last half of the chapter: (1) Can a physicalist ontology with a commitment to causal completion coherently account for mental causation in a way that supports a belief in human agency, personal freedom and moral responsibility? (2) Can NRP affirm a realist position on phenomenal properties that remains consistent with its physical commitments? And, (3) are the options available for developing a physicalist theory of personal identity adequate to establishing the continuity of personal identity through death and resurrection?

On each of these questions we have seen that NRP has developed substantive positions that need to be taken seriously. Each, though, also manifests some significant weaknesses that must be addressed if NRP is to be viewed as a viable christological ontology. With respect to mental causation, although nonreductive physicalists have devoted considerable attention to articulating a nonreductive view of causation that can operate within a physicalist framework, they seem to have paid insufficient attention to the question of whether their answers accord with a commitment to agency and freedom. The NRP account of phenomenal consciousness, on the other hand, offers a coherent account of phenomenal properties. The extent to which this argument is deemed successful, seems to turn largely on intuitive convictions regarding the nature of 'subjectivity' and its compatibility with physical properties. It is on the third question, personal identity, that NRP seems to have the strongest answers. Regardless of whether one finds the various proposals plausible, they seem coherent and christologically adequate.

In general, then, it seems that we can conclude that NRP should be considered a viable candidate for use as a mind-body theory within a christologically adequate anthropology, but that there are a number of unresolved issues that must still be addressed.

6

ACROSS THE CARTESIAN DIVIDE: CHRISTOLOGICAL ADEQUACY AND HOLISTIC FORMS OF DUALISM

I. Moving Beyond the Cartesian Critique: Contemporary Substance Dualism

Having considered in the previous chapter the Christological implications for developing a physicalist ontology of the human person, we now turn our attention to a similar analysis of dualist theories. The prospect of developing any such account, however, seems dim in light of Barth's clear pronouncements against any form of substance dualism. He argues,

> In general, the character and result of this anthropology are marked by a separation of soul and body, an exaltation of the soul over the body, a humiliation of the body under the soul, in which both really become not merely abstractions but in fact two 'co-existing' figments – a picture in which no real man ever recognised himself, and with which one cannot possibly do justice to the biblical view and concept of man. (III/2, 382)

Thus, as long as theology insists on taking the dual nature of humanity as its starting point, 'no real insight is possible' (III/2, 393).

Many contemporary philosophers agree, viewing substance dualism as an inadequate theory of human ontology; and a decisively refuted theory at that.[1]

---

[1] In philosophy of mind, 'dualism' can be used with reference to a duality of substances (as here), properties (i.e. distinct mental and physical properties of a single substance), or predicates (i.e. semantic duality that is not reflected ontologically) (cf. Levin 1979; and Robinson 2004). In this chapter, we will use the term 'dualism' to refer to a dualism of substances in the human person.

Thus, some philosophers contend that we should no longer consider substance dualism to be a serious option in the mind–body debate (e.g. Dennett 1983).[2] According to Himma, then, 'Substance dualism is almost universally rejected among people who work in philosophy of mind and the cognitive sciences' (2005: 81). As Taliaferro indicates, this widespread rejection of mind–body dualism stems from a variety of different criticisms:

> Dualism appears to face intractable problems accounting for mind–body interaction, for the individuation of nonphysical beings, and for our knowledge of the mental life of other persons. Dualism seems vulnerable to private language arguments . . . and dualism is often considered a prime target for Ockham's razor. Moreover, dualism is often considered public enemy number one on religious and ethical grounds. It faces the charge of promoting a life-threatening, body-denigrating asceticism, of encouraging homocentric approaches to the environment, and of favoring an ethic of individualism more generally. It has also been accused of advancing a sexist agenda that privileges a male bias in matters of inquiry and substance. (1995: 567)[3]

Dualism, therefore, is often dismissed as a theory that stems from a simple category mistake (Ryle 1949) resulting in an unfortunate tendency to reify those properties of human persons that we associate with mentality.[4]

Despite this strong consensus, however, Corcoran is able to claim that 'the mind-body problem remains wide open' (2001a: 11). Indeed, discussions of dualism abound in the literature.[5] This may be at least partially because of the continued pervasiveness of dualistic thinking at the popular level.[6] But, it may also stem from a growing realization that *dualism* actually comprises a family of theories, many of which are resistant to some of the

---

[2] Indeed, Moreland and Rae complain, 'most contemporary philosophers and scientists dismiss substance dualism without much serious consideration of the notion and with very little argumentation against it' (2000: 98).

[3] For similar summaries of arguments against dualism see Swinburne 1986; Foster 1989, 1991, 2001; Moreland and Rae 2000; and Moreland 2002.

[4] Murphy 1998a; and Herbert 1998. Similarly, Harre argues that social and linguistic structures have a significant impact on ontologies (1987).

[5] Thus, introductions to philosophy of mind still routinely devote considerable attention to substance dualism (e.g. Graham 1998; Lowe 2000; Cockburn 2001; Crane 2001; Maslin 2001; and Heil 2004a).

[6] Even many non-dualist philosophers affirm that some form of dualism is the common-sense view of most people (e.g. Levin 1979; Shoemaker and Hywel 1984a; Green 2005). Others, though, argue that human persons have an equally strong intuition of our essential physicality and wholeness (van Inwagen 1995; and Corcoran 2005). To a large degree, then, we are dealing here with a conflict of basic intuitions that makes negotiating the various arguments quite difficult (cf. Lowe 2000: 32).

standard criticisms. Historically, dualism has included Platonic, Aristotelian,[7] Thomistic, Cartesian,[8] and Hobbesian dualism.[9] Corresponding to the rapid development of philosophy of mind in the latter part of the twentieth century, these historic forms of dualism have recently been supplemented by more recent formulations. Modern dualist systems thus include basically Cartesian approaches (e.g. H. Lewis, W. Hart, Foster, Robison)[10] along with theories like naturalistic dualism (e.g. Chalmers), emergent dualism (e.g. Hasker, Zimmerman), Thomistic dualism (e.g. Moreland, Stump), and more holistic forms of Cartesian dualism (e.g. Cooper, Goetz, Taliaferro).[11]

This spectrum of positions suggests that any adequate criticism of dualism must engage with more than the Platonic–Cartesian perspective.[12] Unfortunately, much of what passes for a refutation of substance dualism focuses exclusively on this one approach and fails to consider other dualist theories that might be more resistant to criticism. Thus, Taliaferro, contests that 'a fairminded, reasoned case against dualism must take seriously the ways in which a version of dualism may do justice to the unified nature of embodied life' (1994: 568).

Given these newer forms of substance dualism which seek to 'do justice' to the psychophysical nature of the human person, it seems reasonable to engage the question of whether it is possible to formulate a form of substance dualism that is compatible with Barth's christological framework despite Barth's own disavowals. To do this, we will first survey the form of substance dualism that is most often presented in the literature and in response to which most forms of modern dualism have developed – that is, Cartesian dualism. Having offered a definition of Cartesian dualism and a quick survey of the key objections to this ontology, we will look at three significant

---

[7] This is not to say that Aristotle himself was a dualist, but that his philosophy has, at times, been used to support dualist ontologies.

[8] As a subset under Cartesian dualism we would also have to list the parallelistic theories espoused by Leibniz and Malebranch.

[9] Although criticisms have tended to focus on the more Platonic and Cartesian strands of dualism, the Aristotelian and Thomistic branches have actually been far more prominent in much Western philosophy and theology (cf. Crane and Patterson 2000; and MacDonald 2003).

[10] Although Foster and Robinson have presented significant defenses of substance dualism (Foster 1989, 1991, 2001; and Robinson 1989, 2003, 2004), both prefer an idealist approach to human ontology (see esp. Foster 1991).

[11] Locating Swinburne within this spectrum of approaches can be somewhat challenging. As Hasker points out, although his emphasis on evolutionary development would seem to suggest an emergent theory of substance dualism, his creationist perspective on the origin of the soul and some of his language regarding the mind–body relationship suggests a more Cartesian orientation (1999).

[12] Barth himself was well aware of many of these distinctions and took care to comment on several distinct forms of Cartesian and Thomistic dualism (cf. III/2, 383–90).

types of substance dualism that have recently been offered as providing a more holistic view of the human person. Finally, as in the previous chapter, we will consider this more holistic form of substance dualism against the requirements of Barth's christological framework. Specifically, we will look at whether or not even this more holistic approach offers a viable ontology in light of problems surrounding mental causation, embodiment, and contingent personhood.

II. What is Holistic Dualism?

To understand holistic dualism (HD) and the resources that it offers for developing a christologically adequate ontology, it will be helpful to consider briefly the more traditional Cartesian dualism (CD) that serves as the backdrop against which HD developed. There is an ongoing debate regarding the extent to which what is often called 'Cartesian' dualism actually represents the position espoused by Descartes (cf. Baker and Morris 1996). That debate need not concern us at this point. Rather, our focus will remain primarily on CD as it has come to be understood by most philosophers.

a. Understanding the Cartesian Divide

1. The Basic Tenets of Cartesian Dualism

Substance dualism, at its most basic level, involves three claims:

1. There is a mental realm and a physical realm.
2. The mental and physical realms are both fundamental.
3. The mental and physical realms are ontologically distinct.[13]

To understand CD, we will need to unpack each of these further.

According to substance dualists, it is simply evident that any explanation of human persons must account for both physical and mental realities. The recognition of such a basic duality, according to many dualists, has been the common view of human persons throughout history and in all cultures.[14] Given the pervasiveness of this viewpoint, dualists contend that ontological dialogue must begin from this point and that the burden of proof lies on anyone who seeks to deny the reality of either aspect.[15]

Furthermore, not only must we acknowledge both realms, but also, substance dualists argue, we must affirm that both are fundamental and, therefore 'not *reducible* to something else' (Foster 1991: 2). Though property

---

[13] This is adapted from Foster's list of basic dualist assertions (1991: 1).
[14] Foster 1991: 206; Moreland and Rae 2000: 17; and Goetz 2005: 35.
[15] Foster 1991: 150; and Goetz 2005: 43.

dualists are willing to affirm the epistemological nonreduction of mental states, substance dualists argue that mental states must be regarded as completely irreducible if we are to account for their unique properties.

Typically, dualists contend that an examination of these two realms demonstrates that they are so intuitively different from one another that the only plausible option is to conclude that they constitute distinct and irreducible substances.[16] A brief look at these differences will help establish exactly what dualists have in mind.

First, as we saw in the previous chapter, dualists affirm the *qualia* of conscious experiences. As Jackson's famous Knowledge Argument sought to demonstrate (1986), these *qualia* seem very different from the physical properties of human persons. Although the physicalist could respond that these phenomenological experiences only *seem* to be distinct from their physical realizers, Taliaferro rightly points out that even this admission causes problems for the physicalist since the existence of a phenomenological *seeming* is itself a phenomenon in need of explanation (1994: 70). Physicalist attempts to functionalize mental states have similarly failed to convince dualists given the widespread rejection of any attempt to functionalize *qualia*.[17] Thus, we may be able to design a mechanical system that can perform mental functions, but not one that can have phenomenological experiences (Vendler 1994: 319).[18]

Second, mental states can be *about* something – that is, they can be *intentional* (cf. Crane 1998, 2005).[19] According to Crane, 'Mental states like thoughts, beliefs, desires, hopes (and others) exhibit intentionality in the sense that they are always directed on, or at, something' (2005). Physical states, on the other hand, simply *are*, they cannot be *about* anything.[20] Although many physicalists contend that intentional states can be functionally reduced and, therefore, exhibited in complex physical systems (e.g. Fodor 1987), dualists typically reject any attempt to naturalize intentionality in this way, arguing instead that the very nature of intentionality precludes the possibility of its realization in physical states.[21]

---

[16] For example, Swinburne 1984; and Taliaferro 1994.
[17] Cf. Foster 1991; Moreland and Rae 2000; and Zimmerman 2004.
[18] As Swinburne and Padgett argue, attempts to provide reductive explanations of qualia merely separate phenomenality from causality and explain the latter; but, it is the former that is key (1994: 191). Thus, some physicalists, like Kim, agree that qualia cannot be reduced to physical states but argue instead that they must be viewed as the epiphenomenal productions of physical states (cf. Kim 1993c; 2004).
[19] Whether all mental states exhibit intentionality is an open discussion (cf. Pierre 2003). Crane suggestively argues, though, that all mental states have some intentional content even if they cannot all be exhaustively explained in intentional terms (2005).
[20] Crane 1998; though cf. Bontly 2001. Functionalists, though, contend that intentionality can be functionally reduced and, therefore, exhibited in complex physical systems (cf. Fodor 1987).
[21] For example, Moreland 2002; cf. Searle 1983.

And, third, mental states are accessible through first-person introspection and are, therefore, private – that is, only available to the person having them (see Myro 1994). However, physical states are largely thought to be necessarily open and available to analysis from a third-person perspective – that is, they are publicly available to all persons.[22]

As we saw in the previous chapter, though, many physicalists *agree* with substance dualists on these unique properties of mental states. The difference lies in the nature of the substance underlying the properties. While physicalists contend that one need only posit a single, physical substance in all of its complex forms to account for the existence of mental properties (even if we are not able to provide an explanation of how this actually works), dualists argue that the disparate nature of the properties involved requires two, distinct substances, each with different sets of properties. Thus, dualists often favorably cite McGinn's arguments for the essentially mysterious nature of mentality, though disagreeing with his physicalist presuppositions (e.g. Taliaferro 1994: 193). It is important to note, then, that the disagreement does not center on the existence or non-existence of mental properties but on the best possible explanation of those properties.[23]

In addition to dualism's affirmation of distinct substances, CD also affirms that they are (at least) conceivably separable. Indeed, so strongly is the notion of separability linked to substance dualism that many affirm this as its defining characteristic.[24] Thus, one of the primary arguments traditionally used in defense of substance dualism relies entirely on the conceivability of mind–body separation.[25]

We must emphasize, though, that CD need only affirm the *conceivability* of such ontological separation and not necessarily its *actuality*. Thus, Swinburne

---

[22] Several other dualist arguments which could be placed here include the unity-of-consciousness argument (cf. Hasker 1995, 1999, 2001; E. Lowe 1993, 2004; and Goetz 2005) argument and the modal-properties (cf. Taliaferro 1994; Moreland 2002). Each of these identifies ways in which the properties of mental states are irreconcilably different from those of physical states.

[23] Hart 1988: 29; Foster 1989: 8; Hasker 1999: 69; and Taliaferro 2001. As Levin rightly points out, the differences between these two sets of properties do not, then, constitute a decisive argument for substance dualism (1979). Instead, they comprise a data set that needs explanation. Whether the dualist or the physicalist argument represents a better explanation of the data set is what remains to be decided.

[24] For example, Hart 1988; Baker 2004; and Barnes 2004.

[25] Simply stated, the modal argument, in use at least since Descartes, moves from conceivability to metaphysical possibility (see van Cleve 1983; Swinburne 1984, 1998; Bealer 1994; Baker and Morris 1996; and Plantinga 2003). In the context of the mind–body debate, the modal argument contends that the conceivable separability of mind and body entails the metaphysical possibility of such separability and their corresponding non-identity. An analysis of the extensive literature on this argument lies beyond our reach at this point, but see Shoemaker and Hywel 1984a; Alston and Smythe 1994; Hasker 1998; and Goetz 2001.

argues, 'By saying that the person "can" continue if the body is destroyed I mean only that it is *logically* possible, that there is no contradiction in supposing the soul to continue to exist without its present body or indeed any body at all' (Swinburne and Padgett 1994: 146). Similarly, E. J. Lowe asserts, 'though we have to regard [the self] as distinct from its body, we are not required to think of the two as separable (except perhaps purely conceptually, or purely in imagination)' (2004: 853). Consequently, a dualist like Popper can remain agnostic about the actuality of the mind surviving the death of the body (Popper and Eccles 1977).[26]

And, finally, according to CD, the mental and physical substances are capable of entering into causal relationships with one another. The soul possesses a peculiar causal relation with its body such that it is able to act directly upon the body and be acted upon by the body. Although there are forms of substance dualism that do not entail such psychophysical interaction, affirming instead some form of psychophysical parallelism (e.g. pre-established harmony, epiphenomenalism, etc.), most forms of substance dualism support causal transactions between the two substances.[27]

2. *The Cartesian Soul*

Given these two fundamentally distinct and conceivably separable substances in the human person, what does CD believe about the nature of the human soul? For our purposes, we can summarize CD's view of the soul in six assertions.

1. *The soul is simple.* The soul is not a composite entity constructed out of particles that are more basic.[28]
2. *The soul is primitive.* That is, the soul is not an emergent entity. Rather, it is a fundamental substance not derivable from any other substance.[29]
3. *The soul is non-spatial.* The soul is a non-physical substance and is, therefore non-spatial and non-extended. Instead, it is an immaterial substance, which does not inhabit physical space in any way.
4. *The soul is immortal.* By nature the soul is immortal and incapable of destruction.[30]

---

[26] Of course, Popper does not consider himself to be a dualist because he actually posits the existence of *three* separate worlds (1994). Regardless, though, his position is entirely consistent with substance dualism.

[27] We will address this causal relationship later in the chapter.

[28] For good discussions on this point see Zimmerman 2003 and Lowe 2001.

[29] Although some speak of the soul as though it were *made out of* some generic immaterial substance, it is more correct to speak of the dualist soul as a simple substance that is not constructed from any other substance.

[30] Although a variety of arguments have been put forward in support of this position, the most common is that since the soul is a simple substance, it cannot be broken down

5. *The soul is rational.* By this, the Cartesian means that the soul is the substance with which all of the rational faculties of the person are associated. Thus, the soul alone is what thinks, wills, and chooses, even if it must use the body (i.e. the brain) to accomplish this (at least during its embodied state).
6. *The soul is the person.* The person *is* the soul. The body is merely the mechanism by which the person acts and expresses herself in the world. The continuity of the person, therefore, involves only the continuation of the immaterial soul; bodily continuity is not required.

3. Criticizing Cartesian Dualism

The substantial objections that can be raised against substance dualism have been thoroughly addressed many times in the history of philosophy and do not need to be rehearsed again at this point. In this section, then, we will merely list some of the more prominent arguments as a means of understanding the problems that gave rise to more holistic forms of substance dualism.

CD's struggles with mental causation are widely known and often constitute the primary objection against substance dualism.[31] As we will see later in this chapter, dualism's view of mental causation is criticized both for its inability to explain how a causal relation could obtain between such disparate substances and for its alleged scientific inadequacy.

A similar problem is raised by thinkers who contend that CD is unable to account for the extensive psychophysical dependence established by the modern sciences. Recent developments in modern science clearly establish the pervasive link between physical states and mental states like emotions, personality, reasoning, morality, religious experience, and, of course, consciousness itself.[32] Such evidence leads many to conclude that substance dualism, with its premise that body and souls are 'two quite disparate things ... each having almost nothing in common and only the flimsiest connection with the other' (R. Taylor 1983: 13), is simply untenable.[33] After a brief survey of several different ways substance dualism has tried to affirm

---

into its constituent elements (cf. Hasker 1999). But, for something to be destroyed *is* for it to be broken down in this way. Therefore, the soul cannot be destroyed.

[31] Several forms of substance dualism view the mental and physical substances as completely independent such that they do not even interact causally – i.e. parallelism, occasionalism, and epiphenomenalism (cf. Foster 1989; and van Inwagen 2002: 170). These forms of dualism, however, have been much less popular than the traditional Cartesian approach, which maintains the distinctness of the mental and physical substances while still arguing for some level of interaction.

[32] Cf. Gazzaniga 1992, 1997; Damasio 1994, 1999; LeDoux 2002a, 2002b; Ayala 1998; Libet, Freeman, and Sutherland 1999; and Feinberg 2001.

psychophysical interdependence (possession, occupancy, use, and causal interaction), Richard Taylor concludes that substance dualism is simply unable to articulate an ontology that is adequate to these tight psychophysical links (1983: 13–22). Despite substance dualism's appeals to the contrary, critics contend that this approach inevitably leads to an undue separation of the two substances and the ultimate disparagement and devaluation of the principle of embodiment.[34]

Along the same lines, many argue that CD is generally inconsistent with the modern understanding of the physical universe. As we saw in the previous chapter, most contemporary philosophers hold to some form of physicalism with its commitment to the causal and explanatory completeness of the physical universe.[35] Since dualism clearly stands outside this framework, many conclude that it is scientifically unacceptable.[36]

Another problem is raised by those who argue that the Cartesian principle that 'souls are non-spatial and non-extended would make it impossible to individuate one soul from another.[37] As Shoemaker and Hywel point out, Cartesian souls cannot be individuated on the basis of their non-relational properties since they are particulars rather than universals and could, therefore, share their non-relational properties with another particular (1978). Moreover, the possibility of individuating them on the basis of their relational properties is severely weakened by the fact that they are non-spatial and thus cannot be individuated on spatial terms as physical objects typically are. Although the dualist could posit some non-spatial relation to individuate souls, it is not clear what such a relation would be.[38]

---

[33] For example, Jantzen 1984; and Pannenberg 1991.

[34] For example, Ryle 1949; Armstrong 1968; Jantzen 1984; and Thatcher 1987.

[35] Thus Atkins affirms that 'science is all-competent' and that any appeal to an explanation that lies ostensibly outside the reach of the physical sciences is unacceptable (1987: 13).

[36] Some, like Murphy, offer a softer form of this argument which concedes that science does not actually refute substance dualism, but that the physicalist program has, nonetheless, been more successful and progressive (2002b). Therefore, according to this argument, dualism should be rejected as an unnecessary postulate (e.g. Aune 1985; and Crick 1994).

[37] See esp. Strawson 1959; for a more recent presentation of the argument see Carruthers 2004. Taliaferro offers three responses to this argument (1994: 207–9). First, he contends that non-physical entities could be individuated in terms of their qualitative properties. Second, even if such qualitative properties are insufficient for individuation, one could still appeal to some metaphysically deep, though epistemologically unavailable, brute property that individuates such entities, i.e. haecceity. Finally, even if these two arguments fail, it is not clear that the dualist has any more difficulty individuating non-physical entities than the physicalist has individuating physical entities (cf. Swartz 1991; and Hoffman and Rosencrantz 1991).

[38] Shoemaker and Hywel actually affirm the conceivability of such 'quasi-spatial relationships', though he concedes that the notion is problematic (1978).

Finally, since CD affirms a non-physical substance that is completely unavailable to empirical observation, many contend that CD entails that human persons can only be confident in their own mentality and must remain completely agnostic with respect to the existence of other minds (cf. Hyslop 2005).[39] In other words, whether the person across the table is actually a zombie with no mental life at all is something we can never know confidently. This argument, though, is routinely dismissed by dualists, who argue that even though dualism entails that we cannot have indubitable knowledge of other people's mental states, this does not entail that we must, therefore, be skeptical about their existence.[40]

Needless to say, dualists have not been silent on these matters and have offered a number of significant responses to each of these objections.[41] Generally such responses have fallen into one of two categories. Some dualists argue that these objections can all be overcome. Consequently, they affirm the coherence of a largely Cartesian ontology.[42] Others argue that although these objections to Cartesian dualism are not decisive, they do suggest some weaknesses in the Cartesian model, but ones that can be countered by offering an alternate form of dualism.[43] The rest of this chapter will focus on the second response and will consider whether the more holistic forms of substance dualism offered by these thinkers offers a tenable basis upon which to explicate a christologically acceptable anthropological ontology.

b. Understanding the Holistic Alternative

Despite these significant criticisms, then, many dualists have responded by agreeing with many of the concerns that they raise, but denying that they

---

[39] A similar argument, the private language argument presented by Wittgenstein, on the other hand, asserts that private access to mental states causes a problem for understanding the language that we use to refer to them (see Candlish 2004). If such language is based on ostensive reference to completely private mental events, then it would seem to be a 'private language' understandable only to the user. But, according to Wittgenstein, such a language would be incomprehensible to the user herself since the meaningfulness of all language is grounded in particular forms of common life (cf. *Philosophical Investigations* §244–71). Given the incredibly complex nature of the debate surrounding the proper interpretation and evaluation of Wittgenstein's arguments and the fact that the private language argument, though typically addressed to substance dualists, actually touches on any ontology that affirms private access to mental events (including many forms of NRP), we will not address this argument in this study (but see Taliaferro's very helpful account of ostension and private access [1994]).

[40] Cf. Lewis 1982; Foster 1989; and Moreland 2002. Taliaferro thus lays out at least five ways that the problem from other minds can be met (1994: 154–58).

[41] See esp. Lewis 1982; Hart 1988; Swinburne and Padgett 1994; Foster 1991; Taliaferro 1994; Hasker 1999; Moreland 2002; and Moreland and Rae 2000.

[42] For example, Lewis 1982; Hart 1988; and Foster 1991.

[43] For example, Taliaferro 1994; Hasker 1999; and Moreland and Rae 2000.

affect all forms of dualism.[44] By affirming a holistic understanding of human persons, HD seeks an ontology that can maintain the basic commitments of CD (i.e. two ontologically distinct substances that are conceivably separable), while still affirming the functional interdependence of the entire person. Thus, according to Cooper

> Holism ... affirms the functional unity of some entity in its totality, the integration and interrelation of all the parts in the existence and proper operation of the whole. It views an entity as a single primary functional system, not as a compound system constructed by linking two or more primary functional systems. It recognizes entities as phenomenological and existential unities. It implies that the parts do not operate independently within the whole, and that they would not necessarily continue to have all the same properties and functions if the whole were broken up. (2000: 45)

On this understanding, rather than viewing body and soul as disparate ontological 'pieces' and identifying the human person with one 'piece', HD views the human person as one functional whole. Although it is conceivable that the person could survive the death of the body, it would be a truncated existence limited by the demise of the functional psychophysical union. We will, therefore, understand holistic dualism to refer to any ontology that affirms the basic commitments of Cartesian dualism while arguing for a deeper and more integrated body–soul relationship.

1. Different Brands of Holistic Dualism

Cartesian Holism. Holistic dualists typically seek to unpack this psychophysical unity in one of three ways. Some simply retain the Cartesian system but place a greater emphasis on psychophysical interdependence. This would seem to be the best way to understand Taliaferro's 'integrative dualism' (1994, 1995).[45] Taliaferro describes his position as an attempt 'to articulate how a dualist may view the person and body as profoundly unified, while still remaining metaphysically distinct' (1994: 115).[46] Although he thinks that the picture of 'an excessively fragmented version of dualism' has been

---

[44] Hasker argues that all forms of substance dualism are theoretically consistent with the kind of holistic approach argued for by him and others (1999: 149). Taliaferro similarly states that his version of dualism is entirely consistent with the more traditional forms of substance dualism offered by thinkers like Foster or W. Hart; it simply places a greater emphasis on a 'unified understanding' of the person (1994: 115–16). Whether this is actually the case, lies outside the scope of this chapter.

[45] Cf. Cooper 2000; and Goetz 2005.

[46] Taliaferro is, therefore, rightly critical of philosophers like Dennett and Ryle who lampoon substance dualism as entailing a ghostly self floating around the body (1994: 115).

perpetuated primarily by dualism's critics, he nonetheless maintains that traditional dualism has tended toward an unfortunate overemphasis on the disparity between the two substances (1994: 115–16). According to this view, substance dualism is entirely compatible with the idea that persons and bodies 'exist in a profoundly integral union' and, therefore, that they can be treated 'as a single unit in ethical, social, political, and aesthetic contexts, as well as most scientific ones' (1994: 16).[47] He even goes so far as to state 'the body and person form a substantial unity' (1994: 120).

Emergent Dualism. Another approach that has recently received significant attention is the idea that minds and bodies are integrally related because minds are *emergent* entities – that is, mental substances emerge from properly configured physical systems.[48] Thus, Hasker argues that we should view the human mind as something that is 'produced by the human brain and is not a separate element "added to" the brain from outside' (1999: 189). Such properties are emergent in that

> they manifest themselves when the appropriate material constituents are placed in special, highly complex relationships, but these properties are not observable in simpler configurations nor are they derivable from the laws which describe the properties of matter as it behaves in these simpler configurations. (Hasker 1999: 189–90)

While we saw in the previous chapter that there is a form of emergentism that is broadly compatible with physicalist commitments, emergent dualism transcends this framework by arguing that what emerges from the physical substrate are not merely emergent *properties*, but emergent *substances*.[49] Thus, although emergent dualists argue for an ontologically deep relation

---

[47] The mere fact that ontological separation exists as a possibility under the extreme condition of physical death, according to Taliaferro, does not preclude the reality of functional unity (1994: 116).

[48] Cf. Popper and Eccles 1977, Popper 1994; Swinburne 1984; Hasker 1999, 2001, 2005; and Zimmerman 2004. Like other forms of dualism, though, emergent dualism has come under criticism for being unable to explain this emergent relationship. This is because it seems to leave us with the conclusion that either the physical substrate possesses the properties and capacities of the emergent substance, at least in a protoemergent state, or that the properties and capacities of the emergent substance are completely unrelated to its substrate. If the former, we seem to be dealing with some form of protopanpsychism (Hasker suggests this as the primary cost of an emergent dualism [1999: 194]); if the latter, the relationship is brute and inexplicable. Thus, Clayton (2005) notes that one of the primary concerns about emergence is that it is often portrayed as a purely negative ontological thesis with few positive contributions to make to the explanatory task. While neither of these constitutes an insurmountable objection to emergent dualism, they certainly raise some concerns.

between the mental and physical substances, once the mental substance emerges, it is a distinct substance that is at least conceivably divisible from its physical counterpart (see Hasker 1999).[50]

Thomistic Dualism. Finally, a renewed interest in Aristotelian and Thomistic ontologies has generated a number of proposals for understanding substance dualism in terms of the soul as the *form* of the body.[51] We will not be concerned in this chapter with the ontologies of Aristotle or Aquinas themselves, and we certainly will not attempt to resolve the long-standing disagreement about whether they are properly understood as physicalists or dualists.[52] Rather, we will direct our attention to the way in which their philosophy has been used recently to construct a form of HD.

According to Aquinas, as is widely known, the soul is the form of the body.[53] Thus, for thomistic ontologies, all material objects comprise a material composite (i.e. the matter from which the person derives) and a substantial form, which determines the essential nature of the object.[54] For the human person, then, the soul is 'the substantial form . . . in virtue of which the matter informed by it . . . constitutes a living human body' (Stump 1995: 508).[55] Thomists thus view the soul as 'an individuated essence that makes the body a human body and that diffuses, informs, animates, develops, unifies and grounds the biological functions of its body' (Moreland and Rae 2000: 202).[56]

---

[49] Emergent dualists eschew limiting emergence to emergent properties for largely the same reasons that they reject physicalism as a whole, i.e. they do not believe that any form of physicalistic monism is adequate for explaining the data provided by humanity's mental life (cf. Hasker 1999).

[50] Hasker appeals to the analogy of a magnetic field to illustrate this (1999; 2005).

[51] Braine 1992; Stump 1995; Moreland and Rae 2000; and Leftow 2001.

[52] With respect to Aristotle, van der Eijk points out that scholarly consensus on his view of the soul has 'proved impossible' to this point and that this may well stem both from Aristotle's varied philosophical background and from tensions within his philosophy (2000). Similarly, Aquinas' understanding of human ontology has generated significant debate, with some thinkers concluding that his view is simply incoherent (e.g. Hasker 1999, 2005).

[53] *Summa Theologiae* Ia.76.1.

[54] There is some ambiguity in the thomistic approach regarding the nature of the soul as an individuating principle. From one perspective it seems that the soul is an abstract universal (Leftow seems more inclined in this direction [2001]). Since the soul is that which determines the nature of an object, it seems to be something shared by all members of a species. But, thomists generally regard the soul as a particular that serves to individuate the human person (Stump 1995; and Moreland and Rae 2000).

[55] It is important, then, not to confuse *form* with *shape*. The form is that which determines the essential nature of the entity, which certainly has a bearing on its shape, while the shape is a function of its material elements (Stump 1995).

[56] There seems to be some ambiguity regarding how the soul originates. Several thomists argue that forms can be understood as 'configurational states' that emerge from material entities (e.g. Stump 1995; and Leftow 2001). On this view, the material from which

Additionally, thomists generally agree that it is (at least) conceivable that the soul could survive the death of the body, though its existence would be sharply limited.[57]

Although some might prefer to view this more thomistic approach as a non-dualistic understanding of the human person, it fits the general parameters for HD that we have established here – that is, they affirm two ontologically fundamental aspects in the human person that are conceivably divisible such that the soul could continue to exist after physical death, albeit in a limited fashion. Indeed Moreland and Rae explicitly affirm the dualistic implications of the thomistic approach (2000).

2. Not Your Traditional Substance Dualism

These three forms of HD each represent different ways of affirming the basic tenets of CD, while avoiding some of its more negative implications. Of course, since all forms of HD are still varieties of substance dualism, they all maintain that body and soul are ontologically distinct and at least conceivably separable. Additionally, all forms of HD continue to view the soul as ontologically simple and as being that which explains the rational capacities (among other things) of the human person.

There are some marked differences on the other points, however. Thus, holistic dualism maintains CD's view that the soul is primitive while emergent dualists and most thomistic dualists depict the soul as at least somewhat derivative (though cf. Moreland and Rae 2000). Similarly, holistic dualists are more inclined to retain CD's view of the person as identical with the soul, while the other two tend to assert that the person is a composite entity (though again see Moreland and Rae 2000).

The different forms of HD, though, are united in affirming several key differences with the more traditional Cartesian view. First, all three affirm that the soul has a spatial locus.[58] Although the various proposals differ with respect to the precise nature of this spatiality, they all agree that the body provides a spatial locus for the soul in a way that is markedly lacking in CD.[59] Second, holists are united in affirming that, while the soul accounts for the rational capacities of the person, it must be expanded to account for

---

human persons are formed, contain the potentiality for a soul-form that emerges when they enter into the proper configurational state. This seems to conflict, though, with the more traditional view that souls are specially created by God and infused into the material substrate (Aquinas, *Summa Theologiae*, Ia.90.2; cf. Moreland and Rae 2000). Indeed, in a manner very similar to Swinburne, Stump seems to affirm that souls are *both* emergent configurational states *and* that they are specially created by God, without providing any real explanation of how these fit together (1995).

[57] See Stump 1995; and Leftow 2001.
[58] This means that HD is more resistant than CD to the problem of individuation (i.e. that souls cannot be individuated because they are non-spatial).

168

emotional, phenomenal, and sub-conscious factors as well (see especially Taliaferro 1994). Holists are, therefore, careful to present a much broader picture of the soul than is typically associated with CD. And, finally, as we will discuss later, holists are united in affirming that the soul is not naturally immortal.

These three different kinds of holistic dualism go a long way toward easing some of the concerns expressed with respect to substance dualism. All three approaches offer a slightly different understanding of the mind or soul and its relationship to the body, but each contends that its version of dualism maintains their integral union while still affirming their ontological distinctiveness. Thinkers from each camp thus argue that some form of HD is superior to CD in its ability to handle the standard criticisms.[60] While we cannot consider this claim in depth, we will look in the following section at the extent to which HD presents an anthropological ontology that is adequate to Barth's christological criteria.

III. Christology and Coherence: The Viability of Holistic Forms of Dualism

We saw in the previous chapter how the ontological criteria of a christological anthropology could be used to evaluate the adequacy of mind–body theories that rely on some form of nonreductive physicalism. In this section, we will apply the same methodology to determine the viability of HD for developing an anthropological ontology that can operate effectively within this christological framework.

For the purposes of this chapter, we shall focus our discussion on the three ontological criteria that seem most vulnerable on a dualist account of the human person: mental causation, embodiment, and contingent personhood. This is not to say that HD is not susceptible to critiques with respect to the other criteria, but that these are the ones most commonly noted.

a. Making Things Happen: The Problem of Mental Causation (Again)

Since psychophysical causal interaction is part of the very definition of the type of dualism that we are considering in this chapter, questions related to the coherence of its account of mental causation will be critical for determining

---

[59] This spatiality is easier to affirm for emergent and thomistic dualists with their emphasis on the soul as deriving from a particular physical system. Although Cartesian holists tend to affirm that the soul has a unique spatial relation to its body, it is harder to understand *why* this is the case.

[60] Stump 1995: 522–23; Hasker 1999: 317; and Moreland and Rae 2000: 200–1.

its overall adequacy. As we noted earlier, however, the problem of providing an adequate account of the causal relationship between the mental and the physical has long plagued Cartesian dualism. Many philosophers have thus concluded that, despite dualism's long efforts to overcome the problem, the 'scandal of Cartesian Interactionism' (Williams 1978: 287)[61] remains a decisive objection.[62] Thus Murphy states, 'the failure of three hundred years of attempts to solve the problem of mind–body interaction gives good grounds for saying that the problem is essentially insoluble' (2002b: 203).[63]

We cannot possibly hope to resolve such a long-standing debate in this short section. Instead, we will survey the arguments and relevant responses to evaluate the resources that HD has for addressing this problem.

1. The Dissimilarity and Spatiality Problems

Among the oldest and most frequently cited objections to dualist causation, is the claim that the mental and physical substances, according to dualism, are simply so different from one another as to disallow any possibility of causal interaction. Richardson calls this 'the problem of heterogeneity' (1982). In her letter to Descartes, Princess Elizabeth thus noted that causation in the physical realm seems necessarily to involve properties like motion, spatiality, and extension.[64] And, yet, these are the very properties that are excluded by CD.[65] Similarly, Richard Taylor argues:

> However natural it may seem to conceive a person in such terms, as a dual complex of two wholly disparate things, body and mind, it is nonetheless an impossible conception, on the simplest metaphysical grounds. For on this view, the body and the mind *are* wholly disparate things, so that any bodily change wrought by the mind or by some

---

[61] Cf. Richardson 1982.

[62] For example, Armstrong 1968; Levin 1979; Braddon-Mitchell and Jackson 1996; Kim 2001, 2004; and Murphy 2002a. Indeed, this objection to substance dualism has been so well established in the minds of many philosophers that Foster complains, 'many philosophers regard the problem as self-evident and not calling for further elucidation: they take it as just obvious that there is something deeply puzzling, perhaps even 'incoherent' in the dualism account of causation' (1991: 159).

[63] One common response offered by dualists to physicalist criticisms of its account of psychophysical causation is to contend that psychophysical causation is a basic datum of human experience that cannot be simply set aside (Swinburne 1984; Foster 1991; and Taliafferro 1994). As we saw in the last chapter, though, physicalists in no way exclude or ignore this basic datum but take it as an important aspect of any adequate ontology.

[64] Cited in Himma 2005.

[65] We will deal with a specific form of this objection based on the non-spatial nature of the soul in CD a little later when we discuss the causal pairing problem.

nonphysical occurrence transpiring therein is a change that lies quite outside the realm of physical law. This means that human behavior is veritably miraculous. (1983: 18)

It is simply inconceivable, according to Taylor, that an *idea* can cause a physical event to occur: 'Try, I say, to form a conception of this, and then confess that, as soon as the smallest attempt at any description is made, the description becomes unintelligible and the conception an impossible one' (1983: 21).[66]

Holistic dualists are at one with traditional Cartesian dualists, though, in arguing that this particular objection is clearly inadequate for refuting dualism. Descartes responded to this objection in two ways (Richardson 1982). First, Descartes argued that this objection makes an illegitimate comparison between mental and physical causation. Since mental substances are significantly different from their physical counterparts, there is simply no reason to assume that mental causation will be comparable to physical causation. Descartes' second response, was to argue that the psychophysical causal relationship was utterly mysterious and that its ultimate resolution lay beyond our ability to achieve satisfactorily.

These two responses continue to characterize large strands of dualist philosophy. Thus, many dualists similarly contend that mental causation is distinct from physical causation and that physicalist arguments against mental causation are, therefore, invalid (e.g. Richardson 1982).[67] Indeed, Hasker quips, 'The dualist besieged by arguments of this sort would do well to repeat to herself, from time to time, "Psychophysical causation is *not* physical causation"' (1999: 151). Similarly, dualists often follow Descartes in claiming the essentially mysterious nature of psychophysical causation,[68] often arguing that the psychophysical relation is a fundamental (i.e. brute) relation that is simply inexplicable on any other terms (e.g. Foster 1991: 160).[69]

---

[66] Of course, part of the reason that such a concept is unintelligible is because it completely ignores the dualist concept of mental substances as ontologically real entities with causal powers, rather than merely abstract ideas.

[67] Indeed, Foster argues that the influence of physicalist models of causation is the very root of the problem: 'One reason why we may *think* that there is an a priori problem for the dualist is that our conception of the nature of causation tends to be strongly conditioned by the ways in which causality operates in the physical realm' (1991: 159). Similarly, Lowe contends that dualists should jettison 'the Cartesian notion that causation is mechanical and must involve setting bodies in motion' and stop thinking that minds must influence physical events 'by (directly) affecting the state of motion of physical particles' (1992: 271).

[68] For example, Lewis 1982; and Goetz 2005.

[69] For Taliaferro, the mind–body relationship cannot even be understood in terms of some form of necessary correlation (1994: 128).

Such responses, though, have not tended to impress physicalist philosophers. As Richardson notes, these arguments 'seem, jointly, to be little more than an insistence that the interaction of mind and body be accepted, together with the claim that such interaction is inexplicable' (1982: 21). As we saw in the previous chapter, though, and as dualists frequently point out, the physicalist account of causation runs into an equal number of problems (see esp. Himma 2005). Thus, dualists often appeal to Hume's account of causation to point out that all causal relationships are inherently opaque and that physicalist causation is no less fundamentally mysterious than mental causation.[70] Indeed, Kim points out the irony that

> abandoning the substantival dualism of Descartes doesn't get us out of the woods as far as mental causation is concerned. Indeed one notable development in the recent philosophy of mind is the return of the problem of mental causation as a serious challenge to mainstream physicalism, a phenomenon that would have amused Descartes. (1998b: 39)

Another form of the dissimilarity problem that deserves mention is the contention that spatial relations are necessary for causation in the physical world (cf. E. Lowe 1992). Since CD denies that the body is spatial, according to this objection, it cannot enter into causal relations with physical substances. Of course, this objection can also be responded to as before by arguing that mental and physical causation are different.[71] Additionally, since most forms of holistic dualism posit that the soul is spatially located, they do not have a problem at this point (Goetz 1994, 2005; cf. Quinn 1997).

Finally, the argument from dissimilarity fails to provide any traction on the problem because of its failure to provide any defense for its basic intuition. As Kim points out,

> But as an argument this is incomplete and unsatisfying. As it stands, it is not much of an argument – it hardly gets started; rather, it only expresses a vague dissatisfaction of the sort that ought to prompt us to look for a real argument. Why is it incoherent to think that there can be causal relations between 'diverse substances'? (2001: 32)

The other arguments that we will consider, then, seek to provide exactly such an explanation for why dualistic causation is either incoherent or, at least, improbable.

---

[70] Lewis 1982; Swinburne 1984; Foster 1991; Lowe 1992, 2000; and Hasker 1999.
[71] Some have argued that modern science makes the idea of 'causation at a distance' less problematic (e.g. Lewis 1973; and Heil 2004b: 815). The difficulty with this argument, however, is the idea of action across a distance presumes the very kind of spatial location that is precluded on the Cartesian account of the soul.

2. The Causal Pairing Problem

One argument that has recently received significant attention is the contention that dualistic causation is incoherent because it cannot provide any explanation for the causal relation that obtains between particular souls and the relevant bodies.[72] Suppose that we have a situation in which two souls, s_1 and s_2, interact causally with two bodies, b_1 and b_2. What is the precise relationship which establishes that s_1 causally interacts with b_1 and not b_2? Since causal relations are typically understood in terms of the nomological relation of non-causal properties (cf. Foster 1991),[73] the causal pairing argument is a call for dualists to provide just such an account.

As Foster points out, though, such an account is very difficult to provide on dualist terms (1989). Causal laws based on mere temporal correlation are of no use since they would not rule out the possibility of an effect on b_2 that is temporally correlated with the action of s_1. Given the non-spatial soul of CD, Foster argues, the dualist is also prevented from relying on the spatial relationships utilized to explain physical causal pairing.[74] The causal pairing argument, therefore, suggests that the dualist has no way of accounting for the unique causal relation between a soul and its body.

Dualists might try to counter this objection, as before, by arguing that the causal relation is brute.[75] Theists could carry the argument further by simply maintaining that God establishes the proper causal relations when a soul comes into being and that no further explanation is necessary. Kim rightly argues, however, that this misses the point of the argument (2001). The causal pairing argument does not call on dualists to provide an explanation of *how* the causal relation comes into being but *what* the causal relation is. In other words, regardless of how it came into being there must be some causal relation R between a soul and its body. The causal pairing argument is a call for dualists to explain what R is.

Some dualists contend that we should simply reject the premises upon which this argument is based. After a rather thorough discussion of the

---

[72] Cf. esp. Foster 1968, 1989, 1991; and Kim 2001.
[73] On this understanding of causation, as Foster describes it, 'causal relationships between events are always constituted by certain non-causal properties of the situation, together with the relevant covering laws' (1991: 167).
[74] The causal pairing argument should, therefore, not be confused with a naïve appeal to physical 'connection' as an explanation of causation, an argument that is easily defeated by dualists. Rather, the causal pairing argument simply calls for an explanation of the causal relation and argues that any coherent explanation will entail an appeal to spatial relations of some kind. Shoemaker and Hywel's argument that the dualist can simply appeal to 'quasi-spatial' relations to establish causal relations is conceivable, but, as he points out, seems less probable than the spatial account (1978).
[75] Cf. Richardson 1982; Foster 1989, 1991; and Goetz 1994.

problem – indeed, he seems to have introduced the problem (cf. Foster 1968) – Foster contends dualists should either reject the demand for a nomological account of causal pairings, or they should reject the demand for *general* covering laws and rely instead on *particular* laws limited to particular body–soul relations (1989, 1991). Other dualists argue that the whole causal framework built around 'event causation' needs to be discarded in favor of a more substantial view of causation (e.g. Goetz 1994; Moreland and Rae 2000).

The holistic dualist, however, does not need to reconstruct a theory of causality in this way. Causal pairing only appears to be a problem for dualists because of the Cartesian understanding of souls as non-spatial and non-extended. Since causal pairing in a physical system is normally established on the basis of spatial relations, the lack of such relations is what makes it difficult for the dualist to handle the problem.[76] Thus, the causal pairing problem is a problem for dualists only if dualism entails that 'we do not have the slightest hint of any relation holding' between souls and bodies (Hoffman and Rosencrantz 1997: 197). But, HD affirms that the soul has precisely such a spatio-causal relation to a particular body and, therefore, seems to escape the force of the objection (Zimmerman 2004: 319).[77] Even Cartesian Holism, affirms that the soul has such a spatial locus, even if it fails to provide any metaphysically deep explanation for this relation.[78]

3. The 'Principles of Science' Problem

The objections most commonly raised to dualist interactionism are those stemming from the physicalist framework that predominates among contemporary philosophers. As E. J. Lowe notes, 'The more serious area of concern is created by the suspicion that dualist views of the mind-body relation ... are somehow at odds with the findings of modern physical science: not only physiology and neurology, but also, more fundamentally, physics itself' (1992: 263). Along these lines, we can identify objections stemming from at least three different principles: causal completeness, explanatory exclusion, and conservation of energy.

The first two objections (causal completeness and explanatory exclusion) should already be familiar to us from the previous chapter and we will not

---

[76] Kim argues that the causal pairing problem afflicts even soul-to-soul causation on the dualist account (2001). That is, on the Cartesian account of souls, there does not seem to be any way of establishing causal relations between souls that would make soul-to-soul causal interaction coherent.

[77] Goetz disagrees with this causal framework entirely, arguing that causal relations are established on the basis of a basic causal ontology, rather than spatial relations (1994). Regardless of whether this argument is successful, though, it seems that causal pairing is not as significant a problem for HD as for CD.

[78] Cf. Goetz 1994, 2005; and Taliaferro 1994.

rehearse those arguments again. Suffice it to say that these arguments are even more pointed when directed at dualist philosophers, many of whom explicitly reject both principles.[79] Dualists thus contend that although CCP and explanatory exclusion may be valid *methodological* commitments for the physical sciences, we overstep our bounds when we try to make them *metaphysical* theses (Goetz 2005).

In addition to simply setting aside CCP as a metaphysical thesis, dualists offer a number of other responses. Probably the most common is to contend that the objection begs the question.[80] On this argument, the physicalist presumption that physical events can only be caused by and explained in terms of other physical events is precisely what dualism denies. To criticize dualism for failing to maintain these principles, then, simply begs the question.

Some have argued in rejoinder, however, that this counter-argument misses the point of the physicalist objection (e.g. Larmer 1986: 280–81). Physicalists do not merely criticize dualists for failing to maintain the physicalist framework, but primarily for positing a theory that has little or no support from the physical sciences. Thus, as Lowe rightly points out, 'The claim that only the physical can have causal powers – or, at least that only the physical can causally affect the physical – may be seen by many not just as some question-begging antidualist prejudice, but as a cornerstone of modern physical science' (1992: 265; cf. Kim 2004). Given science's superior explanatory track record, physicalists argue, we should assume a scientific framework unless and until it is proven wrong.

A dualist might fairly ask, however, what might qualify as proof in this argument? It seems likely that the only thing such a physicalist would count a 'proof' would be those things that qualify as evidence in a physicalist framework. But this would seem to predetermine the outcome. Thus, many holistic dualists argue that the physical sciences themselves are simply inadequate for addressing the fundamental issues involved in this debate.[81] This does not mean that holistic dualists reject science itself; indeed, many of them rely heavily on the sciences for informing their understanding of how the psychophysical relationship works.[82] But, unlike thinkers who affirm that science is 'all-competent' (Atkins 1987: 13), holistic dualists contend that science is inherently limited in its ability to speak to the existence and nature of the soul.

A second response, however, is to note that the physicalist solution is itself untenable. As we saw in the previous chapter, both reductive and nonreductive forms of physicalism struggle to explain mental causation in a way that maintains the causal significance of the mental while avoiding the problems

---

[79] For example, Popper and Eccles 1977; Foster 1991; Hodgson 1991; and Hasker 1999.
[80] For example, E. Lowe 1993; Hasker 1999; and Moreland 2002.
[81] For example, Moreland and Rae 2000; and Swinburne 2003.
[82] For example, Eccles 1977, 1979; Taliaferro 1994; and Lowe 2004.

of physicalistic determinism. Consequently, some dualists simply note that given a choice between the two, the dualist framework is superior in terms of its ability to affirm the causal efficacy of the mental and the free agency of the human person.[83] As we have seen though, whether the physicalist account of mental causation is as untenable as this response contends remains an open question.[84]

Another objection commonly encountered in the literature is that dualistic psychophysical causation is scientifically untenable because it would violate the Principle of the Conservation of Energy (COE).[85] In other words, dualist interaction entails that mental substances are able to cause changes in physical systems. But, any such change seems to entail a change in the total energy of the physical system, thus violating COE. As Larmer notes, however, 'To many thinkers, this seems too high a price to pay, since to deny the Principle of the Conservation of Energy is to deny one of the most fundamental scientific laws' (1986: 277).

Popper argues that COE should be understood as a statistical principle and suggests that mental causation would not constitute a violation of COE so long as mental acts only involved small amounts of energy (Popper and Eccles 1977). Larmer rightly points out, however, that even if individual mental acts only involve small amounts of energy, the tremendous number of mental acts occurring on a regular basis would certainly constitute a statistically significant contribution to the overall state of the system.

Larmer argues instead that science only entails a weak form of COE, one that holds only for closed systems (cf. Averill 1981). Psychophysical causation, therefore, does not violate COE since mental substances lie outside the physical system. While Larmer is certainly correct that psychophysical causation would not violate a weak form of COE, he does not consider the physicalist's most likely rejoinder – that is, that (1) the lack of evidence for any mental substances outside the physical system and (2) the weight of evidence that the total state of energy of the physical system does not change both support the conclusion that a strong form of COE is justified even if not logically required.

It would seem, then, that the dualist's best response to this objection is to argue again that psychophysical causation is simply different than physical causation.[86] In other words, since mental causation differs from physical causation, there is no reason to suppose that mental causation requires the

---

[83] For example, E. Lowe 1992; Hasker 1999; and Zimmerman 2004.

[84] Two other responses that have been offered by dualists, the possibility of pervasive causal overdetermination (e.g. Mills 1996) and the contention that theistic causation renders these objections untenable (e.g. Zimmerman 2004; and Goetz 2005), were mentioned in the previous chapter and, therefore, will not be pursued here.

[85] Apparently this objection was first formulated by Leibniz (Averill 1981). Versions of the argument can also be found in Armstrong 1968 and Dennett 1983.

transfer of energy. Even though physical-to-physical causation always requires the transfer of energy, it is not necessary to conclude the same for mental-to-mental or mental-to-physical causation. While the physicalist will certainly not be convinced by this argument, it is logically consistent with the dualist's own framework.

The basic dualist rejoinder to objections based on the 'principles of science' to its understanding of mental causation, then, comprises the claim that psychophysical causation is of an inherently different kind than physical causation. Consequently, psychophysical causation cannot be fairly criticized on the basis of physicalist criticisms stemming from causal completeness, explanatory exclusion, and the conservation of energy, since those principles simply do not apply outside the physical realm.

4. *The Explanatory Problem*

One final argument that we should consider is the contention that as long as substance dualism is unable to provide an explanation of psychophysical causation it should be rejected. 'To call one's dualism "integrative" does not help us much', according to Schouten, 'as long as we are kept in the dark as to how this (causal) bridging of the corporeal and mental realms takes place' (2001: 694). In other words, if the mind is able to interact causally with the body and, therefore, cause physical changes in the body, we should be able to provide some theory as to how and where this causal transaction takes place. Thus, Armstrong argues forcefully that the dualist needs to be able to provide some empirically verifiable theory about the locus of causal interaction (1999). This is, of course, the problem that Descartes was attempting to address with his infamous appeal to the pineal gland as the locus of psychophysical interaction (cf. *Treatise of Man and The Passions of the Soul*).

Dualists have offered two responses to this argument.[86] First, one could accept the challenge and attempt to provide a specific and testable theory of causal interaction. The most famous such attempt was put forward by the

---

[86] Larmer also notes that some have suggested that psychophysical causation could be made consistent with COE if one posited that any change in energy caused by a mental action would be balanced by a corresponding change elsewhere in the system (1986). While this is logically conceivable, Larmer rightly questions its plausibility. Additionally, some have argued that quantum science provides support for the idea that physical systems are not 'hermetically sealed off from "outside" forces' (Taliaferro 1994: 221). Whether such appeals to quantum mechanics can provide the necessary support for dualist causation, though, would require a far more extensive understanding and analysis of quantum theory than is possible in this chapter and, indeed, than is normally offered by dualists appealing to it (though cf. Penrose 1989).

[87] Thomistic dualism can actually be read in two different ways on the question of causal transaction. Some thomistic dualists argue for such tight psychophysical relation within the hylomorphic system as to disallow any talk of psychophysical 'interaction' (Stump 1995; cf. Machuga 2002). If thomistic hylomorphism is understood in this

neuroscientist Sir John Eccles.[88] Popper and Eccles' posited that psychophysical interaction could be understood in terms of certain areas of the brain that 'potentially are capable of being in direct liaison with the self-conscious mind' (1977: 358). This 'liaison brain' is a broadly distributed physical system, only a small portion of which is ever actually interacting with the mind at a given moment in time. The self-conscious mind affects psychophysical interaction by scanning the relevant modules of the brain (i.e. the liaison brain) and selectively modifying 'the dynamic spatio-temporal patterns of the neuronal events' (1979: 227).[89] Since this interaction requires very little energy and is broadly distributed throughout the brain, it will be difficult to detect.[90] Nonetheless, Eccles views his theory as 'a kind of research programme' that raises many questions which demand 'detailed theories' (1977: 37). Indeed, much of Eccles work involves a pursuit of just such a scientific analysis.

Evaluating the specifics of Eccles' proposal would take us too far from our task. It does seem significant, however, that his research program has failed to generate any significant following among neuroscientists in general. While his approach exemplifies what a dualist attempt to explicate the locus of psychophysical interaction might look like, it does not seem to have provided an adequate basis upon which to develop such an explanation.[91]

A second response, however, simply dismisses the demand for a scientific theory. Thus, Goetz argues, 'Why, however, think that the dualist needs at all, let alone urgently needs, an empirically testable scientific theory about the location of causal interaction between a soul and its body?' (2005: 53). According to Goetz, the reason dualists do not need such an account is because belief in dualism is not grounded on empirical arguments of this sort. On the contrary, a belief in dualism is grounded in the sorts of intuitively available evidence that we discussed at the beginning of the chapter. While the dualist may choose to posit some theory regarding the locus of causal interaction, such a theory is not necessary, and the refutation of any particular theory would not constitute a decisive refutation of dualism itself (2005: 53). Furthermore, it is not clear what sort of 'proof' the physicalist

---

way, however, it results in an ontology that is little different from the forms of NRP considered in the previous chapter.

[88] See esp. Popper and Eccles 1977; and Eccles 1979.

[89] That this account requires both 'reading' *and* 'modifying' the physical brain is what prevents Eccles' account from being a form of psychophysical parallelism (1979: 229).

[90] Lowe also argues that mental causation should be understood in terms of a broadly distributed engagement with the mind rather than as a direct cause of a specific neuronal event (1992).

[91] If nothing else, Eccles' work demonstrates that those who argue, like Richard Taylor, that any attempt to spell out in detail a scientific account of dualist causation will quickly demonstrate itself to be unintelligible (1983: 22). Surely, even if Eccles' account was ultimately unsuccessful, there is nothing unintelligible about his presentation.

would accept since, by definition, the physicalist is only willing to allow physical causes for physical events.

5. Mind and Matter:
Can Holistic Dualism Cross the Cartesian Divide?

So, what can we say about the adequacy of HD's account of mental causation. First, substance dualists in general seem justified in rejecting the arguments from dissimilarity, causal completeness, and explanatory exclusion. Since their reasons for rejecting these arguments are based on a fundamentally different way of viewing the world, they are unlikely to convince any physicalists by their arguments, but they are, nonetheless, justified in contending that these arguments are inadequate for establishing the falsity of dualism. Additionally, given that the soul has a spatial locus in HD, it is better positioned than more traditional forms of dualism for handling many of these criticisms.[92]

It would seem that the greatest weakness of all dualistic accounts of causation is the pervasive negativity of its arguments. At several points, the dualist position boils down to an affirmation that physicalist arguments do not succeed. While this is helpful, the dearth of positive dualist arguments regarding the nature of psychophysical causation or the empirical basis of dualist interaction is noticeable (Langsam 2001). All too often, one finds the dualist appealing to 'mystery' to explain the mind-body relation.[93] Given the significant difficulties encountered by physicalists in providing their own account of the psychophysical relation, it is difficult to fault dualists overly much on this point. Indeed, from one perspective the HD seems to be on much better footing than NRP at this point since it is less susceptible to charges that its account of mental causation is simply incoherent within its metaphysical system. Nonetheless, even if the dualist rejects the demand for an empirically verifiable theory of the mind-body relation, it would seem reasonable to ask for more work to be done to establish a positive account of the relation that would have some bearing on the data produced by the empirical sciences.

b. Chunks of Matter: The Problem of Personal Embodiment

As we discussed in chapter four, Barth's christological ontology maintains the integral union of body and soul.

> Far from existing as the union of two parts or two 'substances', He is one whole man, embodied soul and besouled body: the one in the other

---

[92] It may be, however, that holistic dualists should be more attentive to concerns raised by Alan Sussman (1981) about attributing properties typically associated with material things to nonmaterial entities. Although such a move increases the explanatory power of dualistic systems, it runs the risk of losing the distinctness of the mental altogether.
[93] For example, Lewis 1973: 118; Swinburne 1986: 195; and Hasker 1999: 200.

and never merely beside it; the one never without the other but only with it, and in it present, active and significant; the one with all its attributes always to be taken as seriously as the other. (III/2, 327)

Consequently, one of his greatest concerns about substance dualism is that it views body and soul as only tentatively united, even though it often tries to affirm the essential unity of the person (III/2, 380–81).

Some modern dualists continue to talk about the body–soul relation in ways that generate such criticisms. Thus, Sydney Shoemaker and Hywel Lewis compare the person's relation to his body with his relation to a mechanical object like a car (1978: 119). Similarly, Swinburne can speak of the body as 'a chunk of matter' through which a person acts in the world (1986: 146). These ways of speaking suggest to some that substance dualism necessarily involves a failure to appreciate the psychophysical intimacy that pervades human experience. As a result, a whole host of problems and objections has been raised against substance dualism. The following concerns, therefore, represent only a sampling of those objections, but they should, nonetheless, serve to raise the kinds of problems the dualist must face and the answers they have offered.

1. The Psychophysical Interdependence Problem

First, how does a dualist account for the integral relation between physical states and such fundamental mental states as consciousness and rationality? According to Jeeves,

At every level of neuroscience research, from single cells and their interactions to the functioning of whole integrated systems coordinating different centers of brain activity, one message is clear. There is interdependence between what is happening at the physical level of brain processes and at the levels of cognition and behavior. On that almost everyone today agrees. (2004b: 173)

As Hasker points out, however, CD seems to provide no explanation for this psychophysical interdependence:

On the dualistic view, why should *consciousness itself* be interrupted by drugs, or a blow on the head, or the need for sleep? And why should reasoning, generally thought of as the distinctive activity of the conscious mind, be interrupted by such physical disturbances? The natural conclusion from Cartesian dualism would seem to be that consciousness should continue unabated during such times – deprived, to be sure, of sensory input and the capacity for motor action ... by making the mind essentially independent of the brain rather than dependent on it, Cartesianism deprives itself of a ready explanation for these kinds of dependence that we actually find. (1999: 154)

Despite this apparent weakness, however, substance dualists have long contended that a person's mental life was dependent on bodily operations (e.g. Hart 1988; Foster 1991: 263). Indeed, as Taliaferro points out, 'the vulnerability of consciousness to material processes . . . is precisely what many dualists expect. Obviously, our whole mental life is causally bound up with the well-being of our material constitution. But this does not mean our mental life is itself material' (1994: 75). Similarly, Swinburne affirms, 'The evidence of neurophysiology and psychology suggests most powerfully that the functioning of the soul depends on the operation of the brain' (1984: 174). Thus, Hywel Lewis, himself a critic of Descartes in many places, points out those who criticize Descartes would do well to remember that he was intensely interested in the natural sciences and the function of the body (1973: 19).

There is, therefore, nothing to prevent a dualist from *affirming* psychophysical dependence. Critics have long maintained, however, that they have no way of *explaining it*. Given the sharp distinction dualists make between physical and mental substances, how can there be any adequate explanation for the intimate connections noted by contemporary science?

At least some forms of HD, however, would seem to fare much better than CD on this point. Since emergent dualism explicitly affirms that the generation and function of the soul is directly dependent (apart from the miraculous intervention of God) on the underlying physical states, it should come as no surprise that damage to one's body would affect one's mental life (Hasker 1999). Similarly, the tight psychophysical connection espoused by thomistic dualism would seem to entail a similarly close connection between physical and mental states (Stump 1995). Cartesian holism, on the other hand, although it certainly affirms a strong psychophysical connection, has a more difficult time providing an adequate account. Thus, although Taliaferro also argues for an integral psychophysical unity, even a substantial union, of body and soul, it is not clear how this approach really explains the connection. It is not sufficient merely to *affirm* such an integral relation; the dualist must also be able to provide some account of that union that fits within his dualist framework. Although the emphasis of the Cartesian holist on the tightly integrated unity of body and soul is incoherent, it is difficult to harmonize with its Cartesian framework. Thus, as Hasker rightly asserts, 'It's not that these phenomena are logically inconsistent with Cartesianism; no doubt they can be accommodated' (1999: 157). Nonetheless, he continues, Cartesianism needs to be able to address these problems 'in a way that exhibits the known facts as plausible consequences of the underlying metaphysical view. A string of ad hoc conjectures will not suffice' (1999: 157).

2. The Biological Continuity Problem

A second, though related, objection stemming from the biological continuity of humans with other animals similarly holds little difficulty for HD (Taliaferro 1995; and Hasker 1999). According to CD, only human persons have a soul (Baker and Morris 1996). The significant mental life of animals must, therefore, be explained in some other way. Such a distinction is, however, very difficult to maintain in light of the growing evidence for the lack of any sharp biological divisions between humans and other animals. That is, if humans and other animals are remarkably similar biologically, why would their mental lives require entirely different explanations?

Once again, though, we can see that HD offers resources for a more adequate response. Both emergent dualism and thomism explicitly incorporate animals in their systems (Moreland 2002) and many affirm the theory of evolution as a reasonable way of understanding the development of human persons.[94] Thus, continuity between animals and humans is exactly what an HD account of human ontology would expect.[95]

3. The Disparagement Problem

Does dualism result in a necessary disparagement of the body and of creation as a whole? One of the more common criticisms espoused by contemporary thinkers,[96] this is also the one most likely to be simply dismissed by dualists. Thus, many dualists point out that there is no necessary relation between dualist ontologies and the disparagement of other aspects of creation (see esp. Taliaferro 1994). While this might be true, given the history of such

---

[94] For example, Popper and Eccles 1977; Swinburne 1984; E. Lowe 1993; Taliaferro 1994; and Hasker 1999; though cf. Moreland and Rae 2000; and Goetz 2005.

[95] Hasker argues, though, that some forms of holism struggle on this question because of their commitment to a creationist view on the origin of the soul (1999: 152). That is, this position would seem to entail that God immediately creates a soul, not only for every human person, but for every animal as well (cf. Swinburne and Padgett 1994: 199). A dualist could try to affirm an agnostic position on the question of animal minds akin to Barth's (e.g. Foster 1991), but this simply raises the problem of biological continuity all over again. As Goetz rightly points out, however, the Cartesian view that God creates each soul immediately is no more problematic than the emergent theists' view that God created the biological world in such a way that each animal would generate its own soul (2005). While one might wonder why he would operate in such an occasionalist manner (Hasker 1999: 153), it is not unintelligible to suppose that he does. Taliaferro argues that even if the dualist rejects the idea that animals have substantial souls, he need not maintain low view of animal mental life (1994: 569). Thus, the dualist could argue that there is significant biological and psychological continuity between animals and humans and still maintain that there is a decisive ontological difference between them (cf. Machuga 2002).

[96] For example, Jantzen 1984; and Thatcher 1987.

disparagement in the dualist tradition, dualists would be wise to provide a much stronger response to this criticism (though see Taliaferro 1994).

Nonetheless, holistic dualists are clear in their emphasis on the importance of the body for life of the whole person. Thus, Taliaferro calls on all those affirming an 'integrative' dualism to 'eschew all suggestions that the person is a "mere" attachment to an object, as though one's body were an accessory' (1994: 233). Given this more holistic emphasis, then, Thatcher is certainly wrong to assume that dualism necessarily disparages the body because it is viewed as 'inessential to mind and to personal identity' (1987: 185). Throughout this discussion, we have seen that HD affirms a much higher view of the body for understanding the human person than is traditionally associated with dualistic ontologies.

4. The Disembodiment Problem

The question of embodiment becomes particularly acute when one turns to more eschatological considerations, specifically the question of whether there will be an 'intermediate state' for human persons between their death and eventual resurrection, in which one aspect of the self continues to exist in a disembodied state.[97] Since dualists all affirm the conceivability of the mind functioning, to some extent, independently of the body, we must ask what this entails about the mind–body relation.[98]

Indeed, most forms of CD view the mind as retaining most or all of its basic functions in its disembodied state (see esp. Hart 1988). Thus able to perceive, think, will, and perform all of the other mental functions of a conscious being, one begins to wonder what role the body actually played in the life of the person prior to disembodiment. Such a view appears to make the body extraneous and unnecessary to the functioning of the person.

---

[97] Following Steven Davis, we will understand the intermediate state to involve a temporary disembodiment that corresponds to the following scenario: 'We human beings are born, live for a time as psychophysical beings, and then die; after death we exist in an incomplete state as immaterial souls; and some time later in the eschaton God miraculously raises our bodies from the ground, transforms them into "glorified bodies", and reunites them with our souls, thus making us complete and whole again' (1989: 121).

[98] Dualists have long contended that the Bible clearly teaches a pre-resurrection intermediate state and that this teaching entails some form of substance dualism. This position is generally supported by holistic dualists as well. Thus Moreland and Rae argue, 'The human soul . . . is capable of entering an intermediate disembodied state upon death, however incomplete and unnatural this state may be, and of eventually being reunited with a resurrected body' (2000: 17). And according to Cooper, 'Any doctrine of the future life—except the theory that we cease to exist from death until the resurrection, traditionally rejected as heretical—requires a dualistic anthropology' (2000: 13; cf. Vallicella 1998). Since, as we noted earlier, the substance dualist need only affirm the conceivability rather than the actuality of mind–body separation, we will assume that substance dualism similarly must only affirm the conceivability of an intermediate state.

As we have seen, though, HD affirms that the mind would only function in a severely truncated manner during such a disembodied state.[99] The issue remains, however, that the mind is still perceived as functioning *in some manner* during this time. Thus, Stephen Davis argues that although the soul's existence during this period constitutes 'a radically attenuated and incomplete form of human existence' (1989: 121), nonetheless, its mental abilities and properties will survive in some form. Thus, 'human persons in the interim state can be spoken of as having experiences, beliefs, wishes, knowledge, memory, inner (rather than bodily) feelings, thoughts, language (assuming memory or earthly existence) – in short, just about everything that makes up what we call personality' (1989: 121). If the mental life of human persons continues without interruption during this period of disembodiment, however, this would seem to raise significant questions regarding HD's emphasis on the integral relationship of the soul to the body.[100]

It would seem that the holistic dualist could offer two responses to this argument. First, HD could affirm the independent functioning of the mind and simply deny that the corresponding implications for understanding the psychophysical relationship constitute decisive objections to its account (e.g. Moreland and Rae 2000). Second, HD could deny the independent functioning of the mind during the intermediate state. This could be accomplished either by arguing that the mind continues to exist but does not continue to function during this time (Robinson 1989), or by asserting the possibility that the mind could be united with some intermediate physical form in connection with which it can continue to function until its eventual resurrection.[101]

Neither of these two arguments is entirely satisfying, however. To the extent that HD relies on the first approach, it seems to entail a slide back toward CD in that the mind is understood to possess a significant degree of independence from its physical embodiment. While this would not constitute a decisive move away from HD, it does signify that the embodiment relation may not be as close as HD appears to affirm. The latter argument, on the other hand, seems to entail a slide in the opposite direction – that is, toward physicalism.[102] In other words, if HD abandons its commitment to the conceivable separability

---

[99] Thus, Davis argues that the abnormality of the intermediate state is 'one of the clear differences' between his position and the immortality of the soul commonly associated with substance dualism (1989: 123).

[100] More sensitive than most dualists to this problem, Robinson notes: 'We are in something of a cleft stick. We want to reconcile the intuition that the mind or self can think and act on the body on its own initiative with the fact that even the most abstract thoughts and decisions appear to depend for their formulation as well as their execution upon the proper operation of the brain. Moreover, the latter fact seems both more certain and more clear in its exact sense than the former intuition. It is, therefore, the dualist's intuition which is most at risk' (1989: 46).

[101] Cf. Harris 1983; and Reichenbach 1983; Baker 1995.

of body and mind, affirming instead that the mind cannot function in any way apart from some form of embodiment, one begins to wonder about the extent to which HD can continue to affirm that they are distinguishable substances.[103]

It may be, then, that the only way that HD can maintain its commitment to *both* the conceivable separability of the two substances *and* their integral interdependence is to appeal to the possibility that God could miraculously sustain some level of functionality for the mind during the intermediate state (e.g. Hasker 1999).

5. Explaining Psychophysical Interdependence: The Prospects of a Dualist Account of Personal Embodiment

Once again we can see that HD is in a much better position to address many of the standard criticisms of traditional substance dualism. Its clear and consistent affirmation of the tight psychophysical relations that pervasively characterize every aspect of human existence, seems to refute decisively any suggestion that all forms of substance dualism necessarily disparage the embodied nature of human persons.

Nevertheless, it does seem that there are at least two remaining weaknesses in HD's portrayal of embodiment. First, while Cartesian holism makes its commitment to human embodiment quite clear, its apparent inability to provide a metaphysically deep explanation of this relationship constitutes a significant drawback as compared to the other forms of HD. Second, we have seen that HD struggles to affirm the conceivable separability of body and soul while still emphasizing the embodiment relation. While neither of these objections suffices to defeat HD as a theory of human ontology, they do suggest that more work needs to be done on this issue.

c. Living Eternally: The Problem of an Immortal Substance

One final area in which substance dualism could be understood to be incompatible with Barth's ontological framework has to do with the nature of the soul and Barth's emphasis that human persons depend on the preserving

---

[102] There are, of course, significant biblical and theological considerations that would also come into play with respect to either soul sleep or intermediate embodiment, which will not be considered in this chapter.

[103] Robinson recognizes the viability of this argument, but apparently does not think that it is incoherent to assert that something entirely comprised of 'unactualized powers' could be understood to 'constitute a real entity' (1989: 56). Given that this constitutes a rejection of the widely held idea that the existence of an entity depends on its causal activity (i.e. 'Alexander's Dictum', see Kim 2003c), though, it would seem that any dualist relying on this approach should offer more of an argument.

work of the Spirit for their existence at every moment.[104] If this is true, substance dualism's historic belief in the natural immortality of the soul would seem to be completely incompatible with Barth's framework.

This objection, though, actually holds very little interest for us at this point. Holistic dualists, most of whom are explicitly Christian theists, clearly insist that the human soul is not inherently immortal and that its existence is fully contingent on God's preserving work.[105] Thus, Swinburne argues that the human soul does not have 'a nature such that it survives "under its own steam"' and, therefore, that is can survive death only if God exercises his power to enable it do to so (Swinburne and Padgett 1994: 308–9).[106] Holistic dualists thus contend that the soul is 'not by nature immortal' (Moreland and Rae 2000: 17) and that it cannot exist 'independently of God's creative activity' (Goetz 2005: 35).[107] Consequently, there seems to be no reason that we should regard HD as inconsistent with Barth's emphasis on the contingent nature of human persons.

IV. Is There Hope for Holistic Forms of Substance Dualism?: Problems and Prospects

From our discussions in this chapter we have seen that 'dualism' is a term that covers a broad range of ontological theories. While some forms of dualism seem clearly unsupportable given Barth's christological framework,

---

[104] That this was one of Barth's primary concerns, if not *the* primary concern, regarding substance dualism is reflected in his statement that the 'central affirmation' of a dualist anthropology is 'the immortality of this rational thing ... which does not come to it by the special grace of God, but dwells within it by nature' (III/2, 380).

[105] Hasker argues that most forms of dualism hold to the natural immortality of the soul (1999: 81). He understands this to mean that 'the soul, like all created beings, needs the sustaining power of God in order to continue its existence. The soul, then, would be annihilated should God cease to sustain it, but otherwise it is indestructible' (1999: 81). While this might have been true for traditional dualists, and may even hold for some Cartesian holists, most holistic dualists affirm that the soul would *not* survive the death of the body unless God actively chooses to sustain its independent existence.

[106] Swinburne and Padgett further argue that this would not be a violation of any natural laws since 'there are no natural laws which dictate what will happen to a soul after death' (1994: 309).

[107] Although the traditional dualist position has been to affirm that the soul is inherently immortal because it is simple (i.e. it has no parts) and, therefore, cannot be broken down into any constituent elements, it is not at all clear why something should be deemed indestructible merely because it is simple (Shoemaker and Hywel 1978: 134). For a nice summary of the philosophical arguments for the natural immortality of the soul as well as a brief refutation, see Swinburne and Padgett 1994: 305–6; cf. van Inwagen 2002: 171.

a number of contemporary dualists have developed forms of substance dualism that express a higher appreciation for the strong psychophysical links that characterize human experience. This more holistic dualism, itself comprising a range of ontological approaches, affirms that human persons comprise two fundamentally distinct substances that are intimately united and integrally interdependent.

As with nonreductive physicalism, though, the christological adequacy of HD, must be evaluated on the basis of its ability to articulate its anthropological ontology in a way that is both consistent with this christological framework and internally coherent. Given these requirements, we have seen that the adequacy of HD has been challenged with respect to its account of mental causation, embodiment, and contingent personhood. On each of these issues, we have also seen that HD is able to offer some serious responses that suggest that HD is an ontological approach that bears serious consideration.

As with NRP, however, there are still some weaknesses to HD's presentation. Thus, we have seen that HD (especially Cartesian holism) needs to do more work developing its positive account of the embodiment relation, spending less time on negative refutations of physicalist arguments. Additionally, we have discussed the problems that arise with respect to the continuing functionality of the soul in any disembodied state. Despite these weaknesses, though, HD has proven itself sufficiently capable of responding to its critics to be considered a christologically viable candidate for developing an anthropological ontology.

7

CONCLUSION: MAKING THE TURN, SHARPENING OUR CHRISTOLOGICAL VISION

I. *Making the Christocentric Turn*

In his theological anthropology, Karl Barth has issued a decisive call for theologians to make what we have been calling the christocentric turn. That is, he has called on Christian theologians to understand the nature of humanity from the unique vantage point provided by the person and work of Jesus Christ. And, indeed it would seem that contemporary theologians have responded to this challenge. Thus, many theologians happily affirm, along with Barth, that the person of Jesus Christ is the key to understanding that which most fundamentally comprises the nature of true humanity. Thus, we see John Zizioulas arguing that 'the mystery of man reveals itself fully only in the light of Christ' (1975: 433). Similarly, John Sherlock states that Jesus is 'the one human being who shows us what true humanity, and true divinity, are like' (1996: 18). And, according to Millard Erickson, Jesus reveals 'what human nature is intended to be' (1998: 532). Such quotes could easily be multiplied as theologians line up to affirm the christocentric turn in theological anthropology. Although each of these thinkers would likely recognize the validity of the data and the interpretive insights generated by other anthropological perspectives, each seems willing to affirm that Christology constitutes a unique approach to the problem of the human person, without which we are lacking something vital to a proper appreciation of all that it means to be human.

Our study has hopefully demonstrated that merely acknowledging the vital significance of Jesus Christ for understanding the nature of human persons does not indicate that one has made the christocentric turn in any meaningful sense. Indeed, we would seem justified in pressing for further clarity as to precisely what is mean by such christological assertions.

CONCLUSION

Thus, we might reasonably press for some explanation as to exactly why Jesus has this central significance (i.e. what is the *ground* of their Christological affirmation?). Does he simply enlighten anthropology in virtue of the fact that he is fully human? If so, it would seem that his ability to explicate the nature of humanity is no more extensive than my own (presuming, of course, that I too am fully human). Or, is it grounded in the fact that he alone is sinlessly human? While this might be rather more helpful, it does raise the question as to whether this might only indicate that he reveals what it means to be sinlessly human in his rather limited historico-cultural location. Though interesting, this would seem to limit the extent to which these insights might be more broadly applicable. This does not mean, of course, that Jesus' full and sinless humanity cannot serve as the ground for a properly christological anthropology, only that anyone affirming the anthropological centrality of Christology owes us some explanation of why this is the case; lacking this we have no way of assessing or interacting with their claim.

Similarly, such a claim requires not only an explanation of why Jesus is anthropologically central, but also the extent to which Christology can and should inform our anthropology (i.e. the *scope* of their christological anthropology). That is, do they understand this claim to apply to every aspect of human existence, or should it be restricted to certain domains? If the latter, in what ways should it be so restricted and how do we make that determination? Again, without providing this kind of analysis, we are left wondering about the extent to which this christological affirmation has any practical value for understanding and analyzing various facets of human existence.

Finally, we might also press for more clarity regarding the way in which one goes about applying christological insights to our anthropological understanding (i.e. the *methodology* of their christological anthropology). Is it legitimate simply to adopt the observable truths of Jesus' person and work as realities generally applicable to all human persons? Surely none of these theologians intends to affirm such an overly simplified methodology. But what methodology do they affirm? What are the guidelines, if any, for moving from Christology to anthropology in a more helpful and enlightening way? Apart from some methodological reflection, it would seem that even a christological anthropology that has been well grounded and whose scope has been clearly delineated has little to offer by way of specific insight. Or, more accurately, it is limited in its ability to discriminate between those insights that are properly derived from its christological premises and those which must be challenged and set aside.

All of these questions clearly point in the same direction. If we are going to move beyond merely asserting the centrality of Jesus for understanding the human person, and engage such a claim in all of its anthropological significance, thus fully making the christocentric turn, we cannot fail to articulate clearly the *ground*, *scope*, and *methodology* of such a christological anthropology. By failing to provide this, those theologians simply affirming the anthropological centrality of Jesus seem open the criticism that they have simply voiced a theological 'slogan' void of any meaningful content.

II. Making the Turn with Barth Driving?

As we have seen, Karl Barth's anthropology is not subject to many of the concerns raised in the previous section as he devotes considerable attention to these very questions. Indeed, the rigorous consistency with which he developed especially the ground of his christological anthropology is impressive. Consequently, we have spent some time exploring the nature of his christological anthropology and some of the implications of his approach for at least one aspect of human existence, hopefully developing along a way a greater understanding of and appreciation for its fundamental anthropological significance.

None of this means, though, that we should simply adopt Barth's particular approach to developing a christological anthropology wholesale. Our primary focus in this study has been on *understanding* and *applying* Barth's anthropology as an exercise in developing a greater awareness of what a specifically christological anthropology might look like, and the resources that it has for engaging the 'mystery' of humanity. Consequently, we have spent little time discussing the adequacy of Barth's particular approach to the ground, scope, and methodology of a christological anthropology. Although a full evaluation lies well beyond the scope of this study, some comments are in order.

Unquestionably, the most thoroughly developed piece of Barth's christological anthropology is his understanding of its basic ground. Consequently, as we discussed in chapter two, he argues forcefully that Jesus is fundamentally significant for understanding all human persons because: (1) human nature is eternally grounded in the divine decree of election in which Jesus is both eternally Elector and eternally Elected; (2) human nature is eternally secure despite the ravages of sin as a result of Jesus' continued covenantal faithfulness; and (3) human nature is continually brought into being and given its covenantal shape in the divine summons that comes in and through Jesus. Together, these three constitute the pillars upon which Barth constructs his christological anthropology.

Although each of these merits a more thorough evaluation, we will restrict ourselves here to making a few interesting observations about what differing from Barth at this point might entail. First, we must recognize that these principles rise and fall together. In other words, without the first, humans would participate in the nature that Jesus faithfully preserves, but there would be no guarantee that it is what God eternally intended or intends. Lacking the second, we would be left with a mere concept of true humanity that has no real value in a sin-ridden world. And apart from the third, we would have a true humanity in which no one other than Jesus actually participates. So, although each of these theological convictions establishes a different principle, Barth's anthropology cannot stand without all three functioning together.

This leads us to a second point. We cannot simply disagree with Barth on one of these issues and continue to affirm his christological approach to anthropology. That is, should we be inclined to reject his christocentric interpretation of the doctrine of election, we *must* reject his christological anthropology as well. This does not mean, of course, that we must reject the hope of developing a christological anthropology in its entirety; it simply means that we cannot continue to affirm *Barth's* christological anthropology. This in turn means, however, that we must then go on to develop our own understanding of the ground, scope, and methodology of a christological anthropology. As we discussed at the beginning of this chapter, we cannot simply neglect this task lest we void our anthropology of any meaningful content. At the same time, we cannot continue to affirm Barth's anthropological methodology after removing the ground upon which it stands. So, we must be aware of the interdependent nature of most theological discourse and realize the implications of differing with Barth at this stage.

With similar rigor, Barth explicates the methodology of his christocentric anthropology. Thus, he argues that we must develop anthropology *from* Christology, but always in such a way that anthropology is not reduced *to* Christology. Although Jesus Christ is fully human, he is also fully divine and, therefore, distinct from all other human persons by virtue of his unique relation to God and his sinless obedience. Thus, while his full humanity means that he provides true insight into human nature, his uniqueness entails that we cannot directly infer general anthropological truths from a consideration of his person and work. Rather, any christocentric anthropology must involve a process with two distinct stages: the christological and the anthropological. Utilizing such a method, Barth is able to develop a series of key christological principles from which anthropological reflection must begin.

However clearly and insightfully explained, though, some important questions must be raised about Barth's methodology as well. First, we might ask about the christological truths that Barth utilizes as the first movement and foundation of his christological anthropology. While he clearly delineates these christological principles, we would do well to press on the extent to which these principles are sufficiently developed and defended. Thus, although Barth believes each of these principles to be biblically justified, the lack of specific exegetical argumentation for any of the principles, leads one to wish that Barth had done more to establish that these are in fact adequately grounded in the biblical testimony regarding the person and work of Christ. If these christological truths, or any other truths for that matter, are going to serve as the touchstone for a theological anthropology, more work needs to be done to ensure that they are properly grounded in the revelation of Christ, and not simply expressions of our own anthropological ideas.

It also seems reasonable to ask Barth to justify why these principles and not others have been chosen. That these are significant aspects of Jesus' life as revealed through his soteriological work is indisputable. But, it is not self-evident that these are the only possible principles or even that they are the best ones for the purposes at hand. Given the foundational role that these principles will play in the development of Barth's anthropology, one would expect a more explicit explanation of why these particular principles should be given pride of place.

Finally, we might have wished that Barth had spent more time discussing the precise way in which we make the move from Christology to anthropology. Although he is quite clear on the fact that the move cannot be a direct one because of the differences between Jesus Christ and other humans, it is this very indirectness that raises the question of the most appropriate ways in which to make this move. That there are two moments in the process is clear, how one moves from one to the other without reducing either to its counterpart is less so. Although most of III/2 can be viewed as particular case studies in the application of this methodology, which provide extensive insights into the precise way in which Barth understood and applied his methodology, a more explicit explanation and defense of the methodology itself would seem necessary if we are to be clear about what we are seeking to accomplish and how we are to go about doing that.

So, it would seem that if we are to continue in the direction that Barth has indicated, more work needs to be done regarding the nature of the methodology that we will use. We must at least determine more certainly that Barth's christological principles are in fact firmly established in the biblical text, while also exploring other christological truths that might serve equally well as fundamental starting points. And we need to work out more fully the way in which one moves from these truths to insights about human persons in general.

Regarding the scope of Barth's christological anthropology, less needs to be said. Throughout this study, we have been arguing that although Barth himself limits the application of his christological insights to certain clearly defined areas of human existence, his christological method itself is amenable to a far more extensive use. Indeed, Barth's own assertions regarding the centrality of Jesus as the starting point for properly understanding *all* the phenomena of humanity clearly indicates his openness to extending these insights far more broadly. As we press on to develop our own christological understanding of human nature, then, we must explore these other facets of human existence in light of Jesus' person and work.

As we consider the precise way in which Barth has rounded the christocentric turn, then, we can affirm that he has done much to clarify the pressing issues surrounding the *ground*, *scope*, and *methodology* of such an approach.

Yet it also seems clear that despite Barth's impressive accomplishments in this area, more work needs to be done at each point. Though a remarkably thorough theologian, Barth's treatment of Christology and its implications for theological anthropology was never intended to be comprehensive. Rather, Barth's theology in general, and his theological anthropology in particular, should be viewed as an invitation to carry on the theological task in new, and often unexpected, ways. Consequently, Barth better serves as guide than driver as we make the christocentric turn.

III. Driving Carefully around the Bend

Moving from these formal and methodological considerations into the substance of our study, we saw how Barth's christological anthropology opens the door for a fruitful engagement with questions related to human ontology. Building off the central affirmations developed from his christological reflections, Barth's approach presents a view of the mind–body relationship in which body and soul are understood to be integrally united and constantly interdependent.

As we have seen, though, his presentation does not comprise a fully worked out theory of human ontology. Throughout Barth seems more interested in presenting what *must* be affirmed about human ontology on the basis of his christological reflections than on developing a theoretically rigorous account of *how* that ontology obtains. Barth's model of the mind–body relationship, then, is better understood as providing an ontological framework within which any particular theory of human ontology must function.

This is precisely what we would expect from Barth's christological methodology. Any attempt to derive a specific theory of human ontology from Barth's christological starting point would seem to violate the principle that one cannot move directly from Christology to anthropology. Indeed, we would expect to find a similar pattern prevailing whenever one develops anthropological insights on the basis of Christology. This approach will always generate a necessary framework within which those insights must function – or, if you prefer, a christological starting point from which the anthropological insights must proceed.

This christological approach, then, should not be understood as constraining the range of human inquiry. If we have applied our christological methodology to some aspects of human experience and determined that certain portrayals of that aspect are christologically inadequate, this does not entail that we must call for the cessation of all attempts to understand the human person from that perspective. A christologically grounded anthropology will forcefully point out the problematic elements in any such theories and consistently reject them as false pictures of true humanity. Nevertheless it will affirm their right to participate in the ongoing conversation about human nature, seeking always to dialogue openly, honestly, and critically in the cooperative endeavor to understand humanity more deeply.

We saw this very form of open-but-critical interaction as we applied our christological methodology to the mind–body debate. The ontological framework derived from Barth's christological anthropology thus proved to be very useful for engaging two contemporary theories of human ontology: *nonreductive physicalism (NRP)* and *holistic dualism (HD)*. In each case, we were able to identify and address a number of salient issues as we sought to establish the christological viability of disparate perspectives on human nature.

Thus, we were able to determine that although physicalist ontologies are routinely dismissed by non-physicalist thinkers for their ostensible inability to provide any coherent account of continuous personal identity and phenomenal consciousness, we saw that this was not necessarily the case. While these are certainly challenging problems for any form of physicalism, physicalist theories do have substantial resources for addressing these issues. We were not able to consider exhaustively all of the available options, but our discussion did provide ample reason to believe that a physicalist ontology may have the necessary resources to address these problems.

A more challenging issue presented itself, however, when we turned to the question of mental causation. Nonreductive versions of mental causation seem caught in the vise created by their commitment both to the principle of a causally closed physical universe and the causal efficacy of mental realities. Although our study did not necessarily lead to the conclusion that this problem is irresolvable within the nonreductive framework, it did raise substantial questions about whether *NRP* can address this problem without sacrificing its commitment either to the causal efficacy of the mental (thus becoming a form of *reductive* physicalism) or to the causal completeness principle (thus sacrificing its standing as a *physicalist* ontology).

We similarly applied our christological analysis to the tenets of *HD*. In doing so we saw that, like *NRP*, *HD* is quite adept at responding to a number of the criticisms typically hurled its way. Nonetheless, our christological starting point pressed us to consider whether *HD* has adequate responses to some of the concerns that surround its account of mental causation and the embodiment relation. Once again we did not attempt to argue that no form of *HD* is capable of responding to these concerns, only that these concerns comprise a continued challenge faced by any theory operating with this broad framework.

Throughout the study, then, we were able to point to some specific challenges faced by *NRP* and *HD* if they are going to offer theories of human ontology that we might consider to be christologically viable. It is important to realize, though, that it is not the task of a christological anthropology to determine that either of these approaches is irredeemably beyond the pale of christological adequacy. It would seem that for it to do so it would need to generate its own particular theory of human nature, and then argue that one or both is incompatible with its own theory. We have argued, however, that this is precisely what a christological anthropology should *not* do. Consequently, rather than definitively establishing the impossibility of developing a particular theory in christologically adequate ways, the task of a christological anthropology should be construed more in terms of identifying that which must be maintained and calling on proponents of the various theories to develop ways in which their theory can do just that.

Consequently, the conclusion to our ontological investigation was necessarily limited. Rather than decisively arguing for the inadequacy of either or both sets of theories, our study simply pointed to some areas in which they seem christologically deficient. Having done this, our study must content itself to wait and see whether either approach is able to make progress toward clarity in those areas. Although this might be less than satisfying for some, it is in keeping with the picture of christological anthropology that has developed over the course of this work – one that is convinced of its christological starting point and committed to its christological conclusions, but which remains open to and constantly engaged in significant conversation with other anthropological perspectives. The task of a christological anthropology, then, is not to close doors, but to identify the doors that seem most promising and the challenges involved in going through them.

IV. *Viewing the Anthropological Panorama from around the Bend*

Once we have rounded the christological turn in our theological anthropologies, the question remains as to what lies around the bend. We have seen that Barth's own study of human nature led him to focus on the questions of ontology, relationality, and time. And certainly no one would deny that these are vital aspects of human nature. Yet, as we noted earlier in this chapter, we do not want to limit the scope of our christological anthropology to these matters alone. Indeed, we argued that a properly christological anthropology should be open to applying its insights across the whole range of human existence and experience. So, before concluding this study, it would seem appropriate to suggest a few ways in which a christological anthropology might profitably be applied to various aspects of human existence.

In our consideration of human ontology, we repeatedly encountered the question of human free will. Determining what exactly 'free' means when applied to human persons has troubled philosophers and theologians endlessly. And yet once again we find little or no effort expending in considering the implications that Christology has for our understanding of human free will. If we maintain that Jesus was fully human, as well as fully divine, and if we are going to maintain the central significance of Jesus' atoning work, what must we affirm about the nature of human free will?[1] How do we understand the relationship of the two natures in the person of Christ (if we assume a Chalcedonian framework) and even of the two wills in Christ (if we assume a dyothelite, or two-will, framework) and what significance does this have for understanding the relationship between divine willing and human freedom? Given the importance of understanding Christ's atoning work as something 'voluntarily' offered to the Father by the Son, what are the implications that this has for evaluating the adequacy of understanding human volitions in terms of their location within a broader nexus of causal events? Clearly these are questions that manifest no easy solutions; but they are, nonetheless, questions well worth exploring as we seek to understand humanity from a christological vantage point.

Drawing on Barth's relational emphasis, especially given the significance of gender for Barth's understanding of relationship, how might the person and work of Christ inform our understanding of human persons as gendered beings? Unlike the question of free will, this is actually an issue that has received some attention as theologians have sought to understand the significance of Jesus' maleness. Thus some theologians have asked whether the fact that the savior came as a man indicates something about the differences (possibly hierarchical differences) between the male and female genders. Others have taken an opposite tack and viewed Jesus' maleness as part of a subversive undermining of patriarchical structures endemic in human society (e.g. Johnson 1991; and Hilkert 1995).[2] And, of course, we could also identify not just other perspectives on this question, but a whole range of other issues relative to our understanding of gender that might usefully be engaged from a christological perspective. Indeed, the very fact that apparently opposite conclusions have resulted from an ostensibly christological perspective indicates that we might do well to reconsider this issue with a more carefully formulated understanding of the nature of a christological anthropology.

Or, we might press further into the insights of the various anthropological sciences, seeking to engage them as anthropological conversation partners. What would it mean if we were to evaluate various perspectives on the psychology of human persons in light of our affirmation that Jesus was and is fully human? How should we engage the burgeoning knowledge of human biology and the influence that it has on nearly every domain of human experience? What implications would Christology have for evaluating claims

---

[1] For a summary of some of the implications that might be raised by a christological consideration of human free will and resources related to the discussion, see Cortez 2007a.

[2] Of course, other thinkers are less positive about the benefits of even a critical appropriation of Christ's maleness as having anthropological significance (e.g. Hampson 1990; and Hopkins 1995).

that our relationship with God is determined by our 'God-gene' (Hamer 2004) or that human moral behavior is ultimately determined by our evolutionary and genetic makeup.[3]

By now it should be clear that we could extend this list indefinitely by raising questions regarding the ways in which Christology might be able to inform our views across the entire anthropological domain. We could press on to enquire about how Christology might shape our understanding of the human person as an economic being, a political being, an ecclesial being, and so forth. The point at every step, though, would be to recognize that we need to broaden the scope of our investigation and sharpen the focus of our christological vision, so that we begin to comprehend fully what it means to say that '[t]he nature of the man Jesus alone is the key to the problem of human nature' (III/2, 136).

---

[3] See esp. Wilson 2000 and Dawkins 2006.

BIBLIOGRAPHY

Abbreviations

Amer Phil Quart	*American Philosophical Quarterly*
Australasian JPhil	*Australasian Journal of Philosophy*
Can JPhil	*Canadian Journal of Philosophy*
Euro JPhil	*European Journal of Philosophy*
EvQ	*Evangelical Quarterly*
FaithPhil	*Faith and Philosophy*
HeyJ	*Heythrop Journal*
IJST	*International Journal of Systematic Theology*
Int Phil Quart	*International Philosophical Quarterly*
JAAR	*Journal of the American Academy of Religion*
JCS	*Journal of Consciousness Studies*
JETS	*Journal of the Evangelical Theological Society*
JPhil	*Journal of Philosophy*
JR	*Journal of Religion*
Midwest Stud Phil	*Midwest Studies in Philosophy*
MindLang	*Mind & Language*
ModTheol	*Modern Theology*
NTS	*New Testament Studies*
Pac Phil Quart	*Pacific Philosophical Quarterly*
Phil Phenomol Res	*Philosophy and Phenomenological Research*
Phil Psych	*Philosophical Psychology*
PhilQuart	*Philosophical Quarterly*
PhilRev	*Philosophical Review*
PhilStud	*Philosophical Studies*
Phil Topics	*Philosophical Topics*
RelS	*Religious Studies*
SJT	*Scottish Journal of Theology*
TTod	*Theology Today*

BIBLIOGRAPHY

References

Alston, William P. and Thomas W. Smythe
1994 'Swinburne's Argument for Dualism', *FaithPhil* 11: 127–33.

Anderson, Clifford
2002 'The Problem of Psychologism in Karl Barth's Doctrine of Sanctification', *Zeitschrift für Dialektische Theologie* 18: 339–52.

Anderson, Ray S.
1982 *On Being Human: Essays in Theological Anthropology* (Grand Rapids: Eerdmans).
1986 'Barth and a New Direction for Natural Theology,' in J. Thompson 1986b: 241–55.
1998 'On Being Human: The Spiritual Saga of a Creaturely Soul', in Brown, Murphy, and Malony 1998: 175–94.

Andrews, Isolde
1996 *Deconstructing Barth: A Study of the Complementary Methods in Karl Barth and Jacques Derrida* (New York: Peter Lang).

Antony, Louise
2003 'Who's Afraid of Disjunctive Properties', in Sosa and Villanueva 2003: 1–21.

Antony, Michael V.
2001 'Is "Consciousness" Ambiguous?', *JCS* 8: 19–44.

Arbib, Michael A.
2002 'Towards a Neuroscience of the Person', in Russell, *et al.* 2002: 77–100.

Armstrong, D. M.
1968 *A Materialist Theory of the Mind* (London: Routledge).
1999 *The Mind–Body Problem* (Oxford: Westview).

Atkins, Peter
1987 'Purposeless People', in Peacocke and Gillett 1987: 12–32.

Audi, Robert
1993 'Mental Causation: Sustaining and Dynamic', in Heil and Mele 1993: 53–74.

Aune, Bruce
1985 *Metaphysics: The Elements* (Minneapolis: University of Minnesota Press).

Averill, Edward and B. F. Keating
1981 'Does Interactionism Violate a Law of Classical Physics?', *Mind* 90: 102–7.

Ayala, Francisco J.
1998 'Biology Precedes, Culture Transcends: An Evolutionist's View of Human Nature', *Zygon* 33: 507–23.

Baker, Gordon and Katherine J. Morris
1996 *Descartes' Dualism* (London: Routledge).

BIBLIOGRAPHY

Baker, Lynne Rudder
- 1993 'Metaphysics and Mental Causation', in Heil and Mele 1993: 75–96.
- 1995 'Need a Christian Be a Mind/Body Dualist?', *FaithPhil* 12: 489–504.
- 1997 'Why Constitution Is Not Identity', *JPhil* 94: 599–621.
- 2000 *Persons and Bodies: A Constitution View* (Cambridge: CUP).
- 2001 'Materialism with a Human Face', in Corcoran 2001c: 159–80.
- 2004 'Christians Should Reject Mind–Body Dualism', in Peterson and VanArragon 2004: 327–37.

Balog, Katalin
- 1999 'Conceivability, Possibility, and the Mind–Body Problem', *PhilRev* 108: 497–528.

Balthasar, Hans Urs von
- 1992 *The Theology of Karl Barth* (trans. Edward T. Oakes, SJ; San Francisco: Communio).

Barbour, Ian G.
- 1974 *Myths, Models, and Paradigms* (New York: Harper & Row).

Barker, Stpehn and Phil Dowe
- 2003 'Paradoxes of Multi-Location', *Analysis* 63: 106–14.
- 2005 'Endurance is Paradoxical', *Analysis* 65: 69–74.

Barnes, Gordon
- 2002 'Conceivability, Explanation, and Defeat', *PhilStud* 108: 327–38.
- 2004 'Is Dualism Religiously and Morally Pernicious?', *American Catholic Philosophical Quarterly* 78: 99–106.

Barr, James
- 1994 *Biblical Faith and Natural Theology: The Gifford lectures for 1991* (Oxford: Clarendon).

Barth, Karl
- 1956–75 *Church Dogmatics* (eds, G. W. Bromiley and T. F. Torrance; trans. G. W. Bromiley; Edinburgh: T&T Clark).
- 1962 A Theological Dialogue. *TTod* 19 (online); http://theologytodayptsem.edu/jul1962/v19-2-article2.htm
- 1979 *Evangelical Theology* (trans. Grover Foley; Grand Rapids: Eerdmans).
- 1981 *Ethics* (trans. Dietrich Braun; Edinburgh: T&T Clark).
- 1982a 'Evangelical Theology in the 19th Century', in *The Humanity of God* (Atlanta: John Knox): 11–33.
- 1982b 'The Humanity of God', in *The Humanity of God* (Atlanta: John Knox): 37–65.
- 1986 'Fate and Idea in Theology', in Martin Rumscheidt (ed.), *The Way of Theology in Karl Barth* (Allison Park: Pickwick): 25–61.
- 1991 *The Göttingen Dogmatics* (trans. Hannelotte Reiffen; Grand Rapids: Eerdmans).
- 1995 *The Theology of John Calvin* (ed. Geoffrey W. Bromiley; Grand Rapids: Eerdmans).

BIBLIOGRAPHY

Barth, Karl and Emil Brunner
 1946 *Natural Theology: Comprising 'Nature and Grace' by Emil Brunner and the Reply 'No!' by Karl Barth* (trans. Peter Fraenkel; London: Centenary).

Baxter, Christina A.
 1986 'The Nature and Place of Scripture in the Church Dogmatics', in J. Thompson 1986b: 33–62.

Bayne, Tim and Levy Neil
 2005 'The Feeling of Doing: Deconstructing the Phenomenology of Agency' (accessed 26 May 2006) http://www.phil.mq.edu.au/staff/tbayne/deconstructing.pdf

Bealer, George
 1994 'The Rejection of the Identity Thesis', in Warner and Szubka 1994: 355–88.

Bechtel, William and Robert C. Richardson
 1998 'Vitalism', in E. Craig (ed.), *Routledge Encyclopedia of Philosophy* (accessed 5 October 2005) http://www.rep.routledge.com/article/Q109SECT4

Beckermann, Ansgar, H. Flohr, and Jaegwon. Kim (eds)
 1992 *Emergence or Reduction? Prospects of Nonreductive Physicalism* (Berlin: Walter de Gruyter).

Bennett, Karen
 2003 'Why the Exclusion Problem Seems Intractable, and How, Just Maybe, to Tract It', *Nous* 37: 471–98.
 2004 'Global Supervnience and Dependence', *Phil Phenomenol Res* LXVIII: 501–29.

Berkouwer, G. C.
 1956 *The Triumph of Grace in the Theology of Karl Barth* (London: Paternoster).
 1962 *Man: The Image of God* (Grand Rapids: Eerdmans).

Bettis, Joseph D.
 1967 'Is Karl Barth a Universalist', *SJT* 20: 423–36.

Betz, Hans Dieter
 2000 'The Concept of the "Inner Human Being" (ὁ ἔσω ἄνθρωπος) in the Anthropology of Paul', *NTS* 46: 315–41.

Bickle, John
 2002 'Multiple Realizability', in Edward N. Zalta (ed.), *Stanford Encyclopedia of Philosophy* (4 July 2006) http://plato.stanford.edu/archives/fall2002/entries/multiple-realizability/

Bielfeldt, Dennis
 2000 'The Peril and Promise of Supervenience for the Science–Theology Discussion', in Gregersen, Drees, and Görman 2000: 117–52.
 2001 'Can Western Monism Avoid Substance Dualism?', *Zygon* 36: 153–77.

BIBLIOGRAPHY

Biggar, Nigel
    1988a 'Hearing God's Command and Thinking about What's Right: With and Beyond Barth', in Biggar 1988b: 101–18.
    1988b (ed.) *Reckoning with Barth: Essays in Commemoration of the Centenary of Karl Barth's Birth* (London: Mowbray).
    1993 *The Hastening That Waits: Karl Barth's Ethics* (Oxford: Clarendon).

Blanshard, Bland
    1964 'Critical Reflections on Karl Barth', in Hick 1964: 159–200.

Block, Ned
    1978 'Troubles with Functionalism', *Minnesota Studies in the Philosophy of Science* 9: 261–325.
    1990 'Can the Mind Change the World?', in George Boolos (ed.), *Meaning and Method: Essays in Honor of Hilary Putnam* (Cambridge: CUP): 137–70.
    1994 'What Is Dennett's Theory a Theory of?', *Phil Topics* 22: 23–40.
    1995a 'How Many Concepts of Consciousness', *Behavioral and Brain Sciences* 18: 272–84.
    1995b 'On a Confusion about a Function of Consciousness', *Behavioral and Brain Sciences* 18: 227–87.
    2001 'Paradox and Cross Purposes in Recent Work on Consciousness', *Cognition* 79: 197–219.
    2002 'The Harder Problem of Consciousness', *JPhil* XCIX: 391–425.
    2003 'Do Causal Powers Drain Away?', *Phil Phenomenol Res* 67: 133–50.
    2004 'What is Functionalism?', in Heil 2004b: 183–99.
    2005 Consciousness (accessed 21 Aug 2006) http://www.nyu.edu/gsas/dept/philo/faculty/block/papers/ecs.pdf

Block, Ned and Robert Stalnaker
    1999 'Conceptual Analysis, Dualism, and the Explanatory Gap', *PhilRev* 108: 1–46.

Bloesch, Donald G.
    1992 *A Theology of Word and Spirit* (Downers Grove, Ill: InterVarsity).

Bonevac, Daniel
    1995 'Reduction in the Mind of God', in Savellos and Yalcin 1995: 124–39.

Bontly, Thomas
    2001 'Should Intentionality be Naturalized?', *Royal Institute of Philosophy Supplement* 49: 43–60.
    2002 'The Supervenience Argument Generalizes', *PhilStud* 109: 75–96.

Borenstein, Daniel B.
    2001 'Presidential Address: Bridging the Millennia: Mind Meets Brain', *American Journal of Psychiatry* 158: 1597–604.

Boyd, Ian R.
    2004 *Dogmatics among the Ruins: German Expressionism and the Enlightenment as Contexts for Karl Barth's Theological Development* (Bern: Peter Lang).

BIBLIOGRAPHY

Boyd, Jeffrey H.
1998   'A History of the Concept of the Soul During the 20th Century', *Journal of Psychology & Theology* 26: 66–82.

Braddon-Mitchell, David and Frank Jackson
1996   *The Philosophy of Mind and Cognition* (Oxford: Blackwell).

Braine, David
1992   *The Human Person: Animal and Spirit* (Notre Dame: University of Notre Dame Press).

Broad, C. D.
1925   *The Mind and its Place in Nature* (New York: Harcourt, Brace & Company).

Bromiley, Geoffrey William
1979   *An Introduction to the Theology of Karl Barth* (Grand Rapids: Eerdmans).

Brooks, D. H. M.
1994   'How to Perform a Reduction', *Phil Phenomenol Res* 54: 803–14.

Brown, Colin
1978   'Barth, Karl', in J. D. Douglas (ed.), *The New International Dictionary of the Christian Church* (2nd edn; Exeter: Paternoster Press).

Brown, Curtis
2002   'Narrow Mental Content', in Edward N. Zalta (ed.), *The Stanford Encyclopedia of Philosophy* (accessed 9 July 2006) http://plato.stanford.edu/archives/win2002/entries/content-narrow/

Brown, Robert F.
1980   'On God's Ontic and Noetic Absoluteness: A Critique of Barth', *SJT* 33: 533–49.

Brown, Warren S.
2004   'Neurobiological Embodiment of Spirituality and Soul', in Jeeves 2004a: 58–76.

Brown, Warren S., Nancey C. Murphy, and H. Newton. Malony (eds)
1998   *Whatever Happened to the Soul? Scientific and Theological Portraits of Human Nature* (Minneapolis: Fortress).

Broz, Ludek
1988   'The Present Task of Theology', *Communio Viatorum* 31: 1–30.

Brunner, Emil
1951   'The New Barth: Observations on Karl Barth's Doctrine of Man', *SJT* 4: 123–35.

Brüntrup, Godehard
1998   'Is Psycho-Physical Emergentism Committed to Dualism? The Causal Efficacy of Emergent Mental Properties', *Erkenntnis* 48: 133–51.

BIBLIOGRAPHY

Budenholzer, Frank E.
2003 'Some Comments on the Problem of Reductionism in Science', *Zygon* 38: 61–69.

Bultmann, Rudolf Karl
1951–55 *Theology of the New Testament* (2 vols; New York: Scribner).

Burge, Tyler
1979 'Individualism and the Mental', *Midwest Stud Phil* 4: 441–58.
1992 'Philosophy of Language and Mind: 1950–1990', *PhilRev* 101: 3–52.
1993 'Mind–Body Causation and Explanatory Practice', in Heil and Mele 1993: 97–120.

Burnyeat, M. F.
1992 'Is an Aristotelian Philosophy of Mind Still Credible? (A Draft)', in Nussbaum and Rorty 1992: 15–26.

Busch, Eberhard
2004 *The Great Passion: Introducing Barth's Theology* (eds, Darrell L. Guder and Judith J. Guder; Grand Rapids: Eerdmans).

Byrne, Alex
1997 'Some Like It HOT: Consciousness and Higher-Order Thoughts', *PhilStud* 86: 103–29.

Camfield, F. W.
1950 'Man in His Time', *SJT* 3: 127–48.

Campbell, Donald T.
1974 '"Downward Causation" in Hierarchically Organized Biological Systems', in F. Ayala and T. Dobzhansky (eds), *Studies in the Philosophy of Biology: Reduction and Related Problems* (Berkeley: University of California Press): 179–86.

Candlish, Stewart
2004 'Private Language', in Edward N. Zalta (ed.), *Stanford Encyclopedia of Philosophy* (accessed 30 May 2006) http://plato.stanford.edu/archives/spr2004/entries/private-language/

Carrithers, Michael, Steven Collins, and Steven Lukes (eds)
1985 *The Category of the Person* (Cambridge: CUP).

Carruthers, Peter
2001a 'Consciousness: Explaining the Phenomena', *Royal Institute of Philosophy Supplement* 49: 61–85.
2001b 'Higher-Order Theories of Consciousness', in Edward N. Zalta (ed.), *The Stanford Encyclopedia of Philosophy* (accessed 3 Sep 2006) http://plato.stanford.edu/archives/sum2001/entries/consciousness-higher/
2004 *The Nature of the Mind: An Introduction* (New York: Routledge).
2005 *Consciousness: Essays from a Higher-Order Perspective* (Oxford: OUP).

Cartwright, Nancy
1999 *The Dappled World: A Study of the Boundaries of Science* (Cambridge: CUP).

BIBLIOGRAPHY

Chalmers, David
1995 'Facing Up to the Problem of Consciousness', *JCS* 2: 200–19.
1996 *The Conscious Mind* (New York: OUP).
2002 'The Puzzle of Conscious Experience', *Scientific American* 12: 90–100.
2003 'Consciousness and its Place in Nature', in Stich and Warfield 2003: 102–42.
2004 'The Representational Character of Experience', in Leiter 2004: 153–81.

Chalmers, David J. and Frank Jackson
2001 'Conceptual Analysis and Reductive Explanation', *PhilRev* 110: 315–61.

Chamblin, J. Knox
1993 'Psychology', in Gerald H. Hawthorne (ed.), *Dictionary of Paul and His Letters* (Downers Grove: InterVarsity): 765–74.

Chisholm, Roderick M.
1976 *Person and Object* (London: Allen and Unwin).

Churchland, Patricia S.
1983 'Consciousness: The Transmutation of a Concept', *Pac Phil Quart* 64: 80–95.

Churchland, Paul
1981 'Eliminative Materialism and Propositional Attitudes', *JPhil* 78: 67–90.

Clark, David K.
2003 *To Know and Love God* (ed. John S. Feinberg; Foundations of Evangelical Theology; Wheaton: Crossway).

Clarke, F. Stuart
1984 'Christocentric Developments in the Reformed Doctrine of Predestination', *Churchman* 98: 229–45.

Clausen, Mattias
1999 'Proclamation and Communication: Apologetics After Barth?', *IJST* 1: 203–19.

Clayton, Philip
2000 'Neuroscience, the Person, and God: An Emergentist Account', *Zygon* 26: 613–53.
2004 'Natural Law and Divine Action: The Search for an Expanded Theory of Causation', *Zygon* 39: 615–37.
2005 *Mind and Emergence: From Quantum to Consciousness* (Oxford: OUP).

Cobb, John B.
1969 *God and the World* (Philadelphia: Westminster).

Cockburn, David
2001 *An Introduction to the Philosophy of Mind* (New York: Palgrave).

Colwell, John
1989 *Actuality and Provisionality: Eternity and Election in the Theology of Karl Barth* (Edinburgh: Rutherford).

BIBLIOGRAPHY

Come, Arnold Bruce
1963 *An Introduction to Barth's 'Dogmatics' for Preachers* (London: SCM).

Cooper, John W.
1982 'Dualism and the Biblical View of Human Beings', *Reformed Journal* 32: 13–6.
1988 'The Identity of Resurrected Persons: Fatal Flaw of Monistic Anthropology', *Calvin Theological Journal* 23: 19–36.
2000 *Body, Soul, and Life Everlasting* (Grand Rapids: Eerdmans).

Corcoran, Kevin
1998 'Persons and Bodies', *FaithPhil* 15: 324–40.
2001a 'Introduction: Soul or Body?', in Corcoran 2001c: 1–11.
2001b 'Physical Persons and Postmortem Survival', in Corcoran 2001c: 201–17.
2001c (ed.) *Soul, Body, and Survival: Essays on the Metaphysics of Human Persons* (Ithaca: Cornell University Press).
2005 'The Constitution View of Persons', in Green and Palmer 2005: 153–76.

Cortez, Marc
2005 'Context and Concept: Contextual Theology and the Nature of Theological Discourse', *Westminster Theological Journal* 67: 85–102.
2007a 'Incarnation and Compatibilism: Christological Implications for a Compatibilist Account of Human Free Will,' Presented at the annual conference of the Evangelical Theological Society; San Diego, CA.
2007b 'What Does It Mean to Call Karl Barth a Christocentric Theologian?', *SJT* 60: 127–43.
2008 'Body, Soul, and (Holy) Spirit: Karl Barth's Theological Framework for Understanding Human Ontology', *IJST* (forthcoming).

Crane, Tim
1994 'Physicalism (2): Against Physicalism', in Samuel D. Guttenplan (ed.), *A Companion to the Philosophy of Mind* (Oxford: Blackwell): 459–83.
1995 'The Mental Causation Debate', *Proceedings of the Aristotelian Society Supplementary Volume*, LXIX: 211–36.
1998 'Intentionality as the Mark of the Mental', in Anthony O'Hear (ed.), *Current Issues in the Philosophy of Mind* (Royal Institute of Philosophy Supplement 43; Cambridge: CUP): 229–51.
2000 'The Origins of Qualia', in Crane and Patterson 2000: 169–94.
2001 *Elements of Mind* (Oxford: OUP).
2003 'Mental Substances', in Anthony O'Hear (ed.), Minds and Persons (Cambridge: CUP): 229–51.
2004 'Mental Substances', in Anthony O'Hear (ed.), *Minds and Persons* (Cambridge: CUP): 229–50.
2005 'Intentionality', in E. Craig (ed.), *Routledge Encyclopedia of Philosophy* (accessed 16 May 2005) http://www.rep.routledge.com/article/V019SECT3

Crane, Tim and Sarah Patterson (eds)
2000 *History of the Mind–Body Problem* (eds, Jonathan Wolff, Tim Crane, M. W. F. Stone, and Tom Pink; London Studies in the History of Philosophy, Vol. 3; London: Routledge).

BIBLIOGRAPHY

Crawford, Robert S.
1972 'Theological Method of Karl Barth', *SJT* 25: 320–36.

Crick, Francis
1994 *The Astonishing Hypothesis* (London: Simon & Schuster).

Crick, Francis and C. Koch
1990 'Toward a Neurobiological Theory of Consciousness', *Seminars in Neuroscience* 2: 263–75.

Cullen, Lindsay
2001 'Nancey Murphy, Supervenience, and Causality', *Science and Christian Belief* 13: 39–50.

Cullmann, Oscar
1958 *Immortality of the Soul or Resurrection of the Dead?* (London: Epworth).

Cunningham, Mary Kathleen
1995 *What is Theological Exegesis? Interpretation and Use of Scripture in Barth's Doctrine of Election* (Valley Forge: Trinity Press International).

Cushman, Robert E.
1981 'The Doctrine of God and Man in the Light of Barth's Pneumatology', in *Faith Seeking Understanding* (Durham: Duke University Press): 156–67.

Dalferth, Ingolf U.
1989 'Karl Barth's Eschatological Realism', in Sykes 1989a: 14–45.

Damasio, Antonio R.
1994 *Descartes' Error: Emotion, Reason, and the Human Brain* (New York: G. P. Putnam).
1999 *The Feeling of What Happens* (San Diego: Harcourt).

Davidson, Donald
1980 *Essays on Actions and Events* (Oxfod: OUP).
1993 'Thinking Causes', in Heil and Mele 1993: 3–18.

Davidson, Ivor
2001 'Theologizing the Human Jesus: An Ancient (and Modern) Approach to Christology Reassessed', *IJST* 3: 129–54.

Davis, Stephen T.
1986 'Is Personal Identity Retained in the Resurrection?', *ModTheol* 2: 329–40.
1989 'The Resurrection of the Dead', in Stephen T. Davis (ed.), *Death and Afterlife* (Basingstoke: Macmillan): 119–44.
2001 'Pysicalism and Resurrection', in Corcoran 2001c: 229–48.

Dawkins, Richard
2006 *The Selfish Gene: 20th Anniversary Edition* (Oxford: OUP).

de Leon, David
2001 'The Qualities of Qualia', *Communication and Cognition* 34: 121–38.

Deddo, Gary W.
1994 'The Grammar of Barth's Theology of Personal Relations', *SJT* 47: 183–222.

BIBLIOGRAPHY

Deegan, Daniel Lee
1961 'Christological Determinant in Barth's Doctrine of Creation', *SJT* 14: 119–35.

Dennett, Daniel
1978 'Current Issues in the Philosophy of Mind', *Amer Phil Quart* 15: 249–61.
1979 'On the Absence of Phenomenology', in Donald F. Gustafson (ed.), *Body, Mind, and Method: Essays in Honor of Virgil Aldrich* (Boston: Reidel): 93–114.
1983 'Current Issues in the Philosophy of Mind', in Kenneth G. Lucey and Tibor R. Machan (eds), *Recent Work in Philosophy* (Totowa: Rowman & Allenheld): 321–46.
1991 *Consciousness Explained* (London: Allen Lane).
1992 'The Self as a Center of Narrative Gravity', in F. Kessel, P. Cole, and D. Johnson (eds), *Self and Consciousness: Multiple Perspectives* (Hillsdale: Erlbaum): 103–115.
2001 'The Zombic Hunch: Extinction of an Intuition?', *Royal Institute of Philosophy Supplement* 48: 27–43.
2003 *Freedom Evolves* (New York: Viking).

Diem, H.
1976 'Karl Barth as a Socialist: Controversy over a New Attempt to Understand Him', in George Hunsinger (ed.), *Karl Barth and Radical Politics* (Philadelphia: Westminster): 121–38.

Dorman, Ted M.
1997 'The Light of God and the Lights of Creation in the Theology of Karl Barth', Paper Presented at the ETS National Convention in Santa Clara, CA (Nov 20–22, 1997; Portland, OR).

Dorrien, Gary J.
1997 'The "Postmodern" Barth', *Christian Century* 114: 338–43.
2000 *The Barthian Revolt in Modern Theology* (Louisville: Westminster John Knox).

Dretske, Fred
1993 'Mental Events as Structuring Causes of Behaviour', in Heil and Mele 1993: 121–36.
1995 *Naturalizing the Mind* (Cambridge: MIT Press).

Duke, James O. and Robert F. Streetman (eds)
1988 *Barth and Schleiermacher: Beyond the Impasse?* (Philadelphia: Fortress).

Dulles, Avery
1974 *Models of the Church* (Garden City: Doubleday).

Ebneter, Albert
1952 *Der Mensch in der Theologie Karl Barths* (Zurich oJ).

Eccles, John C.
1979 *The Human Mystery* (Berlin: Springer-Verlag).

BIBLIOGRAPHY

Ehring, Douglas
    2003   'Part-Whole Physicalism and Mental Causation', *Synthese* 136: 359–88.

Eichrodt, Walther
    1951   *Man in the Old Testament* (London: SCM).

Elder, Crawford L.
    2001   'Mental Causation versus Physical Causation: No Contest', *Phil Phenomenol Res* 62: 111–27.

Ellis, Ralph
    2000   'Consciousness, Self-Organization, and the Process-Substratum Relation: Rethinking Nonreductive Physicalism', *Phil Psych* 13: 173–90.

Erickson, Millard J.
    1998   *Christian Theology* (2nd edn; Grand Rapids: Baker).

Feigl, Herbert
    1958   'The "Mental" and the "Physical" ', in Herbert Feigl, Grover Maxwell and Michael Scriven (eds), *Minnesota Studies in the Philosophy of Science* (Minneapolis: University of Minnesota Press): 370–497

Feinberg, Todd E.
    2001   *Altered Egos: How the Brain Creates the Self* (Oxford: OUP).

Field, Hartry
    2005   'Causation in a Physical World', in Loux and Zimmerman 2003: 435–61.

Fink, Hans
    2006   'Three Sorts of Naturalism', *Euro JPhil* 14.2: 202–21.

Fisher, Simon
    1988   *Revelatory Positivism? Barth's Earliest Theology and the Marbug School* (Oxford: OUP).

Flanagan, Owen J.
    1984   *The Science of the Mind* (Cambridge: MIT Press).
    1992   *Consciousness Reconsidered* (Cambridge: MIT Press).
    2002   *The Problem of the Soul* (New York: Basic).

Flew, Antony
    1967   'Immortality', in Paul Edwards (ed.), *The Encyclopedia of Philosophy* (4 vols; London, New York: Collier Macmillan).

Fodor, Jerry
    1974   'Special Sciences, or the Disunity of Science as a Working Hypothesis', *Synthese* 28: 97–115.
    1981   'The Mind–Body Problem', *Scientific American* 244: 124–32.
    1983   *The Modularity of Mind* (Cambridge: MIT Press).
    1987   *Psychosemantics: The Problem of Meaning in the Philosophy of Mind* (Cambridge: MIT Press).

Ford, D. F.
    1979a   'Barth's Interpretation of the Bible', in Sykes 1979b: 55–87.
    1979b   'Conclusion: Assessing Barth', in Sykes 1979b: 194–202.

BIBLIOGRAPHY

Foster, John
- 1968 'Psychophysical Causal Relations', *Amer Phil Quart* 5: 64–70.
- 1989 'A Defense of Dualism', in Smythies and Beloff 1989: 1–23.
- 1991 *The Immaterial Self: A Defense of the Cartesian Dualist Conception of the Mind* (London: Routledge).
- 1994 'The Token-Identity Thesis', in Warner and Szubka 1994: 299–310.
- 2001 'A Brief Defense of the Cartesian View', in Corcoran 2001c: 15–29.

Frede, Michael
- 1992 'Aristotle's Conception of the Soul', in Nussbaum and Rorty 1992: 93–107.

Frei, Hans
- 1988 'Barth and Schleiermacher: Divergence and Convergence', in Duke and Streetman 1988: 65–87.
- 1993 *Theology and Narrative: Selected Essays* (eds, George Hunsinger and William C. Placher; New York: OUP).
- 2005 'Analogy and the Spirit in the Theology of Karl Barth', (accessed (10 Feb 2005) http://www.library.yale.edu/div/Freiindex.htm

Frey, Christopher
- 1978 'Zur theologischen Anthropologie Karl Barths', *Neue Zeitschrift für systematische Theologie und Religionsphilosophie* 20: 253–77.

Freyer, Von Thomas
- 1991 'Der Mensch "unter dem Himmel auf der Erde": Zur Ontologie des Menschen bei Karl Barth', *Catholica* 45: 192–213.

Friedmann, Edgar Herbert
- 1972 *Christologie und Anthropologie: Methode und Bedeutung der Lehre vom Menschen in der Theologie Karl Barths* (Munsterschwarzach: Vier Turme).

Garcia-Carpintero, Manuel
- 2003 'Qualia that It Is Right to Quine', *Philosophy and Phenomenlogical Research* 68: 357–77.

Gazzaniga, Michael S. (ed.)
- 1997 *Conversations in the Cognitive Neurosciences* (Cambridge: MIT Press).
- 1992 *Nature's Mind: The Biological Roots of Thinking, Sexuality, Language and Intelligence* (New York: Basic).

Geach, Peter
- 1967 'Identity', *The Review of Metaphysics* 21: 3–12.
- 1968 *Reference and Generality: An Examination of Some Medieval and Modern Theories* (3rd edn; Ithaca: Cornell University Press).

Gendler, Tamar and John O'Leary-Hawthorne (eds)
- 2002 *Conceivability and Possibility* (Oxford: OUP).

Gertler, Brie
- 2002 'Explanatory Reduction, Conceptual Analysis, and Conceivability Arguments about the Mind', *Nous* 36: 22–49.

BIBLIOGRAPHY

Gibbs, John G.
1963 'Secondary Point of Reference in Barth's Anthropology', *SJT* 16: 132–5.

Gill, Theodore A.
1986 'Barth and Mozart', *TTod* 43: 403–11.

Gillett, Carl
2003 'Non-Reductive Realization and Non-Reductive Identity: What Physicalism does Not Entail', in Sven Walter and Heinz-Deiter Heckmann (eds), *Physicalism and Mental Causation* (Charlottesville: Imprint Academic): 23–9.

Godlove, Terry
1984 'In What Sense Are Religions Conceptual Frameworks?', *JAAR* 52: 289–305.

Goetz, Stewart
1994 'Dualism, Causation and Supervenience', *FaithPhil* 11: 92–108.
2001 'Modal Dualism: A Critique', in Corcoran 2001c: 89–104.
2005 'Substance Dualism', in Green and Palmer 2005: 33–64.

Gorringe, Timothy
1999 *Karl Barth: Against Hegemony* (Oxford: OUP).
2004 'Culture and Barbarism: Barth amongst the Students of Culture', in McDowell and Higton (2004): 40–52.

Graham, George
1998 *Philosophy of Mind: An Introduction* (2nd edn; Malden: Blackwell).

Green, Clifford
2004 'Freedom for Humanity: Karl Barth and the Politics of the New World Order', in Hunsinger 2004a: 89–108.

Green, Joel B.
1998 '"Bodies—That Is, Human Lives": A Re-Examination of Human Nature in the Bible', in Brown, Murphy and Malony 1998: 149–73.
2002a 'Eschatology and the Nature of Humans: A Reconsideration of Pertinent Biblical Evidence', *Science & Christian Belief* 14: 33–51.
2002b 'Restoring the Human Person: New Testament Voices for a Wholistic and Social Anthropology', in Russell, *et al.* 2002: 3–22.
2004a 'Resurrection of the Body: New Testament Voices Concerning Personal Continuity and the Afterlife', in Green 2004b: 85–100.
2004b (ed.) *What about the Soul? Neuroscience and Christian Anthropology* (Nashville: Abingdon).
2004c 'What Does it Mean to Be Human? Another Chapter in the Ongoing Interaction of Science and Scripture', in Jeeves 2004a: 179–98.
2005 'Body and Soul, Mind and Brain: Critical Issues', in Green and Palmer 2005: 7–32.

Green, Joel B. and Stuart L. Palmer (eds)
2005 *In Search of the Soul: Four Views of the Mind–Body Problem* (Downers Grove: InterVarsity).

BIBLIOGRAPHY

Gregersen, Niels Henrik
2000 'God's Public Traffic: Holist versus Physicalist Supervenience', in Gregersen, Drees, and Görman 2000: 153–88.

Gregersen, Niels Henrik, Willem B. Drees, and Ulf Görman (eds)
2000 *The Human Person in Science and Theology* (Grand Rapids: Eerdmans, 2000).

Grenz, Stanley J.
1994 *Theology for the Community of God* (Carlisle: Paternoster).
2000 *Renewing the Center: Evangelical Theology in a Post-Theological Age* (Grand Rapids: Baker).
2001 *The Social God and the Relational Self* (Louisville: Westminster John Knox).
2004 'Jesus as the Imago Dei: Image-of-God Christology and the Non-Linear Linearity of Theology', *JETS* 47: 617–28.
2005 *The Named God and the Question of Being: A Trinitarian Theo-Ontology* (Lousiville: Westminster John Knox).

Gundry, Robert H.
1976 *Soma in Biblical Theology, with Emphasis on Pauline Anthropology* (Cambridge: CUP).

Gunton, Colin
1989 'The Triune God and the Freedom of the Creature', in Sykes 1989a: 46–68.

Gutenson, Charles E.
2004 'Time, Eternity, and Personal Identity: The Implications of Trinitarian Theology', in Green 2004b: 117–32.

Haldane, John
1991 'Incarnational Anthropology', in D. Cockburn (ed.), *Human Beings* (Cambridge: CUP): 191–212.
2000 'The State and the Fate of Philosophy of Mind', *Amer Phil Quart* 37: 301–12.

Hamer, Dean H.
2004 *The God Gene: How Faith Is Hardwired into our Genes* (New York: Doubleday).

Hampson, Margaret Daphne
1990 *Theology and Feminism* (Oxford: Blackwell).

Hansen, Carsten Martin
2000 'Between a Rock and a Hard Place: Mental Causation and the Mind–Body Problem', *Inquiry* 43: 451–92.

Harre, Rom
1987 'Persons and Selves', in Peacocke and Gillett 1987: 99–115.
2001 'Active Powers and Powerful Actors', *Royal Institute of Philosophy Supplement* 48: 91–109.

BIBLIOGRAPHY

Harris, Murray J.
    1983   *Raised Immortal: Resurrection and Immortality in the New Testament* (London: Marshall, Morgan, & Scott).

Harry, Deutsch
    2002   'Relative Identity', in Edward N. Zalta (ed.), *The Stanford Encyclopedia of Philosophy* (accessed 10 May 2006) http://plato.stanford.edu/archives/sum2002/entries/identity-relative/

Hart, John W.
    2001   *Karl Barth vs. Emil Brunner: The Formation and Dissolution of a Theological Alliance, 1916–1936* (New York: Peter Lang).

Hart, Trevor
    1999   *Regarding Karl Barth: Essays Toward a Reading of His Theology* (Carlisle: Paternoster).

Hart, W. D.
    1988   *The Engines of the Soul* (Cambridge: CUP).

Hartwell, Herbert
    1964   *The Theology of Karl Barth* (London: Gerald Duckworth & Co).

Hasker, William
    1995   'Concerning the Unity of Consciousness', *FaithPhil* 12: 532–47.
    1998   'Swinburne's Modal Argument for Dualism: Epistemically Circular', *FaithPhil* 15: 366–70.
    1999   *The Emergent Self* (Ithaca: Cornell University Press).
    2001   'Persons as Emergent Substances', in Corcoran 2001c: 107–19.
    2005   'On Behalf of Emergent Dualism', in Green and Palmer 2005: 75–100.

Hauerwas, Stanley
    2001   *With the Grain of the Universe: The Church's Witness and Natural Theology: Being the Gifford Lectures Delivered at the University of St. Andrews in 2001* (Grand Rapids: Brazos).

Haugeland, John
    1982   'Weak Supervenience', *Amer Phil Quart* 19: 93–103.

Heckel, Theo K.
    2000   'Body and Soul in Saint Paul', in Wright and Potter 2000: 117–32.

Heil, John
    1987   'Are We Brains in a Vat? Top Philosopher Says, "No!"', *Can JPhil* 17: 427–36.
    2003   'Mental Causation', in Stich and Warfield 2003: 214–34.
    2004a   *Philosophy of Mind: A Contemporary Introduction* (2nd edn; London: Routledge).
    2004b   (ed.) *Philosophy of Mind: A Guide and Anthology* (Oxford: OUP).

Heil, John and Alfred Mele (eds)
    1993   *Mental Causation* (Oxford: Clarendon, 1993).

BIBLIOGRAPHY

Hendry, George
 1984 'The Transcendental Method in the Theology of Karl Barth', *SJT* 37: 213–27.

Herbert, R. T.
 1998 'Dualism/Materialism', *PhilQuart* 48: 145–58.

Hick, John (ed.)
 1964 *Faith and the Philosophers* (London: Macmillan).
 1976 *Death and Eternal Life* (London: Collins).

Higton, Mike
 2004 'The Fulfilment of History in Barth, Frei, Auerbach and Dante', in McDowell and Higton 2004: 120–41.

Hilkert, Mary Catherine
 1995 'Cry Beloved Image: Rethinking the Image of God', in Ann Elizabeth O'Hara Graff (ed.), *In the Embrace of God: Feminist Approaches to Theological Anthropology* (Maryknoll: Orbis): 190–205.

Himma, Kenneth Einar
 2005 'What is a Problem for All is a Problem for None: Substance Dualism, Physicalism, and the Mind–Body Problem', *Amer Phil Quart* 42: 81–92.

Hirst, R. J.
 2004 'Mind and Body', in Heil 2004b: 105–15.

Hodgson, David
 1991 *The Mind Matters: Consciousness and Choice in a Quantum World* (Oxford: Clarendon).

Hoekema, Anthony A.
 1986 *Created in God's Image* (Grand Rapids: Eerdmans).

Hoffman, Joshua and Gary Rosenkrantz
 1991 'Are Souls Unintelligible?', *Philosophical Perspectives* 5: 183–212.
 1997 *Substance: Its Nature and Existence* (London: Routledge).

Holder, Rodney
 2001 'Karl Barth and the Legitimacy of Natural Theology', *Themelios* 26: 22–37.

Honderich, Ted
 1994 'Functionalism, Identity Theories, The Union Theory', in Warner and Szubka 1994: 215–35.
 2001 'Consciousness as Existence, and the End of Intentionality', *Royal Institute of Philosophy Supplement* 48: 1–26.

Hopkins, Julie
 1995 *Towards a Feminist Christology* (London: SPCK).

Horgan, Terrence
 1981 'Token Physicalism, Supervenience, and the Generality of Physics', *Syntheses* 49L: 395–413.
 1982 'Supervenience and Microphysics', *Pac Phil Quart* 63: 29–43.

1993a 'From Supervenience to Superdupervenience: Meeting the Demands of a Material World', *Mind* 102: 555–87.
1993b 'Nonreductive Materialism and the Explanatory Autonomy of Psychology', in Stephen J. Wagner and Richard Warner (eds), *Naturalism: A Critical Appraisal* (Notre Dame: University of Notre Dame Press): 295–320.
1994 'Nonreductive Materialism', in Warner and Szubka 1994: 236–41.
1995 'Supervenience', in Robert Audi (ed.), *The Cambridge Dictionary of Philosophy* (Cambridge: CUP): 778–79.
1997 'Kim on Mental Causation and Causal Exclusion', *Philosophical Perspectives* 11: 165–84.

Hornsby, Jennifer
1993 'Agency and Causal Explanation', in Heil and Mele 1993: 161–88.

Hume, David
1911 *A Treatise on Human Nature* (London: Dent).

Humphrey, Nicholas
1999 *A History of the Mind: Evolution and the Birth of Consciousness* (New York: Copernicus).
2000 'How to Solve the Mind–Body Problem', *JCS* 7: 5–20.

Hunsinger, George
1991 *How to read Karl Barth: The Shape of His Theology* (Oxford: OUP).
2000a 'Beyond Literalism and Expressivism', in *Disruptive Grace: Studies in the Theology of Karl Barth* (Grand Rapids: Eerdmans): 210–25.
2000b 'Karl Barth's Christology: Its Basic Chalcedonian Character', in *Disruptive Grace: Studies in the Theology of Karl Barth* (Grand Rapids: Eerdmans): 131–47.
2000c 'The Mediator of Communion: Karl Barth's Doctrine of the Holy Spirit', in Webster 2000b: 127–42.
2000d 'What Karl Barth Learned from Martin Luther', in *Disruptive Grace: Studies in the Theology of Karl Barth* (Grand Rapids: Eerdmans): 279–304.
2004a (ed.) *For the Sake of the World* (Grand Rapids: Eerdmans).
2004b 'Mysterium Trinitatis: Barth's Conception of Eternity', in Hunsinger 2004a: 165–90.

Hutto, Daniel D.
1997 'The Story of the Self: The Narrative Basis of Self-Development', in Karl Simms (ed.), *Ethics and the Subject* (ed. Myriam Diaz-Diocaretz; Critical Studies, vol. 8; Amsterdam: Rodopi): 61–76.

Hyslop, Alec
2005 'Other Minds', in Edward N. Zalta (ed.), *Stanford Encyclopedia of Philosophy* accessed 16 March 2006) http://plato.stanford.edu/archives/win2005/entries/other-minds/

Jackson, Frank
1982 'Epiphenomenal Qualia', *PhilQuart* 32: 127–36.
1986 'What Mary Didn't Know', *JPhil* 83: 191–5.
1996 'Mental Causation', *Mind* 105: 377–414.

BIBLIOGRAPHY

Jackson, Frank and Philip Pettit
1990 'Program Explanation: A General Perspective', *Analysis* 50: 107–17.

Jantzen, Grace
1984 *God's World, God's Body* (Philadelphia: Westminster).

Jeeves, Malcolm
1998 'Brain, Mind, and Behavior', in Brown, Murphy, and Malony 1998: 73–98.
2004a (ed.) *From Cells to Souls, and Beyond: Changing Portraits of Human Nature* (Grand Rapids: Eerdmans).
2004b 'Human Nature: An Integrated Picture', in Green 2004b: 171–90.
2004c 'Mind Reading and Soul Searching in the Twenty-First Century: The Scientific Evidence', in Green 2004b: 13–30.

Jenson, Robert W.
1969 *God after God: The God of the Future and the God of the Past Seen in the Theology of Karl Barth* (Indianapolis: Bobbs-Merrill).
1997 'Karl Barth', in David Ford (ed.), *The Modern Theologians: An Introduction to Christian Theology in the Twentieth Century* (2nd edn; Cambridge: Blackwell): 23–49.
2003 *On Thinking the Human: Resolutions of Difficult Notions* (Grand Rapids: Eerdmans).

Jewett, Paul K. and Marguerite Shuster
1996 *Who We Are: Our Dignity as Human* (Grand Rapids: Eerdmans).

Jewett, Robert
1971 *Paul's Anthropological Terms* (Leiden: Brill).

Johnson, Elizabeth A.
1991 'The Maleness of Christ', in Anne Carr and Elisabeth Schüssler Fiorenza (eds), *The Special Nature of Women?* (London: SCM): 108–16.

Johnson, William Stacy
1997 *The Mystery of God: Karl Barth and the Postmodern Foundations of Theology* (Louisville: Westminster John Knox).

Jones, Todd
2003 'The Virtues of Nonreduction, Even When Reduction Is a Virtue', *The Philosophical Forum* 34: 121–40.

Jüngel, Eberhard
1986 *Karl Barth, a Theological Legacy* (trans. Garrett E. Paul; Philadelphia: Westminster Press).
2001 *God's Being Is in Becoming: The Trinitarian Being of God in the Theology of Karl Barth* (trans. John Webster; Grand Rapids: Eerdmans).

Kapitan, Tomis
1991 'Agency and Omniscience', *RelS* 27: 105–20.

Kaufman, Gordon D.
1993 *In Face of Mystery: A Constructive Theology* (Cambridge: Havard University Press).

BIBLIOGRAPHY

Kelsey, David
    1975 *The Uses of Scripture in Recent Theology* (Philadelphia: Fortress).

Kerr, Fergus
    2002 'The Modern Philosophy of Self in Recent Theology', in Russell *et al.* 2002: 23–44.

Kim, Jaegwon
    1991 'Supervenience' in Hans Burkhardt and Barry Smith (eds), Handbook of Metaphysics and Ontology (Munich: Philosophia Verlag): 119–138.
    1993a 'Can Supervenience and "Non-Strict Laws" Save Anomalous Monism?', in Heil and Mele 1993: 19–26.
    1993b 'The Non-Reductivist's Troubles with Mental Causation', in Heil and Mele 1993: 189–210.
    1993c *Supervenience and Mind: Selected Philosophical Essays* (Cambridge: CUP).
    1994 'The Myth of Nonreductive Materialism', in Warren and Szubka 1994: 242–60.
    1996 *Philosophy of Mind* (Boulder: Westview).
    1997 'Does the Problem of Mental Causation Generalize?', *Proceedings of the Aristotelian Society* 97: 281–97.
    1998a 'The Mind–Body Problem after Fifty Years', *Royal Institute of Philosophy Supplement* 43: 3–21.
    1998b *Mind in a Physical World* (Cambridge: MIT Press).
    1999 'Making Sense of Emergence', *PhilStud* 95: 3–36.
    2001 'Lonely Souls: Causality and Substance Dualism', in Corcoran 2001c: 30–43.
    2003 'Blocking Causal Drainage and Other Maintenance Chores with Mental Causation', *Phil Phenomenol Res* 67: 151–76.
    2004 'The Mind–Body Problem at Century's Turn', in Leiter 2004: 129–52.

Kincade, James
    1960 'Karl Barth and Philosophy', *JR* 40: 161–9.

Kind, Amy
    2004 'The Metaphysics of Personal Identity and Our Special Concern for the Future', *Metaphilosophy* 35: 536–54.

Kirk, Robert
    1996 'How Physicalists Can Avoid Reductionism', *Synthese* 108: 157–70.
    2000 'Nonreductive Physicalism and Strict Implication', *Australasian JPhil* 79: 544–52.

Knitter, Paul F.
    1983 'Theocentric Christology', *TTod* 40: 130–49.

Knobe, Joshua M.
    2005 'Intentional Action', in *Dictionary of the Philosophy of Mind* (accessed 27 May 2005) http://artsci.wustl.edu/~philos/MindDict/intentionalaction.html

Kripke, Saul A.
    1971 'Identity and Necessity', in Milton Karl Munitz (ed.), *Identity and Individuation* (New York: New York University Press).
    1980 *Naming and Necessity* (Oxford: Blackwell).

BIBLIOGRAPHY

Krötke, Wolf
2000 'The Humanity of the Human Person in Karl Barth's Anthropology', in Webster 2000b: 159–176.

Kuhn, Thomas S.
1970 *The Structure of Scientific Revolutions* (2nd edn; Chicago: University of Chicago Press).

Kümmel, Werner Georg
1963 *Man in the New Testament* (trans. John J. Vincent; London: Epworth).

Lampe, G.
1961 *A Patristic Greek Lexicon Greek–English Lexicon* (Oxford: Clarendon).

Langsam, Harold
2001 'Strategy for Dualism', *Metaphilosophy* 32: 395–418.

Larmer, Robert
1986 'Mind–Body Interaction and the Conservation of Energy', *Int Phil Quart* 26: 277–85.

Latham, Noa
2003 'What is Token Physicalism?', *Pac Phil Quart* 84: 270–91.

Lau, Joe
2004 'Externalism about Mental Content', in Edward N. Zalta (ed.), *The Stanford Encyclopedia of Philosophy* (accessed 6 April 2005). http://plato.stanford.edu/archives/fall2004/entries/content-externalism/

Lauber, David
2004 *Barth on the Descent into Hell: God, Atonement, and the Christian Life* (Aldershot: Ashgate).

LeDoux, Joseph E.
2002a 'Emotions – A View through the Brain', Russell, *et al.* 2002: 101–18.
2002b 'Emotions: How I've Looked for Them in the Brain', Russell, *et al.* 2002: 41–56.

Leftow, Brian
2001 'Souls Dipped in Dust', in Corcoran 2001c: 120–38.

Leiter, Brian (ed.)
2004 *The Future for Philosophy* (Oxford: OUP).

Leiter, Brian and Alexander Miller
1998 'Closet Dualism and Mental Causation', *Can JPhil* 28: 161–82.

LePore, Ernest and Brian Loewer
1989 'More on Making Mind Matter', *Phil Topics* 17: 175–91.

Levin, Michael E.
1979 *Metaphysics and the Mind–Body Problem* (Oxford: Clarendon).

Levine, Joseph
1983 'Materialism and Qualia: The Explanatory Gap', *Pac Phil Quart* 64: 354–61.

1986 'Could Love Be Like a Heatwave?: Physicalism and the Subjective Character of Experience', *PhilStud* 49: 245–61.

Lewis, David
1966 'An Argument for the Identity Theory', *JPhil* 63: 17–25.
1983 *Philosophical Papers, vol. 1* (Oxford: OUP).

Lewis, Gordon R.
2003 'Is Propositional Revelation Essential to Evangelical Spiritual Formation', *JETS* 46: 269–98.

Lewis, Hywel D.
1973 *The Self and Immortality* (London: Macmillan).
1982 *The Elusive Self* (London: Macmillan).

Libet, Benjamin, Anthony Freeman, and Keith Sutherland
1999 *The Volitional Brain: Towards a Neuroscience of Free Will* (Thorverton: Imprint Academic).

Loar, Brian
1997 'Phenomenal States', in Ned Block (ed.), *The Nature of Consciousness: Philosophical Debates* (Cambridge: MIT Press): 597–616.
1990 'Phenomenal States', *Philosophical Perspectives* 4: 81–108.
1999 'David Chalmers' The Conscious Mind', *Phil Phenomenol Res* 59: 465–72.

Lockwood, Michael
1989 *Mind, Brain and the Quantum* (Oxford: Basil Blackwell).

Lormand, Eric
1998 'Consciousness', in E. Craig (ed.), *Routledge Encyclopedia of Philosophy*, edited by E. Craig (accessed 5 June 2005) http://www.rep.routledge.com/article/W011?ssid=119676492&n=1&authstatuscode=202

Loughlin, Gerard
1985 'Persons and Replicas', *ModTheol* 1: 303–19.

Loux, Michael J. and Dean W. Zimmerman (eds)
2003 *The Oxford Handbook of Metaphysics* (Oxford: OUP).

Lowe, E. J.
1992 'The Problem of Psychophysical Causation', *Australasian JPhil* 70: 263–76.
1993 'The Causal Autonomy of the Mental', *Mind* 102: 629–45.
1995 'Self', in Ted Honderich (ed.), *The Oxford Companion to Philosophy* (New York: OUP): 816–7.
2000 *An Introduction to the Philosophy of Mind* (Cambridge: CUP).
2001 'Identity, Composition, and the Simplicity of the Self', in Corcoran 2001c: 139–58.
2003 'Personal Agency', *Royal Institute of Philosophy Supplement* 53: 211–28.
2004 'Non-Cartesian Dualism', in Heil 2004b: 850–65.

Lowe, Walter J.
1988 'Barth as a Critic of Dualism: Re-Reading the Römerbrief', *SJT* 41: 377–95.

1993 *Theology and Difference: The Wound of Difference* (Bloomington: Indiana University Press).

Ludlow, Peter, Yujin Nagasawa, and Daniel. Stoljar (eds)
2004 *There's Something about Mary: Essays on Phenomenal Consciousness and Frank Jackson's Knowledge Argument* (Cambridge: MIT Press).

Lycan, William G.
1987 *Consciousness* (Cambridge: MIT).
1995 'A Limited Defense of Phenomenal Information', in Thomas Metzinger (ed.), *Conscious Experience* (Paderborn Thorverton: Schöningh Imprint Academic): 243–58.
1996 *Consciousness and Experience* (Cambridge: MIT Press).
2001 'Have We Neglected Phenomenal Consciousness?', *Psyche* 7 available at: http://psyche.cs.monash.edu.au/v7/psyche-7-03-lycan.html
2005 'The Plurality of Consciousness' (accessed 25 May 2005) http://www.unc.edu/~ujanel/CogThs.html

Lynch, Michael P. and Joshua M. Glasgow
2003 'The Impossibility of Superdupervenience', *PhilStud* 113: 201–22.

MacDonald, Paul S.
2003 *History of the Concept of Mind: Speculations about Soul, Mind and Spirit from Homer to Hume* (Aldershot: Ashgate).

Machuga, Ric
2002 *In Defense of the Soul: What It Means to Be Human* (Grand Rapids: Brazos).

MacIntyre, Alsadair
1989 'The Virtues, the Unity of a Human Life and the Concept of a Tradition', in Stanley Hauerwas and L. Gregory Jones (eds), *Why Narrative?* (Grand Rapids: Eerdmans).

Macken, John
1990 *The Autonomy Theme in the Church Dogmatics* (Cambridge: CUP).

Macmurray, John
1957 *The Self as Agent* (London: Faber & Faber).
1961 *Persons in Relation* (London: Faber).

Macquarrie, John
1979 'The Humility of God', in Durstan R. McDonald (ed.), *The Myth/Truth of God Incarnate* (Wilton: Morehouse-Barlow Co): 13–25.
1982 *In Search of Humanity: A Theological and Philosophical Approach* (London: SCM).

Madell, Geoffrey
1989 'Personal Identity and the Mind–Body Problem', in Smythies and Beloff 1989: 26–41.

Mangina, Joseph L.
2001 *Karl Barth on the Christian life* (New York: Peter Lang).

2003 'Mediating Theologies: Karl Barth between Radical and Neo-orthodoxy', *SJT* 56: 427–43.
2004 *Karl Barth: Theologian of Christian Witness* (Aldershot: Ashgate).

Marcus, Eric
2004 'Why Zombies are Inconceivable', *Australasian JPhil* 82: 477–90.

Marras, Ausonio
1994 'Nonreductive Materialism and Mental Causation', *Can JPhil* 24: 465–95.
2002 'Kim on Reduction', *Erkenntnis* 57: 231–57.

Marsella, Anthony J., Francis L. K. Hsu, and George A. De Vos (eds)
1985 *Culture and Self: Asian and Western Perspectives* (New York: Tavistock).

Marshall, Bruce D.
1983 'Review of *A Theology on Its Way* by Richard H. Roberts', *Journal of Theological Studies* 44: 453–8.

Martin, Raymond
1995 'Fission Rejuvenation', *PhilStud* 80: 17–40.

Martin, Raymond and John Barresi (eds)
2003 *Personal Identity* (Malden: Blackwell).

Maslin, K. T.
2001 *An Introduction to the Philosophy of Mind* (Cambridge: Blackwell).

Mavrodes, George I.
1977 'The Life Everlasting and the Bodily Criterion of Identity', *Nous* 11: 27–39.

Maxwell, Nicholas
2000 'The Mind–Body Problem and Explanatory Dualism', *Philosophy* 75: 49–71.

McCauley, Robert and William Bechtel
2001 'Explanatory Pluralism and Heuristic Identity Theory', *Theory & Psychology* 11: 736–61.

McCormack, Bruce L.
1997 *Karl Barth's Critically Realistic Dialectical Theology* (Oxford: OUP).
1999 'The Sum of the Gospel: The Doctrine of Election in the Theologies of Alexander Schweizer and Karl Barth', in David Willis-Watkins, Michael Welker, and Mattias Gockel (eds), *Toward the Future of Reformed theology* (Grand Rapids: Eerdmans): 470–93.
2000 'Grace and Being: The Role of God's Gracious Election in Karl Barth's Theological Ontology', in Webster 200b: 92–110.
2002 'Review of *Karl Barth: Against Hegemony*, by Timothy J. Gorringe', *SJT* 55: 236–9.

McDowell, John C.
2002 'A Response to Rodney Holder on Barth on Natural Theology', *Themelios* 27: 32–44.

2003a 'Learning Where to Place One's Hope: The Eschatological Significance of Election in Barth', *SJT* 53: 316–38.
2003b 'Theology as Conversational Event: Karl Barth, the Ending of "Dialogue" and the Beginning of "Conversation"', *ModTheol* 19: 483–510.

McDowell, John C. and Mike Higton (eds)
2004 *Conversing with Barth* (eds John Webster, George Hunsinger, and Hans Anton Drewes; Barth Studies; Aldershot: Ashgate).

McFadyen, Alistair
1990 *The Call to Personhood: A Christian Theory of the Individual in Social Relationship* (Cambridge: CUP).

McFague, Sallie
1987 *Models of God: Theology for an Ecological, Nuclear Age* (London: SCM).
1993 *The Body of God: An Ecological Theology* (London: SCM).

McFarland, Ian A.
2001 *Difference & Identity* (Cleveland: Pilgrim).
2005 *The Divine Image: Envisioning the Invisible God* (Minneapolis: Fortress).

McGinn, Colin
1989 'Can We Solve the Mind–Body Problem', *Mind* 97: 349–66.
1991 *The Problem of Consciousness: Essays Towards a Resolution* (Oxford: Blackwell).
1999 *The Mysterious Flame: Conscious Minds in a Material World* (New York: Basic).
2003 'What Constitutes the Mind–Body Problem?', in Sosa and Villanueva 2003: 148–62.

McGrath, Alister E.
1986 *The Making of Modern German Christology: From the Enlightenment to Pannenberg* (Oxford: Blackwell).
1997 *Christian Theology: An Introduction* (2nd edn; Oxford: Blackwell).
2001 *A Scientific Theology* (vol. 1; Grand Rapids: Eerdmans).

McIntyre, John
1966 *The Shape of Christology* (Philadelphia: Westminster).

McLaughlin, Brian P.
1989 'Type Epiphenomenalism, Type Dualism, and the Causal Priority of the Physical', *Philosophical Perspectives* 3: 109–35.
1992 'The Rise and Fall of British Emergentism', in Beckermann, Florh, and Kim 1992: 49–93.
1993 'On Davidson's Response to the Charge of Epiphenomenalism', in Heil and Mele 1993: 27–40.
1995 'Varieties of Supervenience', in Savellos and Yalcin 1995: 16–59.
2003 'A Naturalist-Phenomenal Realist Response to Block's Harder Problem', *Philosophical Issues* 13: 163–204.

BIBLIOGRAPHY

McLean, Stuart
1975 'The Humanity of Man in Karl Barth's Thought', *SJT* 28: 127–47.
1981 *Humanity in the Thought of Karl Barth* (Edinburgh: T&T Clark).
1986 'Creation and Anthropology', in J. Thompson 1986b: 111–142.

McLelland, Joseph C.
1974 'Philosophy and Theology – a Family Affair (Karl and Heinrich Barth)', in H. Hartin Rumscheidt (ed.), *Footnotes to a Theology* (Waterloo: Corporation for the Publication of Academic Studies in Religion in Canada): 30–52.

Melnyk, Andrew
1995 'Two Cheers for Reductionism: Or, the Dim Prospects for Non-Reductive Materialism', *Philosophy of Science* 62: 370–89.
1997 'How to Keep the "Physical" in Physicalism', *JPhil* 94: 622–38.
2003 'Physicalism', in Stich and Warfield 2003: 65–84.

Merricks, Trenton
1998 There Are No Criteria of Identity over Time. *Nous* 32, 106–124.
1999 Endurance, Psychological Continuity, and the Importance of Personal Identity. *Phil Phenomenol Res* 59, 983–97.
2001a How to Live Forever without Saving Your Soul: Physicalism and Immortality. In, *Soul, Body, and Survival: Essays on the Metaphysics of Human Persons*, edited by Kevin Corcoran 2001c. 183–200. Ithaca: Cornell University Press.
2001b *Objects and Persons*. Oxford: Clarendon.

Metzger, Paul Louis
2003 *The Word of Christ and the World of Culture*. Grand Rapids: Eerdmans.

Meyering, Theo C.
2000 Physicalism and Downward Causation in Psychology and the Special Sciences. *Inquiry* 43, 181–203.
2001 Explanatory Pluralism and Macro-causation. *Theory & Psychology* 11, 761–772.
2002 Mind Matters: Physicalism and the Autonomy of the Person. In *Neuroscience and the Person: Scientific Perspectives on Divine Action*, Russell, et al. 2002: 165–177. Vatican City: Vatican Observatory.

Midgley, Mary
2000 'Consciousness, Fatalism, and Science', In ed. Niels Henrik Gregersen, Willem B. Drees, and Ulf Gorman. *The Human Person in Science and Theology* (Grand Rapids: Eerdmans): 21–40.

Miell, David K.
1989 'Barth on Persons in Relationship: A Case for Further Reflection', *SJT* 42: 541–55.

Migliore, Daniel
2004 'Response to "The Barth-Brunner Correspondence"', in Hunsinger 2004a: 44–51.

BIBLIOGRAPHY

Milbank, John
  1999 'Introduction: Suspending the Material: The Turn of Radical Orthodoxy', in John Milbank, Catherine Pickstock, and Graham Ward (eds), *Radical Orthodoxy: A New Theology* (London: Routledge): 1–20.

Miller, Patrick D.
  2004 'What Is a Human Being? The Anthropology of Scripture', in Green 2004b: 63–74.

Mills, Eugene
  1996 'Interactionism and Overdetermination', *Amer Phil Quart* 33: 105–17.

Molnar, Paul
  1995 'Some Problems with Pannenberg's Solution to Barth's "Faith Subjectivism"', *SJT* 48: 315–39.

Moltmann, Jürgen
  1974 *Man: Christian Anthropology in the Conflicts of the Present* (trans. John Sturdy; London: SPCK).
  1985 *God in Creation: An Ecological Doctrine of Creation* (trans. Margaret Kohl; London: SCM).

Montero, Barbara
  1999 'The Body Problem', *Nous* 33: 183–200.

Moreland, J. P.
  1995 'Humanness, Personhood, and the Right to Die', *FaithPhil* 12: 95–112.
  2002 *What is the Soul?* (Norcross: RZIM).

Moreland, J. P. and Scott B. Rae
  2000 *Body and Soul: Human Nature and the Crisis in Ethics* (Downers Grove: InterVarsity).

Morris, Thomas V.
  1984 'Incarnational Anthropology', *Theology* 87: 344–50.

Muers, Rachel
  1999 'A Question of Two Answers: Difference and Determination in Barth and von Balthasar', *HeyJ* 40: 265–80.

Muller, Richard
  1991 *The Study of Theology: From Biblical Interpretation to Contemporary Formulation* (Grand Rapids: Zondervan).

Murphy, Nancey
  1996 *On the Moral Nature of the Universe: Theology, Cosmology, and Ethics* (Minneapolis: Fortress).
  1998a 'Human Nature: Historical Scientific, and Religious Issues', in Brown, Murphy, and Malony 1998: 1–29.
  1998b 'Nonreductive Physicalism: Philosophical Issues', in Brown, Murphy, and Malony 1998: 127–48.
  1998c 'Supervenience and the Nonreducibility of Ethics to Biology', in Robert J. Russell, William R. Stoeger, and Francisco Ayala (eds), *Evolutionary and Molecular Biology* (Vatican City: Vatican Observatory): 463–89.

1999a 'Downward Causation and Why the Mental Matters', *CTNS Bulletin* 19: 13–21.
1999b 'Physicalism without Reductionism: Toward a Scientifically, Philosophically Sound Portrait of Human Nature', *Zygon* 34, 551–73.
2002a 'The Problem of Mental Causation: How Does Reason Get its Grip on the Brain?', *Science & Christian Belief* 14: 143–58.
2002b 'The Resurrection Body and Personal Identity: Possibilities and Limits of Eschatological Knowledge', in Ted Peters, Robert J. Russell, and Michael Welker (eds), *Resurrection: Theological & Scientific Assessments* (Grand Rapids: Eerdmans): 202–18.
2002c 'Supervenience and the Downward Efficacy of the Mental: A Nonreductuve Physicalist Account of Human Action', in Russell, *et al.* 2002: 147–64.
2005 'Nonreductive Physicalism', in Green and Palmer 2005: 115–38.

Myro, George
1994 'On the Distinctness of the Mental and the Physical', in Warner and Szubka 1994: 329–42.

Nagel, Ernest
1961 *The Structure of Science* (London: Routledge).

Nagel, Thomas and Frank Jackson
1974 'What Is It Like to Be a Bat?', *PhilRev* 83: 435–56.
1986 *The View from Nowhere* (New York: OUP).

Nellas, Panayiotis
1987 *Deification in Christ: The Nature of the Human Person* (Crestwood: St Vladimir's Seminary Press).

Newman, David H.
2001 'Chaos, Emergence, and the Mind–Body Problem', *Australasian JPhil* 79: 180–96.

Newman, Paul W.
1981 'Humanity with Spirit', *SJT* 34: 415–26.

Ng'weshemi, Andrea M.
2002 *Rediscovering the Human: The Quest for a Christo-theological Anthropology in Africa* (New York: Peter Lang).

Nozick, Robert
1981 *Philosophical Explanations* (Oxford: Clarendon).

Nussbaum, Martha C. and Amelie Oksenberg Rorty (eds)
1992 *Essays on Aristotle's De anima* (Oxford: Clarendon).

O'Connor, Timothy
2001 'Causality, Mind, and Free Will', in Corcoran 2001c: 44–58.
2003 'Emergent Individuals', *PhilQuart* 53: 540–55.

O'Connor, Timothy and David Robb (eds)
2003 *Philosophy of Mind: Contemporary Readings* (London: Routledge, 2003).

BIBLIOGRAPHY

O'Connor, Timothy and Hong Yu Wong
  2005 'Emergent Properties', in Edward N. Zalta (ed.), *The Stanford Encyclopedia of Philosophy* (accessed 9 Sep 2005) http://plato.stanford.edu/archives/sum2005/entries/properties-emergent/

O'Donovan, Joan E.
  1986 'Man in the Image of God: The Disagreement Between Barth and Brunner Reconsidered', *SJT* 39: 433-59.

Olson, Eric T.
  2003a 'An Argument for Animalism', in Martin and Barresi 2003: 318-34.
  2003b 'Personal Identity', in Stich and Warfield 2003: 352-68.

O'Neill, Michael
  2004 'Karl Barth's Doctrine of Election', *EvQ* 76: 311-26.

Oomen, Palmyre M. F.
  2003 'On Brain, Soul, Self, and Freedom: An Essay in Bridging Neuroscience and Faith', *Zygon* 38: 377-93.

Osei-Bonsu, Joseph
  1987 'Anthropological Dualism in the New Testament', *SJT* 40: 571-90.

Packer, J. I.
  1975 'Hermeneutics and Biblical Authority', *Themelios* 1: 3-12.

Palma, Robert J.
  1983 *Karl Barth's Theology of Culture: The Freedom of Culture for the Praise of God* (Allison Park: Pickwick).

Pannenberg, Wolfhart
  1985 *Anthropology in Theological Perspective* (trans. Mattew J. O'Connell; Edinburgh: T&T Clark).
  1991 *Systematic Theology* (trans. Geoffrey W. Bromiley; vol. 1; Grand Rapids: Eerdmans).

Papineau, David
  1998 'Mind the Gap', *Nous-Supplement* 12: 373-88.

Parfit, Derek
  1986 *Reasons and Persons* (Oxford: OUP).
  1995 'The Unimportance of Identity', in Henry Harris (ed.), *Identity* (Oxford: OUP): 13-45.

Peacocke, Arthur
  1976 'Reduction: A Review of the Epistemological Issues and their Relevance to Biology and the Problem of Consciousness', *Zygon* 11: 307-31.
  1986 *God and the New Biology* (London: Dent).
  1990 *Theology for a Scientific Age* (Oxford: Blackwell).

Peacocke, Arthur and Grant Gillette (eds)
  1987 *Persons and Personality: A Contemporary Inquiry* (Oxford: Blackwell, 1987).

BIBLIOGRAPHY

Penelhum, Terence
   1970   *Survival and Disembodied Existence* (London: Routledge).

Penrose, Roger
   1989   *The Emperor's New Mind* (Oxford: OUP).

Pereboom, Derek
   2002   'Robust Nonredutive Materialism', *JPhil* 99: 499–531.

Pereboom, Derk and Hilary Kornblith
   1991   'The Metaphysics of Irreducibility', *PhilStud* 63: 125–45. http://www.uvm.edu/~phildept/?Page=pereboom/aajp.htm

Peters, Ted
   2002   'Resurrection of the Very Embodied Soul?', in Russell *et al.* 2002: 305–26.

Peterson, Michael L. and Raymond J. VanArragon (eds)
   2004   *Contemporary Debates in Philosophy of Religion* (Malden: Blackwell).

Pierre, Pierre
   2003   'Intentionality', in Edward N. Zalta (ed.), *Stanford Encyclopedia of Philosophy* (accessed 27 Feb 2005) http://plato.stanford.edu/archives/fall2003/entries/intentionality

Pinnock, Clark
   1977   'Karl Barth and Christian Apologetics', *Themelios* 2: 66–71.

Place, U. T.
   1956   'Is Consciousness a Brain Process?', *British Journal of Psychology* 47: 44–50.

Plantinga, Alvin
   2003   'World and Essence', in Matthew Davidson (ed.), *Essays in the Metaphysics of Modality* (Oxford: OUP): 46–71.

Polkinghorne, J. C.
   1994   *Science and Christian Belief* (London: SPCK).

Popper, Karl
   1994   *Knowledge and the Body–Mind Problem: In Defense of Interaction* (ed. M. A. Notturno; London: Routledge).

Popper, Karl R. and John Carew Eccles
   1977   *The Self and Its Brain: An Argument for Interactionism* (New York: Springer International).

Post, John F.
   1995   '"Global" Supervenient Determination: Too Permissive?', in Savellos and Yalcin 1995: 73–100.

Preece, Gordon
   2001   'Barth's Theology of Work and Vocation for a Postmodern World', in Thompson and Mostert 2001: 147–70.

BIBLIOGRAPHY

Prenter, Regin
1950 'Die Lehre vom Menschen bei Karl Barths', *Theologische Zeitschrift* 6: 211–22.

Price, Daniel J.
2002 *Karl Barth's Anthropology in Light of Modern Thought* (Grand Rapids: Eerdmans).

Putnam, Hilary
1967 'Psychological Predicates', in W. H. Capitan and D. D. Merill (eds), *Art, Mind, and Religion* (Pittsburgh: University of Pittsburgh Press): 37–48.
1975 *Mind, Language, and Reality: Philosophical Papers* (2 vols.; Cambridge: CUP).
1981 'Brains in a Vat', in *Reason, Truth, and History* (Cambridge: CUP).

Quinn, Philip
1978 'Some Problems about Resurrection', *RelS* 14: 343–59.
1997 'Tiny Selves: Chisholm on the Simplicity of the Soul', in Lewis Edwin Hahn (ed.), *The Philosophy of Roderick M. Chisholm* (Peru: Open Court): 55–67.

Radder, Hans
2001 'Psychology, Physicalism and Real Physics', *Theory & Psychology* 11: 773–84.

Rea, Michael C.
2003 'Four-Dimensionalism', in Loux and Zimmerman 2003: 246–80.

Reichenbach, Bruce
1978 'Monism and the Possibility of Life after Death', *RelS* 14: 27–34.
1983 *Is Man the Phoenix?* (Washington: University Press of America).

Rey, Georges
1997 *Contemporary Philosophy of Mind* (Cambridge: Blackwell).

Richardson, R. C.
1982 'The "Scandal" of Cartesian Interactionism', *Mind* 91: 20–37.

Riches, J. K.
1972 'What is "Christocentric" Theology', in S. W. Sykes and J. P. Clayton (eds), *Christ, Faith and History: Cambridge Studies in Christology* (Cambridge: CUP): 223–38.

Richmond, James
1986 'God and the Natural Orders: Is There Permanent Validity in Karl Barth's *Warning to Natural Theology?*', in Alistair Kee and Eugene Thomas Long (ed.), *Being and Truth* (London: SCM): 393–409.

Ricoeur, Paul
1992 *Oneself as Another* (trans. Kathleen Blamey; Chicago: University of Chicago Press).

Ritchie, Jack
2005 'Causal Compatibilism – What Chance?', *Erkenntnis* 63: 119–32.

BIBLIOGRAPHY

Robb, David and John Heil
2005 'Mental Causation', in Edward N. Zalta (ed.), *The Stanford Encyclopedia of Philosophy* (accessed 21 Sep 2005) http://plato.stanford.edu/archives/spr2005/entries/mental-causation/

Roberts, Richard H.
1991 *A Theology on Its Way? Essays on Karl Barth* (Edinburgh: T&T Clark).

Robinson, Howard
1989 'A Dualist Account of Embodiment', in Smythies and Beloff 1989: 43–57.
2003 'Dualism', in Stich and Warfield 2003: 85–101.
2004 'Dualism', in Heil 2004b: 85–101.

Robinson, John A. T.
1952 *The Body: A Study in Pauline Theology* (Chicago: Regnery).

Rockwell, Teed
2004 'Non-Reductive Physicalism', *Dictionary of the Philosophy of Mind* (accessed 4 April 2005) http://philosophy.uwaterloo.ca/MindDict/nonreductivephysicalism.html

Rogers, Eugene F.
1998 'Supplementing Barth on Jews and Gender: Identifying God by Anagogy and the Spirit', *ModTheol* 14: 43–82.
2004 'The Eclipse of the Spirit in Karl Barth', in McDowell and Higton 2004: 173–90.

Rosato, Philip J.
1981 *The Spirit as Lord: The Pneumatology of Karl Barth* (Edinburgh: T&T Clark).

Rose, Steven P. R.
2004 'Introduction: The New Brain Sciences', in David A. Rees and Steven P. R. Rose (eds), *The New Brain Sciences: Perils and Prospects* (New York: CUP): 3–14.

Rosenberg, Alex and D. M. Kaplan
2005 'How to Reconcile Physcalism and Antireductionism about Biology', *Philosophy of Science* 72: 43–69.

Rosenthal, David M.
1986 'Two Concepts of Consciousness', *PhilStud* 49: 329–59.
2002a 'Consciousness and the Mind', *The Jerusalem Philosophical Quarterly* 51: 227–51.
2002b 'How Many Kinds of Consciousness?', *Consciousness and Cognition* 11: 653–65.

Runia, Klaas
1958 'Karl Barth on Man in His Time', *Reformed Theological Review* 17: 1–11.

Rupert, Robert D.
2006 'Functionalism, Mental Causation, and the Problem of Metaphysically Necessary Effects', *Nous* 40: 256–83.

BIBLIOGRAPHY

Russell, Robert, Nancey Murphy, Theo C. Meyering, Michael A. Arbib (eds)
2002 *Neuroscience and the Person* (Vatican City: Vatican Observatory)

Ryle, Gilbert
1949 *The Concept of Mind* (London: Hutchinson).

Savellos, Elias E. and Umit D. Yalcin (eds)
1995 *Supervenience: New Essays* (Cambridge: CUP).

Sawyer, Keith R.
2003 'Nonreductive Individualism Part II – Social Causation', *Philosophy of the Social Sciences* 33: 203–24.

Schechtman, Marya
2003 'Empathetic Access: The Missing Ingredient in Personal Identity', in Martin and Barresi 2003: 238–59.

Schouten, Maurice K. D.
2001 'Theism, Dualism, and the Scientific Image of Humanity', *Zygon* 36: 679–798.

Schrag, Calvin O.
1997 *The Self after Postmodernity* (New Haven: Yale University Press).

Schröder, Jürgen
2002 'The Supervenience Argument and the Generalization Problem', *Erkenntnis* 56: 319–28.

Schwöbel, Christoph
1991 'Human Being as Relational Being: Twelve Theses for a Christian Anthropology', in Christoph Schwöbel and Colin E. Gunton (eds), *Persons, Divine, and Human* (Edinburgh: T&T Clark): 141–65.
2000 'Theology', in Webster 200b: 17–36.

Seager, William and Sean Allen-Hermanson
2005 'Panpsychism', in Edward N. Zalta (ed.), *The Stanford Encyclopedia of Philosophy* (accessed 9 Sep 2005) http://plato.stanford.edu/archives/sum2005/entries/panpsychism.

Searle, John R.
1983 *Intentionality: An Essay in the Philosophy of Mind* (New York: CUP).
1992 *The Rediscovery of the Mind* (Cambridge: MIT).
1997 *The Mystery of Consciousness* (New York: New York Review of Books).
1999 'Consciousness' (accessed 8 Oct 2005) http://humanities.ucsc.edu/NEH/searle1.htm

Sedley, David
2005 'Stoicism', in E. Craig (ed.), *Routledge Encyclopedia of Philosophy* (accessed 10 Oct 2005) http://www.rep.routledge.com/article/A112SECT5

Shagrir, Oron
1999 'More on Global Supervenience', *Philosophy & Phenomenological Research* 59: 691–702.

BIBLIOGRAPHY

Sharp, Douglas R.
1990 *The Hermeneutics of Election: The Significance of the Doctrine in Barth's Church Dogmatics* (Lanham: University Press of America).

Sharpe, Kevin and Jonathan Walgate
2003 'The Emergent Order', *Zygon* 38: 411–33.

Sherlock, Charles
1996 *The Doctrine of Humanity* (Downers Grove: InterVarsity).

Shields, Christopher
2005 'Aristotle's Psychology', in Edward N. Zalta (ed.), *Stanford Encyclopedia of Philosophy* (accessed 1 Oct 2005) http://plato.stanford.edu/archives/sum2005/entries/aristotle-psychology/

Shoemaker Sydney and Lewis D. Hywel
1970 'Persons and Their Pasts', *Amer Phil Quart* 7: 269–85.
1975 'Functionalism and Qualia', *PhilStud* 27: 291–315.
1978 'Immortality and Dualism', in *Persons and Life after Death: Essays by Hywel D. Lewis and Some of His Critics* (London: Macmillan): 110–34.
1981 'Some Varieties of Functionalism', *Phil Topics* 12: 93–119.
1984a 'On an Argument for Dualism', in *Identity, Cause and Mind: Philosophical Essays* (Cambridge: CUP): 287–308.
1984b 'Personal Identity: A Materialist's Account', in Sydney Shoemaker and Richard Swinburne (eds), *Personal Identity* (Oxford: Blackwell).
1994 'Phenomenal Character', *Nous* 28: 21–38.
2003 'Realization, Micro-Realization, and Coincidence', *Phil Phenomenol Res* 67.1: 1–23.

Shults, F. LeRon
2003 *Reforming Theological Anthropology: After the Philosophical Turn to Relationality* (Grand Rapids: Eerdmans).

Sider, Theodore
1997 'Four-Dimensionalism', *PhilRev* 106: 197–231.
2001 *Four-Dimensionalism* (Oxford: Clarendon).

Simon, Caroline J.
2004 'What Wondrous Love Is This? Meditations on Barth, Christian Love, and the Future of Christian Ethics', in Hunsinger 2004a: 143–58.

Smart, J. J. C.
1959 'Sensations and Brain Processes', *PhilRev* 68: 141–56.

Smith, Steven G.
1983 *The Argument to the Other: Reason beyond Reason in the Thought of Karl Barth and Emmanuel Levinas* (Chico: Scholars).
1984 'Karl Barth and Fideism: a Reconsideration', *Anglican Theological Review* 66: 64–78.

Smythies, John R. and John Beloff (eds)
1989 *The Case for Dualism* (Charlottesville: University Press of Virginia).

BIBLIOGRAPHY

Sonderegger, Katherine
    1992 'On Style in Karl Barth', *SJT* 45: 65–83.
    2000 'Barth and Feminism', in Webster 200b: 258–73.

Sosa, Ernest
    1990 'Surviving Matters', *Nous* 24: 306–30.
    1993 'Davidson's Thinking Causes', in Heil and Mele 1993: 41–52.

Sosa, Ernest and Enrique Villanueva (eds)
    2003 *Philosophy of Mind* (Philosophical Issues, 13; Oxford: Blackwell).

Soucek, Josef B.
    1949 'Man in the Light of the Humanity of Jesus', *SJT* 2: 74–82.

Sousa, Ronald de
    1996 'Twelve Varieties of Subjectivity: Dividing in Hopes of Conquest' (accessed 10 Sep 2005) http://www.chass.utoronto.ca/~sousa/subjectivity.html

Spezio, Michael L.
    2004 'Freedom in the Body: The Physical, the Causal, and the Possibility of Choice', *Zygon* 39: 577–91.

Stalnaker, Robert
    1996 'Varieties of Supervenience', *Philosophical Perspectives* 10: 221–41.

Stephan, Achim
    1992 'Emergence – A Systematic View on its Historical Facets', in Beckermann, Flohr, and Kim 1992: 25–48.

Stevenson, Leslie and David L. Haberman
    1998 *Ten Theories of Human Nature* (3rd edn; Oxford: OUP).

Stich, Stephen P. and Ted A. Warfield (eds)
    2003 *The Blackwell Guide to Philosophy of Mind* (Oxford: Blackwell).

Stock, Konrad
    1980 *Anthropologie der Verheissung: Karl Barths Lehre vom Menschen als dogmatisches Problem* (Munchen: Kaiser).

Stoeger, William R., S. J.
    2002 'The Mind–Brain Problem, the Laws of Nature, and Constitutive Relationships', in Russell, *et al.* 2003: 129–46.

Stoljar, Daniel
    2001a 'The Conceivability Argument and Two Conceptions of the Physical', *Nous Supplement* 15: 393–413.
    2001b 'Physicalism', in Edward N. Zalta, *Stanford Encyclopedia of Philosophy* (accessed 10 Jan 2005) http://plato.stanford.edu/archives/spr2001/entries/physicalism/
    2001c 'Two Conceptions of the Physical', *Phil Phenomenol Res* 62: 253–82.
    2005 'Physicalism and Phenomenal Concepts', *MindLang* 20: 469–94.

BIBLIOGRAPHY

Stone, Lawson G.
  2004 'The Soul: Possession, Part, or Person? The Genesis of Human Nature in Genesis 2:7', in Green 2004b: 47–62.

Strawson, Galen
  1994 'The Experiential and the Non-Experiential', in Warner and Szubka 1994: 69–86.

Strawson, P. F.
  1959 *Individuals* (London: Methuen).

Stubenberg, Leopold
  2005 'Neutral Monism', in Edward N. Zalta (ed.), *The Stanford Encyclopedia of Philosophy* (accessed 4 April 2006) http://plato.stanford.edu/archives/spr2005/entries/neutral-monism

Stump, Eleanore
  1995 'Non-Cartesian Substance Dualism and Materialism without Reductionism', *FaithPhil* 12: 505–31.

Sturgeon, Scott
  1998 'Physicalism and Overdetermination', *Mind* 107: 411–33.

Surin, Kenneth
  1990 'A Politics of Speech', in Gavin D'Costa (ed.), *Christian Uniqueness Reconsidered: The Myth of a Pluralistic Theology of Religions* (New York: Orbis): 191–212.

Sussman, Alan N.
  1981 'Reflections on the Chances for a Scientific Dualism', *JPhil* 78: 95–118.

Swartz, Norman
  1991 *Beyond Experience: Metaphysical Theories and Philosophical Constraints* (Toronto: University of Toronto Press).

Swinburne, Richard
  1984 'Personal Identity: A Materialist's Account', in Sydney Shoemaker and Richard Swinburne, *Personal Identity* (Oxford: Blackwell): 158–81.
  1986 *The Evolution of the Soul* (Oxford: Clarendon).
  1998 'The Modal Argument Is Not Circular', *FaithPhil* 15: 371–2.
  2003 'The Soul', in O'Connor and Robb 2003: 30–46.

Swinburne, Richard and Alan G. Padgett (eds)
  1994 *Reason and the Christian religion* (Oxford: Clarendon).

Sykes, S. W.
  1979a 'Barth on the Centre of Theology', in Sykes 1979b: 17–54.
  1979b (ed.) *Karl Barth, Studies of His Theological Method* (Oxford: Clarendon).
  1979c 'The Study of Barth', in Sykes 1979b: 1–16.
  1988 'Schleiermacher and Barth on the Essence of Christianity: An Instructive Disagreement', in Duke and Streetman 1988: 88–107.
  1989a (ed.) *Karl Barth: Centenary Essays* (Cambridge: CUP).
  1989b 'Introduction', in Sykes 1989a: 1–13.

BIBLIOGRAPHY

Taliaferro, Charles
- 1986 'Pollock's Body-Switching', *PhilQuart* 36: 57–61.
- 1994 *Consciousness and the Mind of God* (Cambridge: CUP).
- 1995 'Animals, Brains, and Spirits', *FaithPhil* 12: 567–81.
- 2001 'Emergentism and Consciousness: Going Beyond Property Dualism', in Corcoran 2001c: 59–72.

Tanner, Kathryn
- 2000 'Creation and Providence', in Webster 200b: 111–126.
- 2001 *Jesus, Humanity and the Trinity* (Minneapolis: Fortress).

Taylor, Charles
- 1989 *Sources of the Self* (Cambridge: CUP).

Taylor, John V.
- 1981 'The Theological Basis for Interfaith Dialogue', in John Hick and Brian Hebblethwaite (eds), *Christianity and the Other Religions: Selected Readings* (Philadelphia: Fortress): 93–110.

Taylor, Richard
- 1983 *Metaphysics* (3rd edn; Englewood Cliffs: Prentice-Hall).

TeSelle, Eugene
- 1975 *Christ in Context: Divine Purpose and Human Possibility* (Philadelphia: Fortress).

Teske, John A.
- 2000 'The Social Construction of the Human Spirit', in Gregersen, Drees, and Görman 2000: 189–211.

Thatcher, Adrian
- 1987 'Christian Theism and the Concept of a Person', in Peacocke and Gillett 1987: 180–196.

Thiemann, Ronald F.
- 1981 'Toward a Theology of Creation: A Response to Gustaf Wingren', in Vander Goot 1981: 119–36

Thiselton, Anthony C.
- 1994 'Barr on Barth and Natural Theology: A Plea for Hermeneutics in Historical Theology', *SJT* 47: 519–28.

Thompson, Geoff
- 2001 '"Our lines and concepts continually break apart": Language, Mystery and God in Barth', in G. Thompson and Mostert 2001: 191–209.

Thompson, Geoff and Christiaan Mostert (eds)
- 2001 *Karl Barth: A Future for Postmodern Theology?* (Hindmarsh: Australian Theological Forum).

Thompson, John
- 1976 'Humanity of God in the Thought of Karl Barth', *SJT* 29: 249–69.
- 1986a 'On the Trinity', in J. Thompson 1986b.

1986b (ed.) *Theology beyond Christendom: Essays on the Centenary of the Birth of Karl Barth* (Allison Park: Pickwick).
1991 *The Holy Spirit in the Theology of Karl Barth* (Allison Park: Pickwick).

Tooley, Michael
2003 'Causation and Supervenience', in Loux and Zimmerman 2003: 386–434.

Torrance, Alan J.
1996 *Persons in Communion: An Essay on Trinitarian Description and Human Participation* (Edinburgh: T&T Clark).
2003 'Developments in Neuroscience and Human Freedom: Some Theological and Philosophical Questions', *Science & Christian Belief* 16: 123–37.
2004 'What Is a Person?', in Jeeves 2004a: 199–222.

Torrance, Thomas. F.
1947 'The Word of God and the Nature of Man', in Frederick William Camfield (ed.), *Reformation Old and New: a Tribute to Karl Barth* (London: Lutterworth): 121–41.
1962 *Karl Barth: An Introduction to His Early Theology, 1910–1931* (London: SCM).
1970 'The Problem of Natural Theology in the Thought of Karl Barth', *RelS* 6: 121–35.
1986 'The Legacy of Karl Barth (1886–1986)', *SJT* 39: 289–308.
1989 'The Soul and Person, in Theological Perspective', in Stewart R. Sutherland and T. A. Roberts (eds), *Religion, Reason and the Self* (Cardiff: University of Wales Press): 103–18.
1990 *Karl Barth, Biblical and Evangelical Theologian* (Edinburgh: T&T Clark).

Trigg, Roger
1998 *Rationality and Religion: Does Faith Need Reason?* (Oxford: Blackwell).

Tye, Michael
1995 *Ten Problems of Consciousness* (Cambridge: MIT Press).
1999 'Phenomenal Consciousness: The Explanatory Gap as Cognitive Illusion', *Mind* 108: 705–25.
2003 'Qualia', in Edward N. Zalta (ed.), *Stanford Encyclopedia of Philosophy* (accessed 26 Feb 2005) http://plato.stanford.edu/archives/sum2003/entries/qualia/

Unger, Peter
1990 *Identity, Consciousness, and Value* (New York: OUP).

Urban, Linwood
1964 'Barth's Epistemology', in Hick 1964: 218–222.

Vallicella, William F.
1998 'Could a Classical Theist Be a Physicalist?', *FaithPhil* 15: 160–80.

Van Cleve, James
1983 'Conceivability and the Cartesian Argument for Dualism', *Pac Phil Quart* 64: 35–45.

1990 'Mind-Dust or Magic? Panpsychism Versus Emergence', Philosophical Perspectives 4: 215–26.

Van der Eijk, Philip J.
2000 'Aristotle's Psycho-Physiological Account of the Soul–Body Relationship', in Wright and Potter 2000: 57–78.

Van Gelder, Tim
1998 'Monism, Dualism, Pluralism', *MindLang* 13: 76–97.

Van Gulick, Robert
1992 'Nonreductive Materialism and the Nature of Intertheoretic Constraint', in Beckermann, Flohr, and Kim 1992: 157–79.
1993a 'Understanding the Phenomenal Mind: Are We All Just Armadillos?', in Martin Davies and Glyn W. Humphreys (eds), *Consciousness* (Oxford: Blackwell): 137–54.
1993b 'Who's in Charge Here? And Who's Doing All the Work?', in Heil and Mele 1993: 233–58.
2000 'Inward and Upward: Reflection, Introspection, and Self-Awareness', *Phil Topics* 28: 275–305.
2004 'Consciousness', in Edward N. Zalta, *Stanford Encyclopedia of Philosophy* (accessed 6 Jan 2005) http://plato.stanford.edu/archives/fall2004/entries/consciousness/

Van Inwagen, Peter
1978 'Possibility of Resurrection', *International Journal for Philosophy of Religion* 9: 114–21.
1983 *An Essay on Free Will* (Oxford: Clarendon).
1990 *Material Beings* (Ithaca: Cornell University Press).
1992 'The Possibility of Resurrection', in Paul Edwards (ed.), *Immortality* (New York: Macmillan): 242–47.
1995 'Dualism and Materialism: Athens and Jerusalem?', *FaithPhil* 12: 475–88.
1997 'Materialism and the Psychological-Continuity Account of Personal Identity', *Nous-Supplement* 11: 305–19.
2001 *Ontology, Identity, and Modality* (Cambridge: CUP).
2002 *Metaphysics* (Cambridge: Westview).

Vander Goot, Henry (ed.)
1981 *Creation and Method: Critical Essays on Christocentric Theology* (Washington: University Press of America).

Vendler, Zeno
1994 'The Ineffable Soul', in Warner and Szubka 1994: 317–28.

Verghese, Paul
1972 *The Freedom of Man* (Philadelphia: Westminster).

Wacome, Donald H.
2004 'Reductionism's Demise: Cold Comfort', *Zygon* 39: 321–37.

Waldrop, Charles T.
1984 *Karl Barth's Christology* (Berlin: Mouton).

Ward, Graham
1993a 'Barth and Postmodernism', *New Blackfriars* 74: 550–56.
1993b 'The Revelation of the Holy Other as the Wholly Other: Between Barth's Theology of the Word and Levinas' Philosophy of Saying', *ModTheol* 9: 159–80.
1995 *Barth, Derrida and the Language of Theology* (Cambridge: CUP).
2004 'Barth, Hegel, and the Possibility for Christian Apologetics', in McDowell and Higton 2004: 53–67.

Warner, Richard and Tadeusz Szubka (eds)
1994 *The Mind–Body Problem: A Guide to the Contemporary Debate* (Oxford: Blackwell).

Watson, Francis
1997 *Text and Truth* (Edinburgh: T&T Clark).
2000 'The Bible', in Webster 2000b: 57–71.

Webb, Stephen H.
1991 *Re-figuring theology: The Rhetoric of Karl Barth* (Albany: State University of New York Press).

Webster, John B.
1995 *Barth's Ethics of Reconciliation* (Cambridge: CUP).
1998 *Barth's Moral Theology: Human Action in Barth's Thought* (Edinburgh: T&T Clark).
2000a *Barth* (2nd edn; London: Continuum).
2000b (ed.) *The Cambridge Companion to Karl Barth* (Cambridge: CUP).
2000c 'Introducing Barth', in Webster 2000b: 1–16.
2001a 'Barth, Modernity, and Postmodernity', in G. Thompson and Mostert 2001: 1–28.
2001b 'The Grand Narrative of Jesus Christ: Barth's Christology', in G. Thompson and Mostert 2001: 29–48.
2001c 'Rescuing the Subject: Barth and Postmodern Anthropology', in G. Thompson and Mostert 2001: 49–69.
2004a 'Response to What Wondrous Love is This?', in Hunsinger 2004a: 159–64.
2004 '"There is no past in the church, so there is no past in theology": Barth on the History of Modern Protestant Theology', in McDowell and Higton 2004: 14–39.

Wetzel, Linda
2005 'Type/Token Distinction', in E. Craig (ed.), *Routledge Encyclopedia of Philosophy* (accessed 1 Dec 2004) http://www.rep.routledge.com/article/X044

White, Graham
1984 'Karl Barth's Theological Realism', *Neue Zeitschrift für systematische Theologie und Religionsphilosophie* 26: 54–70.

Whitehouse, Walter
1949 'The Christian View of Man: An Examination of Karl Barth's Doctrine', *SJT* 2: 57–74.

BIBLIOGRAPHY

Williams, Bernard
    1970   'The Self and the Future', *Philosohpical Review* 79: 161–80.
    1973   *Problems of the Self* (Cambridge: CUP).
    1978   *Descartes: The Project of Pure Inquiry* (Atlantic Highlands: Humanities).

Williams, Daniel D.
    1947   'Brunner and Barth on Philosophy', *JR* 27: 241–54.

Willis, Robert E.
    1971   *The Ethics of Karl Barth* (Leiden: Brill).

Wilson, Edward O.
    2000   *Sociobiology: The New Synthesis, Twenty-fifth Anniversary Edition* (Cambridge: Belknap).

Wilson, Jessica
    1999   'How Superduper Does a Physicalist Supervenience Need to Be?', *Phil Quart* 49: 33–53.

Wimsatt, William C.
    1976   'Reductionism, Levels of Organization, and the Mind–Body Problem', in Gordon G. Globus, Grover Maxwell, and Irwin Savodnik (eds), *Consciousness and the Brain* (New York: Plenum).
    1994   'The Ontology of Complex Systems: Levels of Organization, Perspectives, and Causal Thickets', *Can JPhil* Supplementary Volume 20: 207–74.

Witmer, Gene D.
    2003   'Functionalism and Causal Exclusion', *Pac Phil Quart* 84: 198–215.
    2004   'Multiple Realizability', *Dictionary of Philosophy of Mind* (accessed 4 May 2005) http://www.artsci.wustl.edu/~philos/MindDict/identitytheory.html

Wolff, Hans Walter
    1974   *Anthropology of the Old Testament* (trans. Margaret Kohl; London: SCM).

Woolhead, Linda
    1999   'Theology and the Fragmented Self', *IJST* 1: 53–72.

Wright, John P. and Paul Potter (eds)
    2000   *Psyche and Soma: Physicians and Metaphysicians on the Mind–Body Problem from Antiquity to Enlightenment* (Oxford: Clarendon).

Wright, N. T.
    2003   *The Resurrection of the Son of God* (London: SPCK).

Yablo, Stephen
    1992   'Mental Causation', *PhilRev* 101: 245–80.
    1999   'Concepts and Consciousness', *Phil Phenomenol Res* 59: 455–63.
    2003   'Causal Relevance', *Philosophical Issues* 13: 316–28.

Zimmerman, Dean W.
    1998   'Criteria of Identity and the "Identity Mystics"', *Erkenntis* 48: 281–301.
    1999   'Compatibility of Materialism and Survival', *FaithPhil* 16: 194–212.

2003 'Two Cartesian Arguments for the Simplicity of the Soul', in O'Connor and Robb 2003: 15–29.
2004 'Christians Should Affirm Mind–Body Dualism', in Peterson and VanArragon 2004: 315–326.

Zizioulas, John D.
1975 'Human Capacity and Human Incapacity: A Theological Exploration of Personhood', *SJT* 28: 401–48.
1985 *Being as Communion: Studies in Personhood and the Church* (Crestwood: St Vladimir's Seminary Press).

INDEX

Anderson, Ray S. 4, 5, 8, 71, 77, 93–4, 104
Armstrong, D. M. 122, 163, 170, 176, 177

Baker, Lynne Rudder 14, 96, 120, 124, 132, 136, 148, 149, 151, 152, 153, 160, 184
Balthasar, Hans Urs von 7, 18, 19, 25, 27, 42, 43, 48, 51
Barr, James 44, 76
Bennett, Karen 116, 124, 131
Berkouwer, G. C. 6, 22, 25, 31, 49–50, 76, 77, 78, 99
Bielfeldt, Dennis 113, 123, 124, 133, 135
Biggar, Nigel 25, 36, 43, 48, 72
Block, Ned 102, 103, 119–20, 122, 123, 133, 139, 140, 141, 144
and Robert Stalnaker 113, 143–4
Bromiley, Geoffrey William 52, 89
Brown, Warren S. 115, 116, 126
Brunner, Emil 9, 25, 44, 59, 62, 71
Burge, Tyler 10, 117, 128, 132, 135, 136
Busch, Eberhard 72, 105

Carruthers, Peter 113, 141, 142, 163
Chalmers, David 11, 103, 124, 140, 143, 144, 145, 146, 157
Churchland, Patricia S. 10, 11, 140
Churchland, Paul 10, 11, 111, 114, 141
Clayton, Philip 104, 125, 139, 166
Colwell, John 23, 25
Come, Arnold Bruce 14, 25, 43, 44, 94
Cooper, John W. 11, 14, 78, 98, 147, 157, 165, 183
Corcoran, Kevin 11, 96, 120, 137, 138–9, 148, 149, 150, 156

Cortez, Marc 41, 75, 108, 196
Crane, Tim 102, 116, 125, 138, 156, 159
and Sarah Patterson (eds) 2, 157
Crawford, Robert S. 43, 44, 71, 76
Crick, Francis 113, 145, 163

Davidson, Donald 123, 124, 128, 134
Davis, Stephen T. 146, 149, 152, 153, 183, 184
Dennett, Daniel 10, 11, 102, 103, 122, 138, 140, 145, 156, 165, 176
Dorrien, Gary J. 43, 44
Dretske, Fred 134, 141

Ebneter, Albert 9, 23, 25, 27, 43
Eccles, John C. 78, 175, 178

Feigl, Herbert 2, 118
Flanagan, Owen J. 100, 138, 144
Fodor, Jerry 119, 120, 122, 159
Ford, D. F. 44, 47, 51, 76
Foster, John 11, 118, 143, 156, 157, 158, 159, 160, 162, 164, 170, 171, 172, 173, 174, 175, 181, 182
Frei, Hans 43, 48, 55
Frey, Christopher 9, 59, 76, 89
Freyer, Von Thomas 45, 48, 59, 102
Friedmann, Edgar Herbert 9, 14

Goetz, Stewart 5, 107, 124, 157, 158, 160, 165, 171, 172, 173, 174, 175, 176, 178, 182, 186
Gorringe, Timothy 48, 95, 100
Green, Joel B. 2, 11, 13, 14, 76, 78, 89, 152, 156
Grenz, Stanley J. 4, 49, 76, 101, 102

INDEX

Haldane, John 4, 10, 11–12
Hansen, Carsten Martin 125, 128, 130, 131, 132
Harre, Rom 105, 128, 156
Hart, W. D. 157, 160, 164, 165, 181, 183
Hasker, William 11, 107, 138, 157, 160, 162, 164, 165, 166, 167, 169, 171, 172, 175, 176, 179, 180–1, 182, 185, 186
Heil, John 113–14, 128, 156, 172
Hick, John 147, 149
Hoekema, Anthony A. 77, 89
Honderich, Ted 116, 122, 123
Horgan, Terrence 116, 118, 119–20, 123, 124, 125, 129–30, 135, 136
Hunsinger, George 14, 21, 34, 42, 44, 53, 56, 71–2, 74, 76, 79, 93

Jackson, Frank 141, 159
Jeeves, Malcolm 2, 11, 180
Jenson, Robert W. 4, 14, 18
Jewett, Paul K. and Marguerite Shuster 57, 86
Johnson, William Stacy 31, 38, 42, 45, 47, 50, 52, 70, 72, 74
Jüngel, Eberhard 24, 38, 50

Kim, Jaegwon 2, 10, 78, 111, 112, 113–14, 115, 116, 118, 119–20, 121, 122, 123, 124, 125, 126–7, 128, 129, 130, 131, 132, 133, 134, 135, 136, 138, 142, 159, 170, 172, 173, 174, 175, 185
Kirk, Robert 114, 117
Kripke, Saul A. 11, 119, 150
Kümmel, Werner Georg 13, 76, 89, 100

Larmer, Robert 175, 176, 177
Leftow, Brian 167, 168
Levine, Joseph 140, 142
Lewis, David 43, 114, 119, 122, 146, 150, 151
Lewis, Hywel D. 157, 164, 171, 172, 179, 180, 181
Loar, Brian 142, 144
Lowe, E. J. 101, 105, 116, 118, 128, 131, 134, 156, 160, 161, 171, 172, 174, 175, 176, 178, 182
Lycan, William G. 103, 141, 142

Macmurray, John 98, 102
Macquarrie, John 4, 57, 78, 79, 86, 87, 94, 95, 98
Mangina, Joseph L. 42, 44, 47, 48, 53, 81, 86, 94, 101, 105
Marras, Ausonio 114, 120
McCormack, Bruce L. 18, 22, 23, 25, 36, 38, 42, 44, 45, 46, 47, 49, 51, 52, 60, 80
McDowell, John C. 23, 44, 47, 48, 49, 69
McFarland, Ian A. 4, 6
McGinn, Colin 84, 117, 125, 143, 144, 146, 160
McGrath, Alister E. 25, 43, 44, 50
McLaughlin, Brian P. 118, 121, 124, 125, 128, 142, 144
McLean, Stuart 9, 18, 25, 51, 73, 76, 77, 80, 88, 94
Melnyk, Andrew 107, 113, 114, 116, 117, 118, 120, 123, 124, 125
Merricks, Trenton 96, 150, 152
Meyering, Theo C. 113, 114, 115, 118, 122, 134
Moltmann, Jürgen 60, 78, 81, 83, 85, 87–8, 94, 98
Moreland, J. P. 11, 78, 84, 156, 157, 159, 160, 164, 175, 182
and Scott B. Rae 14, 89, 92, 107, 143, 156, 158, 159, 164, 167, 168, 169, 174, 175, 182, 183, 184, 186
Murphy, Nancey 5, 112, 113, 115, 116, 118, 126, 134, 135, 152, 156, 163, 170

Nagel, Thomas 102, 141, 142, 143, 148

O'Connor, Timothy 11, 125
Olson, Eric T. 103, 147, 148, 149, 150

Pannenberg, Wolfhart 4, 44, 71, 79, 163
Parfit, Derek 146, 150, 151, 153
Peacocke, Arthur 113, 115, 126, 134, 135
Penrose, Roger 145, 177

242

INDEX

Pereboom, Derek 122, 126, 136, 137, 142
  and Hilary Kornblith 120, 132, 136, 142
Popper, Karl 161, 166
  and John Carew Eccles 161, 166, 175, 176, 178, 182
Price, Daniel J. 2, 9, 18, 47, 66, 69–70, 71, 75, 76, 77, 78, 83, 85, 96, 100
Putnam, Hilary 119–20, 122, 123, 128

Reichenbach, Bruce 152, 184
Riches, J. K. 41, 43, 44
Robb, David and John Heil 118, 128
Roberts, Richard H. 18, 43
Robinson, Howard 155, 157, 184, 185
Rosato, Philip J. 43, 53, 93, 99–100
Rosenthal, David M. 102, 139, 141
Ryle, Gilbert 2, 156, 163, 165

Schwöbel, Christoph 6, 71
Searle, John R. 103, 104, 125, 126, 131, 134, 139, 140, 143, 144, 146, 159
Sharpe, Kevin and Jonathan Walgate 112, 115, 135
Shoemaker, Sydney and Lewis D. Hywel 11, 103, 122, 141, 145, 150–1, 156, 160, 163, 173, 180, 186
Shults, F. LeRon 6, 21
Smith, Steven G. 45, 48
Sonderegger, Katherine 9, 38, 48
Sosa, Ernest 128, 146
Stock, Konrad 9, 47, 58, 65–6
Stoljar, Daniel 107, 116, 142, 144, 146
Stump, Eleanore 157, 167–8, 169, 177, 181

Swinburne, Richard 143, 156, 157, 159, 160, 166, 168, 170, 172, 175, 179, 180, 181, 182
Sykes, S. W. 14, 42, 43, 44, 50–2

Taliaferro, Charles 5, 11, 92, 107, 156, 157, 159, 160, 163, 164, 165, 166, 169, 171, 174, 175, 177, 181, 182
Tanner, Kathryn 25, 47, 54
Taylor, Richard 162, 163, 170–1, 178
Thompson, John 22, 24, 25, 27, 36, 53
Torrance, Alan J. 4, 8, 21, 128
Torrance, Thomas F. 9, 16, 25, 42, 44, 47, 51, 53, 71, 76, 94
Tye, Michael 102, 139, 140, 141, 142

Van Gulick, Robert 11, 84, 102, 103, 114, 115, 122, 132, 133–4, 136, 139, 143, 144, 145
Van Inwagen, Peter 89, 116, 117, 138, 148, 149, 150, 151, 156, 162

Ward, Graham 44, 45
Webster, John B. 9, 10, 14, 19, 20, 25, 36, 38, 43, 46, 47, 49, 50, 51, 54, 69–70, 72, 99, 100, 101, 105, 108
Williams, Bernard 148, 170
Witmer, Gene D. 119, 131, 136, 138

Yablo, Stephen 128, 134, 136–7, 144

Zimmerman, Dean W. 150, 153, 157, 159, 161, 166, 174, 176
Zizioulas, John D. 4, 36, 57, 59, 102, 188

But the music is closer to the earth, more like the winds from which the stick came, than ever before. he has run it thin, & the rain & the wind have bent it & closed some of the holes. It no longer sounds the same. Yet he is snow person, & he keeps blowing anyway. He could have grown up. The sounds are not so big. The sound is worn & twisted & sweet. The pipe is worn &

Imagine a man in the woods, long ago, who discovers a hollow wooden stick & turns it into a flute by poking some holes & gratefully in it. He blows & blows & learns to make the most beautiful sounds from it. The creatures of the forest follow him wherever he goes, because his sound fills up the woods, making the leaves flutter, the trees sway, & the sky brighten. After yrs. of playing on the stick,

Daniel J. Price

Barth's Anthropology
in light of modern
Thought

Eerdmans 2002

[signature]